658.001
P76d

92466

| DATE DUE | | | |
|---|---|---|---|
| May19'75 | | | |
| | | | |
| | | | |
| | | | |
| | | | |
| | | | |
| | | | |
| | | | |
| | | | |
| | | | |
| | | | |
| | | | |

t

# DEVELOPMENTS IN
# MANAGEMENT THOUGHT

BY THE SAME AUTHOR

*Hospitex* – a hospital ward management exercise
(Management Games Ltd, Weybridge)

# DEVELOPMENTS IN MANAGEMENT THOUGHT

## Harold R. Pollard

*B. Com., F.I. Sc.B.,*
*Formerly Senior Lecturer in Management Studies*
*Peterborough Technical College*

CRANE, RUSSAK & COMPANY, INC.
NEW YORK

*Published in the United States by:*
Crane, Russak & Company, Inc.
52 Vanderbilt Avenue
New York, N.Y.10017


© Harold R. Pollard 1974

First published 1974



Library of Congress Catalog No. 72-84394
ISBN 0-8448-0069-4

Printed in Great Britain

# Preface

At a time when books on management are coming out almost by the hundred it may seem impertinent and unnecessary to write yet another. But as the idea for this book took form in my mind the very fact that there were so many others led me to believe that it could fill an important gap.

Originally the idea arose because in the course of my teaching duties I needed a book like this for a particular course of students and I failed to find one. But further reflection led me to think that if students could not be expected to read twenty or thirty books to find how management thought had been developed, how much less likely would a busy, practising manager be expected to do so. And yet both students and managers ought to know something of the background to management theory. My aim is to help them to do so.

In order to keep the book within reasonable (and economic) bounds it was necessary to do three things. The first was to restrict its time coverage. With the exception of the second chapter on Peter Drucker, the book deals only with developments up to 1960 or thereabouts. This is not entirely arbitrary. It is my experience that a period of about ten years is needed for new ideas to become widely accepted.

The second restriction will inevitably create disagreement. Only a limited number of authors could be included. The final choice is my personal one, for which I bear full responsibility. There can be no valid answer to the argument that so and so should have been left out and someone else ought to have been included. After forty years' reading on management topics and fifteen years of teaching the subject I can only hope that I have given a reasonable cross-section of the possibles. Similarly the vast range of techniques which developed after about 1930 has been left out. To do them even moderate justice would require a book in itself. Further, while I should be the last to decry the importance of techniques in management, the vital aspect of management, whatever its setting,

v

is the management of people. This book, therefore, concentrates on management thought as it has developed in relation to people.

The third restriction is in the very nature of the book itself. Each chapter is a personal summary of my ideas of the most significant parts of each author's contribution. Necessarily they contain a large subjective element, and leave out much. They are intended to present a broad picture, to arouse interest, and, I hope, to lead the reader on to study the original versions. Specific references and bibliographies are collected at the ends of chapters. The particular editions of the books consulted for quotation are shown there but it will be appreciated that further editions of some of them may have been published.

As anyone who has ever tried to write a book knows, it cannot be done without the co-operation of other people. I must record my very grateful appreciation of my wife's tolerance of the disturbance which I have caused and of her help in reading much of the script and making many helpful suggestions and even typing some of it. My thanks are due, too, to the many publishers who have allowed me to use direct quotations (separate acknowledgments appear elsewhere), to Mr G. B. Smith of Peterborough Technical College, who read the whole of the script and produced many useful comments, and to Mrs D. Kaye of Denby Dale, who coped valiantly with the bulk of the work of translating a near illegible script into acceptable typewritten form. I think also that I should thank the many hundreds of students and managers who by their questions, their arguments, and their disagreements have done so much to give me what small understanding I may have of a most difficult subject.

The errors of omission, of interpretation, of opinion are mine alone, and for these I must ask the indulgence of the reader.

*Denby Dale*                                                   H. R. POLLARD

# Acknowledgments

The author wishes to acknowledge his indebtedness to the following for kind permission to include extracts from the books quoted:

American Management Association, Inc.
*Classics in Management*, edited by H. F. Merrill.

Harper & Row, Publishers, Inc.
*Personality and the Organization*, by C. Argyris.
*The Principles of Organization*, by James D. Mooney.
*Scientific Management*, by F. W. Taylor.

Harper & Row, Publishers, Inc. and William Heinemann Ltd
*Managing for Results*, by Peter F. Drucker.
*The Practice of Management*, by Peter F. Drucker.

Division of Research, Harvard Business School, Boston, 1946
*The Human Problems of an Industrial Civilization*, by Elton Mayo.

Division of Research, Harvard Business School, 1945, and Routledge & Kegan Paul Ltd
*The Social Problems of an Industrial Civilization*, by Elton Mayo.

Harvard University Press
*The Functions of the Executive*, by Chester I. Barnard.

Heinemann Educational Books Ltd
*Exploration in Management*, by Lord Wilfred Brown.

Richard D. Irwin, Inc.
*The Writings of the Gilbreths*, edited by W. R. Spriegel and C. E. Myers.

Longman Group Ltd
*The Human Factor in Business: Experiments in Industrial Democracy*, by B. S. Rowntree.

McGraw-Hill Book Company
*New Patterns of Management*, by Rensis Likert. Copyright McGraw-Hill Book Company, 1961.
*The Human Side of Enterprise*, by Douglas McGregor. Copyright McGraw-Hill Book Company, 1960.
Extracts used with permission of the copyright holders.

## Acknowledgments

Penguin Books Ltd
> *The Social Psychology of Industry*, by J. A. C. Brown. Copyright the Estate of J. A. C. Brown, 1954.

Sir Isaac Pitman & Sons Ltd
> *General and Industrial Management*, by Henri Fayol.
> *Dynamic Administration*, edited by H. C. Metcalf and L. Urwick.
> *The Philosophy of Management*, by Oliver Sheldon.

Tavistock Publications Ltd
> *Group Dynamics*, by D. Cartwright and A. Zander.

# Contents

# PART I

## The Work Approach

# Frederick Winslow Taylor
## 1911-15

*Introduction*

Any book which attempts to show how management thought has developed must inevitably start with Frederick Winslow Taylor. Such books as had been written on management topics before his time were so far removed from modern management as to have little significance today. Taylor, on the other hand, has become generally known as the 'father of scientific management'. He, if he had known, would probably have disputed this title, for, as he said, 'Every one of us realizes that this [scientific management] has been the work of 100 men or more, and that the work which any one of us may have done is but a small fraction of the whole.'[1] No doubt he was too modest, for the ideas he put to use, the work he did and the papers he wrote were of the greatest importance.

Born in 1856 at Boston, Massachusetts, of middle-class parents, Taylor should have gone on to the university and a career in law. It must have seemed to him the greatest misfortune that at the end of his school career his doctor advised against further study on account of weakness in his eyesight. So he looked for a job which did not involve much reading or writing and obtained one as an apprentice machinist with a small firm of engineers. During the next four years he became not only a journeyman machinist but also a journeyman pattern-maker.

Leaving this firm at the end of his apprenticeship in 1878, he joined Midvale Steel Company, first as a labourer. He was then appointed clerk and later worked as a machinist. No doubt because of his high intelligence and education he was promoted to 'gang boss' within two months of joining. In the eleven years he stayed there he rose from machinist to shop superintendent. It was here that scientific management was born, and Taylor himself puts the date precisely as 1882. In 1889 he left Midvale to join the Bethlehem Steel Company and to continue his work on scientific management there. In all he estimated that he spent about thirty years on it.

First as an apprentice, then as a machinist, Taylor realized that no one who was working a machine ever worked at anything near the speed that he could achieve if he wanted to. Deliberate restriction of output on the part of the men was the normal pattern. Taylor described this as 'soldiering', either natural soldiering due to 'the natural instinct and tendency of man to take it easy'[2], or systematic soldiering due to 'more intricate second thought and reasoning caused by their relationships with other men'.[3] This behaviour was in the nature of self-protection in relationships with other workers, and of opposition to bad management in relationships with managers.

As a worker Taylor was prepared to go along with others and to 'soldier' with the rest, as under the current style of management he felt and admitted that it was in the workers' own best interests to do so.

When he became a foreman, however, things were different. He was now on the management side and determined at whatever cost to get more work out of his men – in fact, to get a reasonable day's work. But what was a reasonable day's work, and what was necessary to achieve it? Although he fought hard and with some success to increase output, Taylor realized that not until he really knew the proper answers to these two questions could he hope to succeed. Finding these answers took years of work and produced 'scientific management'.

### Scientific Management

Describing the type of management which prevailed in the best of industry at this time, Taylor called it 'the management of *"initiative and incentive"* '. Under this system management provided an incentive to the worker in the form of piece-rates or a bonus, but left the responsibility for initiative as to how and when the work was done to the worker. At the same time low wages and low costs of production were regarded as synonymous, so if workers earned too much (according to management) on a piece-rate the rate was immediately cut. To combat this the workers resorted to systematic soldiering. Conditions such as these could only lead to a state of affairs where workers regarded employers and managers as enemies and the work situation as an arena for a power struggle.

This struggle could only be resolved by the discovery of facts to replace opinions, both those of management and those of workers. Assembling the facts may sound a simple enough task: actually it took Taylor thirty years of painstaking, detailed work. In brief, it involved the following:

(i) Always securing the full, wholehearted support of top managers and directors.

(ii) A complete mental revolution on the part of both management and workers.

(iii) The substitution of friendly co-operation for fighting between management and workers.

(iv) The determination of the correct feeds and speeds for cutting metals.

(v) The discovery of the one best way of doing each job, and the time it should take.

(vi) The determination of the extra pay required to call forth the effort required.

(vii) The selection and training of 'first-class' men to do it.

(viii) Breaking down the foreman's job into those of eight functional foremen.

(ix) Finding the correct method for installing the new system, and the right men to do it.

For Taylor as an engineer in charge of a machine shop the starting point was, of course, how long it should take to do any particular job in the shop. He did not know the answer for a fact and neither did anyone else. So he started a careful series of experiments, recording all variables and all information. The first fact to come out was the fundamental complexity of the problem. In all Taylor found no less than twelve independent variables, each of which affected the answer.

When he started this work Taylor expected that it would be completed in six months. At the end of that time he had some useful information and a much better idea of how big the problem was. In fact experimental work on it continued in all for twenty-six years. The results of all this work were his first book, *The Art of Cutting Metals*; invention of a set of slide-rules which enabled any machinist who was trained to use them to answer any problem on the speed at which his machine should run; the discovery of high-speed steel; and a revolution in machining practice throughout the world.

This work was important to Scientific Management in two ways. First, it showed a complete change of heart on the part of top management in allowing 'unproductive' work to be done and money to be spent on establishing facts. Secondly, it was the first real attempt to analyse work in a scientific way, to substitute fact for opinion, and was, therefore, the basis of Scientific Management.

As a foreman Taylor soon realized that under the existing system of 'initiative and incentive' the greater part of the responsibility for getting the work done was left to the workers, whereas he believed that all responsibility for planning and arranging work should rest with management, leaving the doing of it to the worker. This involved a complete change in attitude, a 'mental revolution', on the part of both managers and workers.

In a very well-known statement to the Special Committee of the House of Representatives to investigate the 'Taylor and Other Systems of Shop Management', he says:

Scientific Management is not any efficiency device; not any device of any kind for securing efficiency; nor is it any bunch or group of efficiency devices. It is not a new system of figuring costs; it is not a new scheme of paying men; it is not a piecework system; it is not a bonus system; it is not a premium system; it is no scheme for paying men; it is not holding a stop watch on a man and writing things down about him; it is not time study; it is not motion study nor an analysis of the movements of men; it is not the printing and ruling and unloading of a ton or two of blanks on a set of men and saying 'Here's your system; go use it.'

It is not divided foremanship or functional foremanship; it is not any of the devices which the average man calls to mind when scientific management is spoken of. (These things) . . . are useful adjuncts to scientific management, so are they also useful adjuncts of other systems of management.

Now, in its essence, scientific management involves a complete mental revolution on the part of the working man engaged in any particular establishment or industry – a complete mental revolution on the part of these men as to their duties toward their work, toward their fellow men and toward their employers. And it involves the equally complete mental revolution on the part of those on the management's side – the foreman, the superintendent, the owner of the business, the board of directors – a complete mental revolution on their part as to their duties toward their fellow workers in the management, toward their workmen and toward all of their daily problems. *And without this complete mental revolution on both sides scientific management does not exist.*[4]

As Taylor saw it the real basis of scientific management was this mental revolution. The worker was to
  (i) cease worrying about and fighting over the division between wages and profits of the surplus from industrial production;
 (ii) accept an increase, scientifically determined by experiment, of between 30 per cent and 100 per cent in his wages in return for effort on the scale determined by the facts;
(iii) give up all idea of soldiering and help management to establish scientifically the facts about production;
 (iv) accept that management would determine scientifically what was to be done, when, where and how, and how long it should take;
  (v) agree to be trained in and follow the new methods prescribed by management.

On the part of management the revolution was as great, if not greater. Management was to

7

   (i) develop a science for each operation to replace opinion and rule of thumb;

  (ii) determine accurately from the science the correct time and method for each job;

 (iii) select and train workers so that each was in the job for which he was best suited, i.e. the most difficult work of which he was capable (after suitable training) and on which he could still be a 'first-class man';

 (iv) set up a suitable organization which would take all responsibility from the worker except that of actual performance of the job;

  (v) itself agree to be governed by the science developed for each operation and by facts and in so doing surrender its arbitrary power over the workers.

There does, however, seem to be some contradiction between the above and a statement which Taylor made on several occasions. The division of responsibility here set out for both sides would seem to imply the removal of almost all responsibility from the workers' shoulders. This reduces the job to merely carrying out instructions and operations. And, in fact, as much of industry has developed over the period 1900–70 along the lines pioneered by Taylor this is just what has happened – the virtually complete separation of planning and doing. As this process has gone on to its logical conclusion, where, as the psycho-sociologists argue, work has become a meaningless chore, it has produced a new series of problems, which will be discussed in Part III of this book.

In practice, then, scientific management removes almost all responsibility from the worker. Perhaps Taylor was deluding himself when he said 'under Scientific Management fully one half of the problem is "up to the management" ',[5] ' . . . and each man at the same time loses none of his originality and proper personal initiative'.[6]

Having defined scientific management, how did Taylor suggest it should be introduced, and what techniques did he recommend in operating it? On the question of installation he laid the greatest stress on two major aspects – the provision of the right background conditions and the need to make haste slowly. First and foremost the directors or owners of the business had to be convinced of the value of scientific management and determined to introduce it whatever the apparent cost and the difficulties met *en route*. Without this conviction at the top the new method would fail. The next preliminary step was to find the right man who could be entrusted with the job of installing the system. This would call for an independent specialist, and could not be done by a line manager, such as the Works or Shop Manager, whose job was to keep the rest of the plant running while the installation took place. Then it was necessary to find the man or men with the ability and the right frame of mind to carry out the detailed work of analysis and building up the science of the job.

*Scientific Approach*

The next stages of investigation and installation can best be illustrated by the method used by Taylor himself in carrying out his work on the job of shovelling. The first thing was to select a single job which was eminently suitable for study, which had sufficient variety, without being complex, which employed enough men to be worth while, and which would provide an 'object lesson' to all when installed. Two men were selected who were good, steady workers and who were expected to be willing to co-operate in experiments. They were told that if they would help with the experiments, do exactly as they were told, and be prepared to have a man with a piece of paper, a pencil and a stop-watch standing over them all the time and telling them to do 'damn fool things' they would be given double pay as long as, but only as long as, the experiments lasted. They agreed and the study commenced. A start was made with a large shovel and heavy material and for each day the total amount shovelled was weighed and recorded. Then gradually the size of the shovel was cut down so that the weight of a shovel load decreased but the total amount shovelled per day increased. This was continued until the total per day began to fall. This determined the best weight per shovel-load and the size of the shovel for that particular material. The right size of shovel or fork was then determined for all the other kinds of material handled, from iron ore to rice coal. The actual movements of shovelling, the use of hands, arms and legs were studied in detail, as were the different types of base on which the material could lie, for example earth, wood, metal, and so on.

From all this study emerged a 'science of shovelling', which showed the correct method for each material, the correct shovel-load, the correct tool for each type of work, and the amount which should be shovelled per day by a 'first-class man'.

Although Taylor does not say so in his description of these experiments, the next step would be to determine scientifically the rate of bonus to be paid to get the required effort, day in and day out, while still satisfying the worker. Elsewhere he describes it as follows. A number of good men were carefully selected and trained by the observers in the new method. They were told the quantity of work to be done per day, and offered a bonus of 10 per cent above their normal day-rate if they achieved it. At this rate of bonus probably all the men, after trying it, would say that they preferred to go back to the old system, so the bonus would be increased by stages until at 30 per cent, 40 per cent, 60 per cent or even 100 per cent in some cases all the men expressed themselves as satisfied with the new way of working and the new higher pay. The bonus was then fixed at whatever rate was the minimum required to achieve this result.

*Installation*

At this point the system was ready for installation. Taylor insisted on three principles being observed. First, that a new system must never be introduced on a trial basis. This foredoomed it to failure. Secondly, that it must be put in on the basis of individual work-men, never on a group basis. Thirdly, that each stage of installation must provide an 'object lesson' to everyone around. To start, then, a single workman who appeared likely to succeed would be offered the chance of working on the new system and earning a bonus of *x* per cent. If he agreed, he would be trained by the observer (later a functional foreman), and when fully competent he would be put to work by himself. Each day he would be told whether he had achieved his bonus; if he failed the observer would return for one or more days to help him with further teaching. When the first man was consistently earning bonus the same procedure would be followed with a second, then a third, and so on. Eventually, and this might take up to two years, everyone would want to be on the new system and the whole yard, shop or whatever could be changed over.

Parallel with the increase of the number of men on the new system there would be a system for providing the right tools, materials, and so on, at the right time and place, and a clerical office system for planning daily in advance what was to be done, notifying individuals of their task for the day and their achievement on the previous day. Also, once a fair number of men were on the new system a number of 'teachers' would be required to install and maintain it.

Two aspects of Taylor's scientific management deserve further consideration: the wage system and functional foremen.

## Wages

On the question of a wage system Taylor seems to have changed his mind between the time when he started this work and the time when he gave his testimony before the Congressional Committee. In this it seems that he may have been influenced by his friend and co-worker for a number of years, Henry Gantt. To begin with he suggested and used what became known as the Taylor Differential Piece Rate System, referred to in his paper 'A Piece Rate System' presented to the American Society of Mechanical Engineers in 1895. On this system there were two different piece-rates in operation, one for use if the target or task was reached and another low (penal) one for use when it was not. For example, if the task was twenty pieces per day there might be two piece-rates of 10 and 7 cents per piece. If the man reached or passed his task of twenty pieces he would be paid for them all at the rate of 10 cents per piece, that is, $2 or more for the day's work. If, however, he failed to reach his task and produced less than twenty pieces he would only get 7 cents per piece for those he had produced, so nineteen pieces would give him a day's pay of $1.33 as against $2 for twenty. In fact, of course, it was never Taylor's intention that the lower rate should be used. The whole idea was that the man reached his target and achieved the higher rate. If he did not then something was wrong and it was management's job to put it right, either by more teaching or by transferring the man to a job where he could achieve the target, assuming that he was not just lazy. If he was, there was just no room for him under this system.

In his paper on 'Shop Management' Taylor refers to both the 'Differential Piece Rate' system and the 'Task and Bonus' system. The latter would appear to have been developed by Gantt and adopted by Taylor. Under this system the worker was given a guaranteed day-wage, irrespective of the amount produced. If the task was accomplished he was given a bonus on his day-rate of anything between 30 per cent and 100 per cent according to the nature of the work and the amount of bonus required to call forth the extra effort. Certainly the effect of failure to reach the task was not so harsh under the Task and Bonus system, and Gantt developed it because he considered it more humane.

## Foremanship

No doubt because he had been a foreman himself Taylor knew that it was quite impossible for the general foreman to have all the knowledge and to exercise all the responsibility required by his new system of management. He therefore abolished the job of general foreman and in its place substituted a system of eight functional foremen. These were:

> Order of Work and Route Clerk
> Instruction Card Clerk
> Time and Cost Clerk
> Shop Disciplinarian
> Gang Boss
> Speed Boss
> Repair Boss
> Inspector

Of these eight 'foremen' some were obviously not foremen in the strict sense of the word, although they all performed functions which to a greater or lesser extent had been carried out by the general foreman.

The first three were largely concerned with the new managerial responsibility of detailed planning of the work. The Order of Work and Route Clerk decided the priorities for jobs and specified the machines on which they should be done. The Instruction Card Clerk wrote out from the records the precise details of what to do and, if necessary, how to do it. The Time and Cost Clerk was concerned with the time the job should take and, on the return of the completed documents, with determining what the job had cost.

The Shop Disciplinarian was concerned with problems of discipline, complaints and grievances wherever they arose. The Gang Boss would be responsible for providing the right men for the machines that were working or the jobs that wanted doing. The job of the Speed Boss was to guide the worker as to the correct feeds and speeds for his machine for the job in hand. The Repair Boss had to keep an eye on all machines and decide when they should be taken out of service for repair or maintenance. Finally the Inspector or Inspectors were responsible for checking the quality of the finished product and accepting or rejecting it. This system was obviously developed with the machine shop in mind, but it could be adapted to any form of work.

*Conclusion*

To assess the value and validity of Taylor's contribution to management thought and its effect on practice is indeed a difficult task. However, an attempt will be made to give a balanced assessment, taking in various points of view.

There can be no doubt that it set in train the development of modern management thought. Taylor started the ball rolling. Whether or not he started it in the right direction may be a matter of opinion. It seems reasonably certain that Taylor himself was what might be called an intellectual perfectionist. It is also reasonably certain that he was a good deal cleverer than most of his contemporary managers and much more able to take a detached view. His entire work rests upon the concept of a 'complete mental revolution' on the part of both managers *and* workers. How far this was ever achieved or even could be achieved generally is another matter. It is probable that while he was first at Midvale Steel Co. and later at Bethlehem Steel Works it did take place to a very considerable extent. But he was under no illusions as to what happened elsewhere, and that his system could be grossly misused. In fact it was the misuse of the system that led to the Congressional Enquiry into it. When Taylor was giving evidence to the Enquiry he was asked by the Chairman, 'How many concerns, to your knowledge, use your system in its entirety?' To which Taylor replied, 'In its entirety – none, not one.' He did go on to say however that 'a very great many' substantially used the system.

In the United Kingdom attempts to use Taylor's methods met with the greatest opposition from the trade unions and, in fact, Taylorism is still (in 1971) a 'dirty word' in the folk-lore of British trade unionism, despite the fact that many of his ideas have been adopted in modified form and accepted by the unions.

It would appear that the 'body' of his ideas has grown and developed without the 'spirit'. The perfectionist attitude, the philosophy, the mental revolution died with Taylor. The techniques, the study of work and method, set times for the job, the bonus for achieving it, the functional foreman (now the functional department) survived and grew.

But with the growth of these practices has come a new series of problems. Perhaps workers no longer generally systematically 'soldier' to prevent the rate being cut, but there are more arguments in industry over times for jobs than over anything else. The time is no longer a scientifically demonstrable *fact* but a compromise based on struggle, or what, if he is honest enough to admit it, the time-study expert thinks the workers will accept. And the worker? If he is on bonus rates he has a 'kitty' or 'bank' of spare hours collected from jobs with loose timings to cover the next tight job. No sign of a mental revolution here! Again in post-war Britain the pernicious practice of overtime as a means, mutually recognized by both management and workers, of bringing a low base-rate up to a living wage has meant that few workers today work at a speed which Taylor would have recognized as worthy of bonus.

There is another side too which is worthy of mention. Although this point does not appear in the book *Scientific Management*, Taylor did once admit that there might be psychological aspects relating to his ideas which he was not competent to assess and which, he hoped, someone would study. Although Sheldon makes some reference to the human implications of scientific management (*see* Part II, Chapter 9), and ideas on it can be inferred from Follett's papers (*see* Part III, Chapter 12), a really serious study of the subject was not undertaken for almost fifty years, and it is still going on.

Taylor himself put the main emphasis on the bonus, the pay packet as the motivating factor. Perhaps it would be fairer to say that this is how it worked out in practice. Taylor himself did insist that at the same time men should constantly be trained and up-graded to the highest level of work they could do. This, if carried out, would have met to some extent the need for self-realization and self-actualization. But the combination of the economic theories of the nineteenth century on 'economic man' and the emphasis of scientific management on 'task and bonus' have over the past seventy years produced in most managers the firm belief that the worker is interested only in the pay packet. This belief and the practices to which scientific management has led are, according to the psycho-sociological school, the main causes of our ills and troubles in industry and management today.

It is very easy to be wise seventy years later and to condemn Taylor out of hand on the basis of present knowledge. But in twenty years from now our current knowledge may seem as out-dated as Taylor does today.

Let it be said that he was a great pioneer. He led the way in the application of detailed scientific method to the study of management, and for that we must always be grateful to him.

### References

*Note:* These references are from *Scientific Management*, 1964. This reprints and combines in one volume the verbatim record of Taylor's testimony at the Congressional hearing (headed 'Testimony') and his book *The Principles of Scientific Management*. Both sections are separately page numbered.

## The Work Approach

(1) Taylor, F. W. *Scientific Management* (Harper & Bros, London 1964) 'Testimony', p. 282.

(2) ibid., p. 117.

(3) ibid., p. 117.

(4) ibid., p. 26 (the italics are the author's).

(5) Taylor, F. W. *The Principles of Scientific Management* (Harper & Bros, New York 1915), p. 39.

(6) ibid., p. 140.

*Bibliography*

BOOKS BY F. W. TAYLOR

*Shop Management* (Harper & Bros., New York 1911).

*The Principles of Scientific Management* (Harper & Bros, New York 1915).

*Scientific Management* (Harper & Bros, New York 1947; London 1964).

# 2

# Frank B. and Lilian M. Gilbreth
## 1908-20

*Introduction*

Was it just coincidence that two men alike in so many ways as
Taylor and Gilbreth, both living in America, should apply their
minds to the problems of work and management so nearly at the
same time? Like Taylor, Gilbreth had a middle-class background
and yet started work right at the bottom, this time as a bricklayer's
apprentice. Like Taylor he met the problems of a superior intellect
looking at manual work and decided that neither men nor management really knew what they were doing, or why. Like Taylor he
rose rapidly to foreman, to manager, then to his own construction
business, and finally to consultancy.

Differences there were, however. Gilbreth came some years
after Taylor and was therefore able to accept and to develop
Taylor's ideas. Secondly, his wife, Lilian M. Gilbreth, was a
trained psychologist and was able to help him in his work, and
indeed to develop certain aspects on her own. Finally, although
Gilbreth developed the management-responsibility aspects of
Taylor's work into elaborate 'systems' for his own business, he is
remembered almost entirely for his work in developing the science
of motion study. This he did in such depth and detail that few
major alterations have been made to it since.

Much of the original work of the Gilbreths seems to have been
published as articles in American scientific and technical journals
or in books which are now out of print. It is now hard to come by
in Britain in its original form. However, Dean Spriegel and Pro-
fessor Myers of Texas University edited in one volume (*The
Writings of the Gilbreths* published by Richard D. Irwin Inc. in

1953) the works of the Gilbreths which they considered had lasting value. It is from this book that the ideas for this chapter are drawn, and my debt to them is obvious and is here acknowledged.

## Systems Management

While the word 'system' has a number of different meanings today, at the time and in the work of Gilbreth it meant one thing only – an ordered and prescribed way of doing things down to the very last detail. If there is one phrase more than any other which is associated with Gilbreth it is 'the one best way'. As an apprentice bricklayer he very soon found that experienced craftsmen had different ways of doing the same job; not only were they different from each other, but each man had two or three different ways of working, depending on circumstances and his immediate objective. To young Gilbreth this was not good enough. One way or some combination of the different ways must be the best. Finding it, whether it was for bricklaying or for management, became his life's work.

Management in the construction industry has always faced one major difficulty which does not exist in the self-contained factory. There is a central head office, working in conjunction with operating sites which might be on the doorstep or a thousand miles away, or anywhere in between. To cope with this situation when he had his own business Gilbreth set down for all his managers, foremen and workers what he called the 'Field System'. This was a set of rules and procedures reduced to writing and applicable to all work sites. Their purpose was uniformity of practice, and to ensure this the Introduction included the following: 'All employees must follow these rules to the letter unless they receive written permission to suspend certain rules.'[1] The possibility of change in the rules was allowed for by the proviso that 'We shall appreciate and will pay money for suggestions that will improve this system.'[2] But until the rules were changed they had to be followed.

The system as described can be divided into various parts:
  (i) A description of the general form of contract with the customer.
  (ii) Emphasis on the need for speed of work without losing

accuracy, and the suggestion of division of work into equal portions and the use of 'athletic contests' between teams.

(iii) General Rules: thirty-four rules on a variety of topics which seem, on the face of it, to vary from the very detailed to the very general and must have left many aspects uncovered. Rule 16, 'Do not bother the Office unnecessarily', must have left a lot of room for interpretation!

(iv) Rules for suggestions and reports, including a suggestions scheme with small cash prizes, and publicity within the firm for the monthly winners.

(v) Rules for 'steady pay men' and apprentices, presumably non-casual labour, which appear to be meant to ensure that they were occupied for every minute of the day whatever the weather.

(vi) Detailed instructions for taking and using photographs as permanent records.

(vii) 'White List Cards': these were a form of testimonial given to men who had proved themselves 'superior' workers on a job. They ensured priority of employment on another job.

It is impossible at this distance to tell whether management in this form was unique to Gilbreth's own business. Certainly as one of the keenest supporters of Taylor's ideas on the responsibilities of management Gilbreth put them into practice. His main problem, from a management point of view, was to ensure performance and control at a distance. His answer would today put him in the category of 'benevolent autocrat'. Autocratic because although he welcomed and encouraged suggestions they could only be put into practice with his own personal approval. He laid down the system and insisted on rigid adherence to it. He insisted on a maximum day's work at all times and under all circumstances. Benevolent because he seems to have been scrupulously fair and to have ensured a 'good deal', financial and otherwise, for all his employees.

The two other systems were more technical in character, although they did also contain many rules for the detailed management of the system. One was the Concrete System and the other the Bricklaying System. Both were built up gradually by incorporating 'the written ideas of the most successful men in our organization'.[3] Again, '. . . these rules must be carried out to the letter'.[4]

The Concrete System consisted of General Rules, Mixing and Transportation. The Bricklaying System had sections on Training Apprentices, Methods of Management, Scaffolding, the Packet System of handling bricks, and details of the motion study on bricklaying.

It is presumably fair to assume that in the construction industry Gilbreth found, as Taylor had done in engineering, that the actual doing of the work was entirely a matter of handed-down tradition and personal preference, and that the speed of most workers, if not all, was a long way below what they could reasonably accomplish. To deal with this situation he took Taylor's concept of the separation of planning from doing to its extreme logical conclusion.

Two examples may illustrate the point. On mixing concrete there are 231 rules to follow! Rule 198 reads 'When men shovel against a plank, always use a square pointed shovel. Use a round pointed shovel at all other times.'[5]

In the section on 'Methods of Management in the Bricklaying System' there is the following:

Take for example a wall of nine piers, separated by eight windows. On this wall there should be nine bricklayers, if the piers are of about the same size. If the piers are not the same size the number of bricklayers should be increased or reduced, so that their work will be equal, and the slow man will be shown up quickly. The foreman should watch the bricklayers to see which man is standing up idle. He is standing up for one of three reasons: (a) he is loafing; (b) he is out of stock; (c) he has finished his bit.

If it is for the first reason, he should be dealt with. If he is out of stock, the leader of tenders needs attention. If it is for the third reason, his speed should be recognized, and the mason who is behind and delaying the raising of the line to the next course should be investigated.[6]

It would be difficult to find more detailed planning than that shown in these two items.

The relatively short section on motion study in the Bricklaying System is interesting because it seems to show an early stage in the development of the science, and also because it shows an understanding of human nature which the Gilbreths may always have had but which seems to have become lost later on. Right at the end of the section Gilbreth says, 'In the selection of these methods as adopted here for the training of our young men, we have followed the best of the working methods of the men in our organization.'[7] This statement, together with the charts, which show the normal motions used and those that can and should be eliminated, would seem to imply that, at this stage, the method used was largely a study of existing practices, the choice of the best and the elimination from it of unnecessary motions by improving the work-place layout or the position of the worker.

The new set of motions were to be taught to apprentices from the very beginning. They were not to be allowed to learn old fashioned inferior ways from people using other methods. But it was appreciated that it might be difficult to teach old dogs new tricks. Those who could adapt to the new system and achieve the new rates of output, expected to be at least double the old, would receive a 'substantial increase above the minimum rate of pay'. Those who could adapt in part would get 'more than the minimum'. Those who could not adapt but could by intense effort achieve 'a fair day's work' by their own methods could continue to use them and receive the minimum rate. Finally, those who would not attempt to try the system were only to be employed in an emergency when better men were not available. Despite the possible inconsistency between the rulings on the last two groups, it does look as if Gilbreth appreciated that the 'one best method' might not suit everybody and that allowances and variations might be necessary.

*Motion Study*

The first definitive account of the more detailed development of motion study appeared as a series of articles in the American journal *Industrial Engineering* in 1911. It was published in book form a year later.

In the Introduction to the book R. T. Kent, the editor of *Industrial Engineering*, says of the articles, 'It now appears, however, that the apparent lack of interest was due to the fact that we had presented a subject so entirely new that it required some little time for people to comprehend its importance and to realize its value.'[8]

Gilbreth himself is in no doubt about its importance and wastes no time before he stresses it. 'There is no waste of any kind in the world that equals the waste from needless, ill-directed, and ineffective motions.'[9] But he also says that he has only reached the first stage of motion study, discovering and classifying the best practice.

This analysis is to be carried out by following these steps:[10]

1. Reduce *present* practice to writing
2. Enumerate motions used
3. Enumerate variables which effect each motion
4. Reduce best practice to writing
5. Enumerate motions used
6. Enumerate variables which affect each motion.

The variables are classified as those of the worker, those of the surroundings, equipment and tools, and those of the motion, in all forty-two different aspects. Each of these is discussed in some detail, showing the way they might or do affect the work.

Points which are emphasized in developing the idea of moving from present practice to best practice are:

  (i) The use of written charts to record the two methods.

 (ii) The determination of the variables of motion applicable and their use to set up standard motions, standard tools, standard conditions and standard methods.

(iii) The deduction of standard methods before tools etc. are standardized.

(iv) Improvement to the best method implies more than just the elimination of the unnecessary. It must come from re constructing the method from basic motions.

(v) Observation and analysis must be by a trained scientific observer.

(vi) Comparison between two methods can be made by timing the motion elements in each.

Gilbreth suggests that once a time study of an element has been done it becomes a standard which could be used by anyone and that the greatest need is for as many people as possible in all trades to be trained in time study and then to exchange data. He also suggests the setting up of a Government agency to collect, analyse and publish data for all concerned, and asks trade schools and colleges to produce and publish information.

Six years later, in 1917, Frank and Lilian Gilbreth jointly published a book entitled *Applied Motion Study*. While the principle remains unchanged, this second book shows the development of techniques which had taken place in the meantime and includes some discussion of the effects of motion study. Motion study itself is defined as: '. . . dividing the work into the most fundamental elements possible; studying these elements separately and in relation to one another; and from these studied elements, when timed, building methods of least waste'.[11] Detailed study such as this would seem to have progressed a long way from an analysis of the ways used by existing workmen. And indeed it has. It now includes three elements: determining the elements to be measured, the methods to be used, and the devices to be used.

Although he does not give them at this point, nor, in fact, are they mentioned anywhere in this book, the elements are presumably what he called 'therbligs'. These consist of eighteen items which are illustrated in various texts as in Figure 1.

Although other people have produced slightly more extensive versions of these elements because it was felt that some items were not included, Gilbreth's version represents a tremendous advance in the detail which could be shown as compared with the original five elements used in visual written analysis. These were operation, transport, inspection, delay and filing. But because they were so detailed they depended on new methods of observation. It was no longer possible for an adequate job to be done by an observer manually recording the operation as it was being done.

| SYMBOL | NAME | COLOUR |
|---|---|---|
| (search eye) | Search | Black |
| (find eye) | Find | Grey |
| → | Select | Light grey |
| ∩ | Grasp | Red |
| ⊓ | Hold | Gold ochre |
| ⌣ | Transport loaded | Green |
| 9 | Position | Blue |
| # | Assemble | Violet |
| ∪ | Use | Purple |
| # | Disassemble | Light violet |
| ○ | Inspect | Burnt ochre |
| ⚲ | Pre-position | Pale blue |
| ⌒ | Release load | Carmine red |
| ⌣ | Transport empty | Olive green |
| ℓ | Rest for overcoming fatigue | Orange |
| ⌃ | Unavoidable delay | Yellow |
| ⌐ₒ | Avoidable delay | Lemon yellow |
| ℘ | Plan | Brown |

*Figure 1*. Therblig symbols and colours

Ordinary still photography seems to have been the first method used. This, done from various angles, gave a permanent record of work-place layout and position of the work and the worker. Stereoscopic photography followed to give three-dimensional pictures. The real break-through came with the use of the cine-camera. Basically the idea was to photograph the motions of the worker and to show the result on a screen at normal speed, at slow speed and even frame by frame for analysis. Again stereoscopic methods were developed to give depth. This still left two important items unmeasured – time and distance. Time was dealt with by the development of special clocks which could show divisions down to whatever unit was required. For one job it was as small as one millionth part of an hour. This special clock was placed within the area to be photographed so that a simultaneous record of movement and time was obtained. This method was called micro-motion study.

An early method of dealing with distance was to have a squared chart as a background to the operation. Later this was developed into double-exposure photography so that the chart, photographed first, became an integral part of the picture. Methods of recording such as these made much more detailed analysis possible, and for this purpose special analysis forms were developed. These were the transfer form for a first analysis, the simo-motion chart for recording the simultaneous motions of both arms in detail from the shoulder to each of the fingers separately, and the man-machine chart for linking manual and machine operations.

Still Gilbreth was not satisfied. Even with stereoscopic photography it was difficult to analyse the path of motions. A start was made with the cyclegraph. This method involved attaching small lights to the hand or arm which, when photographed on a single plate, showed up as a continuous path of light, thus avoiding the small time-breaks in the motion-picture film. Further work on the lights converted them into regularly flashing lights, with a known time-gap between the flashes, and the light coming on suddenly and fading out gradually. This increased the value of the result enormously. The flashes showed as a modified oval with a blunt end as they came on and a pointed end as they faded out, thus showing the direction of movement and the distance moved in the time between flashes. The cyclegraph had become the chrono-cyclegraph and from this permanent records in the form of bent wire models could be constructed for analysis and teaching.

Motion study had reached a peak, never to be surpassed and, so far as can be gathered, seldom to be equalled. It seems that in practice very few people had ever gone to the lengths developed by Gilbreth and that visual manual recording has remained the most usual method. It is one thing, however, to record even in the minutest detail, it is quite another to develop 'the one best way'. Part of the answer is to eliminate unnecessary motions and work, the rest is invention and developing new and better ways. Gilbreth's criteria appear to have been the minimum number of motions, the required motions being balanced and requiring the minimum time, and the fatigue, mental or physical, resulting from the work. Automatically these led into time study and the development of the standard time for the job, made up of the times for the various elements, an allowance to compensate for fatigue, and other allowances for such things as unavoidable delay, personal needs, degree of concentration required and so on.

Time study and the development of standard times have remained with us and developed in two ways; first and foremost as the basis of wage-payment systems, and secondly into predetermined standards for building up synthetic times. It is perhaps ironical that the 'scientific' determination of standard times has, perhaps, led to more arguments and trouble between management and workers than any other single subject and that for the workers themselves one result has been the development of an infinite capacity for 'beating the system'. The 'kitty' or 'bank' is one such development where on soft jobs, where a worker can easily complete them in less than standard time, he will book the standard time and so have a few hours 'in hand' so that a tight job can be still booked within the time allowed. No doubt Gilbreth would have said that this was just bad timing.

*Fatigue Study*
The development of motion study must have led inevitably to the question of fatigue. The elimination of unnecessary and wasteful motions would, of itself, reduce the amount of fatigue, but it left untouched the more basic problem that, as all work necessarily produces fatigue and the only answer to fatigue is rest, it is

necessary to find out the best combination of work and rest to make the work most productive for the firm and the worker. Mr and Mrs Gilbreth jointly published *Fatigue Study* in 1916. It approached the problem at two levels: first, what might be called the elementary, commonsense level, and secondly, the analytical level, although they stressed that this was very much in its infancy. They started by making the distinction between unnecessary fatigue, which arises from unnecessary effort, and necessary fatigue resulting from necessary work. The first must be eliminated, they said, by removing the unnecessary work, the second must be minimized by providing adequate rest periods at the correct intervals.

The commonsense approach attacks the problem from various angles. The working day can be shortened by a longer dinner break, recognized 'tea breaks', or by shorter overall hours. These may, they said, be dangerous unless the problem is studied as a whole, because the worker may suspect that a shorter day means lower wages. Management must, therefore, make sure that the shorter hours will at least produce the same output, and then guarantee no reduction in wages. Ideally they should produce greater output and be matched by increased wages voluntarily given by management.

Apart from taking recognized breaks, workers should be allowed to rest when rest is needed. To make this rest most effective ideally special reclining chairs with leg-rests should be provided. In addition to special 'rest chairs' all workers whose work is mainly done standing should be provided with a chair of some sort for use at any time when standing is not essential.

The third line of attack they called 'betterment work'. They disliked the term 'welfare work' as it was so often taken by the workers to imply charity. 'Betterment work' is done because it is good for the business as well as the employee. Rest rooms, canteens, entertainment, all come into this category. In another work Frank Gilbreth suggests early forms of 'Music while you work'. It took the Second World War and the technology of radio to popularize this idea.

Moving on to what might be called a semi-scientific approach, they deal with aspects other than the work itself which might be contributory factors in increasing fatigue. These are lighting (both inadequate and glaring), heating and ventilation, fire and safety hazards, the individual work-place, the work chair, the positioning of work and tools, and clothing. All of these should be studied, and for all there is usually ample room for improvement.

Parallel with this approach is the emphasis all the time that the workers themselves must appreciate that there is something in it for them, that increased output will be matched by increased wages, and that they themselves should become as interested in and concerned with reducing fatigue as management should be.

The second analytical level involves more scientific study of the incidence and extent of fatigue. In essence it appears to consist of two stages, first a proper motion-study of the job to standardize the best way of doing it, followed by a detailed study of performance and output against time. Any falling off in output is regarded as the measure of fatigue, and experiments with various work and rest periods must be carried out to discover the combination which produces maximum output with minimum fatigue.

An interesting example of the extent to which Gilbreth was prepared to go in prescribing detailed working conditions is given by the account of the handkerchief folders. Presumably this belonged to Gilbreth's days as a consultant, as it is far removed from laying bricks or mixing concrete. After a detailed study which standardized working conditions and methods the following is the substance of the working timetable laid down:

For each hour, except the last before lunch and the last before closing time

First six minutes, work five minutes, rest one seated.

Next eighteen minutes, repeat above three times.

Next six minutes, work five minutes, rest one standing.

Next six minutes, repeat above.

Next eighteen minutes, repeat above, sitting or standing at will.

Last six minutes, complete rest, walking, talking, etc.

For the last hour before lunch and knocking off the first fifty-four minutes were the same as for the other hours, but the last six minutes were spent in working as a long break followed in any case.

Gilbreth claims that the new way of working produced three times the output of the old one, with no more fatigue. Incidentally the purpose of this study was not to decrease fatigue, which had not been excessive under the old way, but to increase output and earnings. He does not give one fact which would be very interesting indeed – a comparison of the non-working time under the old method, consisting of collecting work, taking it up for inspection and voluntary rests taken when the girls wished to stop, with the 15 minutes per hour (9 minutes for two of the hours) compulsory rest under the new method.

When fatigue elimination has been seriously attempted Gilbreth claims that its success should show in a number of ways which can be measured. These are improvements in the general health of the work force, increased output over a prolonged period, better posture, whether sitting, standing or walking, an improvement in the general behaviour and attitudes of the workers, better transfer of skill between workers, and an increased number of individual and social 'happiness minutes'. Although he describes these as 'general measurement tests' he does not in any way suggest how they are to be measured.

This short work finished with an impassioned appeal to workers, to management, to the Colleges, to the Government and to the people at large to make the elimination of fatigue a top priority.

## Motion Study and the Worker

One sometimes hears the reply to the criticism that Christianity has never worked: 'Because it has never been tried.' Would it be fair to draw a parallel and suggest that motion study has seldom been as effective as it might have been because it has rarely been used correctly? A short paper by Gilbreth entitled 'The Effect of Motion Study upon the Workers', published in 1916, would seem to justify the argument.

The paper appears to be based on experience in his own firm and to set out his ideas on how motion study should be applied and what results it should, in his case did, produce. It starts with the bald statement 'The process of motion study is such as to interest the worker.'[12] In showing how this interest was aroused he says that it was found 'of utmost importance and mutually advantageous from every standpoint, to gain the full and hearty co-operation of the worker at once, and to enlist him as a co-worker in the motion study from the moment the first investigation is made'.[13] The worker will then show initiative in helping to derive the best method, and will become extremely interested in the methods and techniques used and in the final result, which he knows is for his benefit as well as the management's. It is claimed also that motion studies have a long-term educative effect on the worker in that he learns to observe his own work even when not being studied. Also it becomes easier for him to learn new methods.

Motion study, together with fatigue study, and the two must always go together, provide for the worker's physical and mental well-being. Against the argument that standard methods produce monotony Gilbreth thunders

> Now psychology, as well as the results in actual practice, proves that monotony comes not from performing the activity the same way every time, but from a *lack of interest involved in, or associated with, the activity*. This interest is supplied not only directly by motion study, but indirectly by the other parts of measured functional management . . .[14]

This new situation is brought about by co-operation between management and workers on an entirely new scale. And co-operation is essential. Management must now provide permanent employment because it cannot afford to lose workers trained in this way; the workers gain with greater skills, greater interest in and a better attitude to work, bigger pay-packets, more promotion and less fatigue; the firm gains with more and better suggestions for improvements, better-attended workers' and foremens' meetings, more co-operation, and voluntary study of the science of management. It sounds like Utopia. Is it, or hasn't it been properly tried out since Gilbreth's day?

## The Psychology of Management

In 1914 Lilian Gilbreth published her own book under the title

*The Psychology of Management.* The book deserves a mention, though as a factor in the development of management thought it was probably of little importance. It is unfair to be too harsh on the book as the psychology of 1914 was very different from that of today. Basically the idea was to compare the three types of management of the day, i.e. Traditional (or, as Taylor called it, Initiative and Incentive), Interim or Transitional, i.e. moving towards Scientific Management, and Scientific Management itself. They were compared under the different headings of Individuality, Functionalization, Measurement, Analysis and Synthesis, Standardization, Records and Programmes, Teaching, Incentives and Welfare.

In summary, under each heading discussed in terms of the psychology of the day, Traditional management generally had little in its favour. Transitional management was moving in the right direction and Scientific Management as portrayed by Dr Taylor was perfection itself.

### Conclusion

It is interesting to speculate how far Gilbreth's ideas and work were a product of his time and situation and therefore not of general application. His basic ideas of method study, of finding a better way, have stood the test of time in that in their simpler forms they have been used ever since by an increasing number of firms, although it is equally true to say that even in the early 1970s many firms still do not use these techniques and others are only just reaching the stage of wanting to learn about them. The more complex methods of chrono-cyclegraphs, stereoscopic photography and so on have very seldom been used.

Neither do the detailed management systems seem to have survived in anything like their original form. Even a casual observation today of any building or construction site shows the very conditions which Gilbreth set out to prevent. A suggestion made by me to a group of people in the construction industry that they should prescribe for their bricklayers the foot positions, the movements to be used and the number of bricks to be laid was greeted with derision. They insisted that its only effect would be to cause the bricklayers to get another job! Perhaps one could do this in the earlier part of this century when there was no unemployment pay, no social security, and jobs were often hard to come by. While the larger companies in the construction industry do issue manuals of procedure for their site staff, none of them are thought to go into the sort of detail which Gilbreth considered appropriate. His concept of the one (and only) best way depends fundamentally on the power of adaptation of the individual or on the assumption that all workers are alike. Both ideas are challenged by the psycho-sociological school.

Over Gilbreth must hang the same question as hangs over Taylor. Was he right in principle – if there is a better way, find it and use it ? But has the misapplication and misuse of the principle by others created more problems than it has solved ?

### References

(1) *The Writings of the Gilbreths* ed. Spriegel, W. R. and Myers, C. E. (Richard D. Irwin Inc., Homewood, Ill. 1953), p. 6.
(2) ibid., p. 6.
(3) ibid., p. 22.
(4) ibid., p. 23.
(5) ibid., p. 30.
(6) ibid., p. 45.
(7) ibid., p. 65.
(8) ibid., p. 142.
(9) ibid., p. 149.
(10) ibid., pp. 151–2.
(11) ibid., p. 220.
(12) ibid., p. 268.
(13) ibid., p. 268.
(14) ibid., p. 270.

### Bibliography

BOOKS BY F. B. GILBRETH
*Field System* (The M.C. Clark Publishing Co., New York 1908).
*Concrete System* (Engineering News Publishing Co., New York 1908).
*Bricklaying System* (The M.C. Clark Publishing Co., New York 1909).
*Motion Study* (Constable, London 1911).
*Management* (Constable, London 1912).
*Primer of Scientific Management* (Van Nostrand, New York 1912).

## Frank B. and Lilian M. Gilbreth

BOOKS BY F. B. GILBRETH AND L. M. GILBRETH

Pamphlets on Motion Study, 1915.

*Fatigue Study* (Sturgess and Walton, New York 1916; Routledge, London 1916). Second Edition, revised (Macmillan Co., New York 1919).

*Applied Motion Study* (Sturgess and Walton, New York 1917).

*Motion Study for the Handicapped* (Routledge, London 1920).

# 3

# Henry L. Gantt
## 1901-08

*Introduction*
It is, perhaps, debatable whether Henry Gantt justifies a separate chapter in this book. At the most it will be a short one, and will be included on the grounds that by modifying to some extent the rigours of the Taylor system he did develop scientific management in a way which made it somewhat more acceptable to workers.

As a colleague of Taylor at the Bethlehem Steel Works, Gantt can be described as a helper in the development of scientific management, and, at first, as a whole-hearted disciple. Later when he became a consultant in his own right he had second thoughts on the differential piece-rate system and developed his own payment system. He developed, too, a philosophy of consideration for and fair dealings with workers which became an integral part of his consultancy service. The explicit acceptance of this philosophy on the part of management was a pre-requisite of his taking a consultancy assignment, and where he was unconvinced that the management would live up to it he would refuse the job.

This was a reflection not so much on Taylor's own ideas and work but on the fact that in practice as applied by others scientific management was often used as a means of oppression and extortion by unscrupulous management. In an attempt to make this less easy to do Gantt developed his own variations on the principle.

*A Bonus System of Rewarding Labour*
The first full account of the new system was given as a paper presented in December 1901 to the American Society of Mechanical

Engineers.[1] The system follows normal scientific management methods in that a detailed instruction card is issued to the worker with the work, showing the operations, methods, and time allowed. Beyond this point modifications begin to creep in.

Gantt stresses heavily that the analysis and determination of the very best way to do the work generally takes too much time and effort to be really worth while, and that the setting of piece-rates on anything less than this can only cause trouble. The basis must therefore be the best known method at the moment. This, of course, is liable to change as the result of improvements suggested by management or workers.

Piece-rates, whether straight or differential, are inappropriate because of this possibility of change and the suspicion aroused by the often unscrupulous cutting of piece-rates by employers. Gantt's solution is to set the time for the job, as above, and to pay the day-rate for the time worked plus a bonus of between 20 per cent and 50 per cent of day wages if the job is completed in the time set. The time set consists of detailed times for each part of the total job, and if a worker finds that he is unable to complete any part of the job in the time set he is required to notify the foreman or gang boss immediately. The latter must forthwith demonstrate that the operation can be done in the time allowed or, if he is unable to do so, call the engineer who set the time. Again, the engineer must be able to demonstrate or, if he cannot do so, he must set a new, more realistic time.

It seems that Gantt recoils from Taylor's idea of removing the maximum possible responsibility from the worker. While he says that the gains of management under his system are so great that managers must do their jobs efficiently to realize them, he still leaves a good deal to the worker. The worker will not receive his bonus if for *any reason*, other than proof that the job cannot be done in the time set, he fails to make his target. Either directly or by implication the worker is required to maintain his machine in peak condition or to see that it is maintained, to see that breakdowns are dealt with immediately, to see that he is not left waiting for any reason at all, to teach himself how to improve his work methods, to criticize foremen and management when they let him down, and to suggest better methods of work provided he has used the current official method.

At the same time responsibility and incentives are given to the foreman or gang boss to see that all his men earn their bonus. He is given a bonus for each man that achieves his target and an additional one if all of them do it. Gantt says that in this way the foremen are encouraged to help and train the weaker ones in their teams.

Naturally Gantt is enthusiastic about his own system and claims that it has marked advantages over other methods. The compensation to the worker '. . . is quite large for the maximum amount of work obtainable, and quite small for anything less than this amount'.[2] The increase in output is claimed as 200 to 300 per cent, and is rapidly reached after installing the system. Relations between management and workers improve to a very great extent. Accidents and breakdowns are reduced. There is 'a quickening of the intelligence of the men'.[3] Once a few men in a shop show that bonus can be earned the rest will rapidly learn or insist on being taught how to follow their example.

There is a very interesting comment on the question of worker responsibility at the end of this paper. Gantt points out that his system leads men to do the best which is already known. 'The next and most obvious step is to make it in the interests of the *men to learn more than their cards can teach them*.'[4] To do this he believes in

paying a liberal compensation for improved methods of work, and in offering special inducements to a workman to make out instruction cards, by which others are enabled to carry out his methods. The compensation should be sufficiently liberal not only to induce him to part with what information he may have, but to use his ingenuity to devise better methods.[5]

*Training Workmen in Industry and Co-operation*
Seven years after presenting this paper, in December 1908 Gantt read a further paper to the American Society of Mechanical Engineers entitled 'Training Workmen in Habits of Industry and Cooperation'.[6]

The content of the paper is basically similar to that of the earlier one. The interest lies in the marked change of emphasis. While the 1901 paper is concerned largely with the Task and Bonus System as a means of increasing output, this paper is intended to show the system as a means of creating habits of hard work and of co-operation between workers and management. In addition it is claimed that many unskilled workers will be trained up by the system to the point where they become skilled operators. A great deal of the material in the paper is purely repetitive, so attention here will be concentrated on significant differences.

First, the importance of habits of industry, of working hard, is stressed. Such habits are of value to the employer for obvious reasons, but also they are claimed as being of value to the worker. Not only does he earn more, but by working harder he improves his health, his intelligence and his interest in his job. It is suggested that the technical training schools should not only teach what to do but how to do it as well. By 'how' Gantt means faster and more efficiently.

A further point not made clear in the earlier paper is that in Gantt's Task and Bonus System there are instructors. Their existence is now emphasized but their role is not clearly defined. Presumably their job would be to teach workmen to carry out the various operations in the way described and at the speed required.

Gantt goes on to state that the policy of management generally had been that of driving the workers, but that this must give way to teaching and training based on scientific knowledge 'to the advantage of all concerned'.[7] With systematic training in habits of industry 'it has been found possible ... to develop an effective system of cooperation between workmen and foremen'.[8] Training in faster methods is claimed to produce not only more work but better quality work, with fewer mistakes and less scrap. This is due to the increased attention and concentration required.

### The Gantt Chart

There can be no doubt that Gantt's greatest contribution to posterity and his greatest claim to fame was, to begin with, simply an offshoot of his main work. The central core of his system was the completion of a given amount of work in a given time. Simple graphical presentation in a form which emphasized the facts and which could be understood by anyone was obviously desirable, and to do this he developed the Gantt Chart.

In essence the task was represented on the chart by a straight line proportional to the time allowed for it. The chart would be divided horizontally into hours, days and weeks. The actual achievement was shown by a further line above the task line. If less than the task had been accomplished then the line fell short of the task line and the gap was plain for all to see. If the task had been achieved then the performance line was drawn to the full length of the task line and the surplus shown as an additional line above. Again, this was an indication of the situation so obvious that none could miss it. The cumulative position could be shown by further continuous lines below the task line.

In one form or another and with many variations on the basic theme the Gantt Chart has been in constant use from the day of its invention to today as the most universal means of planning work and recording performance.

*Conclusion*

Historically Gantt is not a giant of the stature of Taylor or Gilbreth, but he deserves his place among the early pioneers. To his credit he realized, more perhaps than Taylor or Gilbreth, that the worker was a human being. His insistence on the basic day-wage as a minimum and, perhaps more important, on the acceptance of his philosophy by managements who wanted him as a consultant showed a consideration that was frequently lacking in early scientific management.

As with most, if not all, of his contemporaries Gantt made the simple, basic assumption that the chance to earn more money was all that was needed to motivate workers to accept improved methods, and provided management set up the conditions which made this possible then industry's problems would be solved. Today this seems very naïve to those who know something of later developments and ideas. Gantt must bear his share of responsibility for sowing the seeds of ideas which at best are only half-truths, but which still persist in the folk-lore of practising management today.

# Henry L. Gantt

## References

(1) Printed in *Transactions of the American Society of Mechanical Engineers*, vol. 23, pp. 341–60, and reprinted in *Classics in Management* ed. Merrill, H. F. (American Management Association, New York 1960).

(2) *Classics in Management* ed. Merrill, H. F., p. 119.

(3) ibid., p. 128.

(4) ibid., p. 134.

(5) ibid., pp. 134–35.

(6) Printed in *Transactions of the American Society of Mechanical Engineers*, vol. 30, pp. 1037–48, and reprinted in *Classics in Management* ed. Merrill, H. F., op. cit.

(7) *Classics in Management* ed. Merrill, H. F., p. 137.

(8) ibid., p. 136.

## Bibliography

BOOKS BY H. L. GANTT

*Industrial Leadership* (Yale University Press, New Haven; Humphrey Milford, London 1916).

*Organizing for Work* (Harcourt, Brace and Howe, New York 1919; Allen and Unwin, London 1920).

*Gantt on Management* ed. Rathe, A. W. (American Management Association, New York 1961).

# 4

# James D. Mooney
## 1939-47

*Introduction*

The first edition of *Principles of Organization* was written by James D. Mooney and Alan C. Reilly in 1939. Eight years later, and again in 1954, Mooney wrote revised editions which were brought up to date with illustrative material mostly related to changes in the American system of government.

The book appears to have two main objectives: to set out what are called 'principles', which relate to all forms of organization, and to illustrate the truth of these 'principles' by detailed accounts of the structure of the Catholic church, the army, government, and finally business. It is an abstract book in its attempt to elucidate a theory. It is extremely difficult to read. Its inclusion in this volume is justified on the grounds that it is a recognized early attempt to set out a theory of organization.

*The Meaning of Organization*

Before defining the 'principles' of organization it is necessary to decide what organization really means. Once again it is one of those words which too often mean only what the writer or speaker intends them to mean. Mooney develops his own meaning at some length, and he intends it to be precise and definitive.

Organization is claimed to be a necessity to mankind simply because it is absolutely universal. The moment that the aim and objectives of human beings became too big or too diverse for one individual to carry out by himself, organization came into existence. But aims and objectives are only the 'psychics' of organization, and by themselves are only the fringe of the subject. Organization without them is impossible, but beyond them 'Organization in the formal sense means order, and its corollary, an organized and orderly procedure.'[1] But when a formal definition of organization is wanted he goes back to the idea of a common aim: 'organization is the form of every human association for the attainment of a common purpose'.[2]

A formal definition is, of course, only a starting point. A definition inevitably carries with it other implications, and these are set out in detail. Firstly, organization is 'pure process', that is, *doing* something. As such it is related to people, who are the doers, and also to an aim or purpose which the activity is intended to achieve. To study this phenomenon means studying the internal structure of organization. Secondly, it is partially true that organization is the machinery of administration (which here appears to mean the process of management), that it is the framework of any group with a common purpose, but also it is more than these. 'It refers to the complete body, with all its correlated functions',[3] it relates to the co-ordination of all these different aspects and functions. Thirdly, organization may be said to be subordinate to administration (management), as it is the means through which the latter works, but on the other hand organization must exist before day-by-day administration can take place. Finally, organization must involve a careful and proper division of duties so that it is possible for administration to co-ordinate effectively the efforts involved in carrying out the duties.

Having in this way defined and explained what he means by organization, Mooney turns his attention to determining the 'principles' relating to it.

## The Co-ordinative Principle

Co-ordination involves people acting together in unity of action in the pursuit of a common purpose. The vital importance of this principle is stressed by the following quotation: 'When we call *coordination* the first principle, we mean that this term expresses the principles of organization *in toto*; nothing less.'[4] In order to get co-ordination it must itself have a foundation, which is given as authority vested in some central power. This power may be autocratic or it may be democratic. In the former case it rests in an individual, in the latter in the group itself.

Authority must be distinguished from leadership, and both must be distinguished from power. Authority is a right, the right to command. Leadership must exercise authority and can only exist in an organization. Power is the ability to do things, whether existing in the individual or in the group.

The basis of organization is community of interest or aim, which involves mutual duties and mutual service. In order to obtain these there must also be, on the part of all involved, a common understanding of purpose. Understanding will not come about of itself, so it is a major task of administration (management) to see that conditions for it are favourable.

Mooney pushes this question of understanding still further, and illustrates it from church and army spheres. Both have at their centre what can be called doctrine – a recognized pattern of ideas and beliefs which everyone in the organization should accept, if he is to remain a loyal and useful member of it, and which explains the meaning and purpose of the organization. Perhaps the general aura surrounding the word 'doctrine' makes it seem not altogether applicable to modern business or industrial organization, so the phrase 'mode of thought' has come to be used in its place in management literature. Later Mooney suggests that it could well be that the lack of common or mutual understanding on both sides of industry will lead to the breakdown of co-ordination and of the present patterns of organization. There would seem to be grounds to justify this point of view.

Finally, the principle of co-ordination involves discipline. This must take two forms: the discipline imposed (*sic*) on the majority by those with authority, and the self-discipline imposed on themselves by those in authority.

### The Scalar Principle

The second 'principle' of organization is the scalar principle, or the principle of hierarchy. Mooney considers the term 'hierarchy' to be capable of different and misleading interpretations, and so insists on 'scalar' as the correct word. Scalar is taken as meaning the grading of the duties involved for different members of the organization according to 'degrees of authority and corresponding responsibility'.[5] This type of division is universal and appears in every type and every size of organization. Its essential feature is the superior–subordinate relationship, that of the manager to the managed. It is the means by which the supreme authority gets the task accomplished at the grass roots.

The scalar process, which is the 'principle' in action, itself has its own principle, process and effect. In brief, the principle is that of leadership based on the possession of the authority necessary for its place in the scalar chain. The process by which this principle is put to work is delegation. This means that a person higher in the scalar chain confers the right to exercise a lower degree of authority on, and assigns duties to, a subordinate rank. The subordinate thus becomes responsible to his superior for carrying out his assignment. The superior can and does surrender authority which he can now only exercise by withdrawing it explicitly or implicitly from his subordinate, but he does not and cannot surrender the ultimate responsibility for the achievement of the task. As the organization becomes larger and larger so those to whom authority has been delegated themselves have to sub-delegate parts of it to their subordinates. The effect of the 'principle' finally is functional definition, whereby the actual task for the individual is specified, defined and assigned.

It is in the process of delegation that many of the problems of organization arise. Some people in high positions are unwilling or incapable of delegating. Perhaps most frequently this happens with the man who has started a small organization. He has made it grow to the point where, if it is to remain under control, he must delegate to others. It is too big for him to manage, but he cannot bring himself to believe that others can do even a part of what he has done, and so he strangles his own organization. Others are only too glad to delegate, not only what they should delegate but also those things which they should keep to themselves. They shed and avoid the responsibilities inherent in their positions.

Yet again, delegation should be done in such a way that it

produces order, that subordinates have logical and meaningful tasks. This is what should happen, but often delegation is of the wrong things to the wrong people; there are things which are not delegated, leaving gaps; and others which are delegated twice, resulting in overlapping. The art of successful delegation is the supreme test of management's ability.

## The Functional Principle

Having just mentioned functional definition as the effect of the scalar 'principle', Mooney then has to take care to insist that the 'Functional Principle' is not the same thing. The 'Functional Principle' means 'the distinction between kinds of duties'.[6] It is probably fair to say that another, and more readily recognized, word for it would be specialization. Modern industry has probably taken it to the greatest extremes so far known.

Following the previous pattern, this 'principle' should itself be broken down into principle, process and effect. It is, but with some apparent confusion both as to terminology and as to the precise connection between the breakdown and its origin. Mooney writes of three 'functions' – the determinative, the applicative, and the interpretative. In other words these mean deciding what to do, getting it done, and resolving differences and problems in doing it. Later in the book in a summary shown as a logical square these three 'functions' reappear as principle, process, and effect. While these three aspects are claimed as being logically distinct, it is admitted that within organizations they are often found combined in the same person.

In developing the idea of functionalism great stress is laid on four essentials. The first is the need for the exact specification of tasks if harmonious working is to be achieved. The second insists that active harmony can only come from real understanding of the purpose as a whole. The third and fourth are centred on correlation – correlation of tasks by the organizer and of understanding by the leader. To get these two forms of correlation the organizer must work through the scalar chain vertically and the leader through horizontal contacts across the functional divisions.

## The Staff Phase of Functionalism

Here the analysis seems to be based almost entirely on developed military concepts of organization. The logic is complete; its subsequent application to the realities of industrial organization seems, looking back, to have caused only chaos and confusion in management thought and terminology.

Logically the position can be briefly and clearly stated. The staff function in organization is carried out by the giving of advice or counsel, based on specialist knowledge, to those in the scalar chain who exercise authority. The latter may use or disregard this advice in making decisions and giving orders. The choice is theirs. The staff function never issues orders or makes decisions.

The need for a staff function has arisen because of the vastly increased amount of specialized knowledge available and required to manage a modern organization. It operates in three different ways. These are:

(i) Collecting and passing on information.
(ii) Giving advice, including generating new ideas.
(iii) Supervising performance to ensure that the best known ways are followed.

## Illustration

The main central part of Mooney's book is devoted to a historical review of organization in practice in government, in the church and in the army. When the book was originally written in 1939 there was little material available to illustrate the 'principles' put forward, and Mooney and Reilly felt that they must develop their own. While it makes interesting reading and has commanded much, perhaps too much, attention, lack of space prevents its inclusion in this book.

## Industrial Organization

Because of its direct connection with the management of industry some brief reference must be made to Mooney's comments on industrial problems.

Great stress is laid upon the tremendously rapid pace of the evolution of industry through the period of the industrial revolution and beyond. At the same time it is claimed that those responsible for the development of organization patterns to cope with the situation had little, if any, previous knowledge to help them. With the pace as rapid as it was, trial and error were the order of the day, with little time for study and reflection. Under these circumstances diversity in practice is perhaps the most significant feature of modern industry.

Three types of problems are given in industrial organization.

   (i) Internal problems, which relate to the structure and conduct of the firm itself.
  (ii) External problems, which relate to the firm and its contacts with the outside world.
 (iii) Intermediate problems, caused by the interrelation of (i) and (ii).

Writing in 1947, Mooney considers (somewhat optimistically) that great progress has already been made in solving internal problems, and that, although many still remain, the future will take care of them. Intermediate problems and external problems, it is suggested, perhaps prophesied would be a better word, are likely to be the most difficult.

Among the intermediate problems that of the trade union is given the place of honour and, indeed, a chapter to itself. Essentially trade-union membership, if the 'principles' of organization are correct, places the worker in an impossible situation. He is required to accept two opposing 'doctrines' with different and opposite aims. The one calls for loyalty to the firm and the satisfaction of customer needs. The other, owing to history and the oppression of workers by employers, calls for loyalty to the union and opposition to the firm.

That this conflict exists and that it will get worse unless something is done about it Mooney is in no doubt whatever. And yet he says, 'That there is any inherent necessity for conflict between capital and labour in industry is inconceivable in the light of the principles reiterated in this book.'[7]

His answer is to put on one side the idea of an industry as the unit and to substitute for it the individual firm. When this is done,

capital, management and labour become complementary members
of the same unit and the attainment of their own individual purposes can only be achieved through the success of the firm in
attaining its own ends – i.e. meeting the needs of its customers.
This, then, becomes the paramount aim of *all* within the firm, or at
least it is the chief job of top management to bring this about by
indoctrination. The job of the trade unions in these circumstances
is to act as advisers to top management, giving counsel as to how
the job can best be done. This, however good it might be for the
firm, would no doubt seem like an invitation to hara-kiri to a trade-
union leader!

External problems again are correctly diagnosed as revolving
around the increasing involvement of government in industry and
the pressure for some countervailing force to the enormous power
of industry itself.

## Conclusion

Mooney says in his Foreword in 1954 'It is the hope of the author
that the identification here of the principles of organization will
make some slight contribution to the development of more effective
American organizations.'[8] It is, in other words, intended to be a
practical book.

It must be admitted that it is a most difficult book to follow and
comprehend. It is almost impossible to imagine that the sections
which deal with 'principles' ever became popular reading. There
has also been the complaint that the theory of organization has
laid too much emphasis on what has happened in the church and
the army, and that this has tended to be misleading because conditions there are very different from those in industry.

There is probably some truth in the complaint. If so, it leads to
the suspicion that the illustrative material in the book has received
more attention than the much more difficult 'principles' themselves. In this chapter a very modest attempt has been made to
restate these 'principles'.

*References*

(1) Mooney, James D. *The Principles of Organization* (Harper & Row,
New York 1954), p. x.

(2) ibid., p. 1.
(3) ibid., p. 3.
(4) ibid., p. 5.
(5) ibid., p. 14.
(6) ibid., p. 25.
(7) ibid., p. 193.
(8) ibid., p. xi.

*Bibliography*
BOOKS BY J. D. MOONEY AND A. C. REILLY
*Onward Industry* (Harper & Bros, New York 1931).
*The Principles of Organization* (Harper & Bros, New York 1939); revised by Mooney, J. D. (Harper & Row, New York 1947).

# Peter F. Drucker – I
## 1955

*Introduction*

If the extent of a man's influence on the development of management thought can be assessed by the quantity of his writings and their popularity as shown by sales, no one can have exercised a greater influence than Peter Drucker. But popularity and success at the bookshops do not, of themselves, prove that new ideas and approaches have been developed. Popularity may come from good (or lucky) timing, and new ideas may languish because they are too far ahead of their time.

Drucker, one might say, 'pulled off a double'. He developed new ideas on and a new approach to management, and also did it just at the right time: a time when the old ideas and beliefs of the 'classical' management approach were being challenged, were crumbling, and a new credo was needed to take their place.

Inevitably he has his critics who maintain, chiefly, that he provides, not a theory on which to build a coherent structure, but a practical 'do-it-yourself' kit on what he considers to be good management practice. It is true he does not theorize, and he would probably regard it as a compliment to be called a pragmatist, using the Concise Oxford Dictionary definition of (one who) 'estimates any assertion by its practical bearing upon human interests'.

Space and the limitation of not going beyond the early 1960s in this book restrict the field to two of his books, the first, published in 1955, being *The Practice of Management*. At the time of writing many still consider it his major and most important work. Essentially it is a practical book, as its title implies, written for managers and managers-to-be, and not as a text-book. Skilfully it avoids the two dangers of the 'practical' book – the tendency to over-simplify, and the approach of 'Here are a score of rules – follow these and you will be a good manager.' The task of reducing it to a chapter in this book without doing it injustice is indeed a daunting one, but the alternative of leaving it out is impossible.

The book is divided into five parts and a conclusion, and these will be dealt with in the order and under the headings which Drucker himself uses.

*The Nature of Management*
This is by far the shortest section, but absolutely essential in that it sets the stage for the rest of the book. It answers in a new form the old question 'What is management?' To answer the question he re-phrases it: 'What is the role of the manager? What does he do?' And then he gives the answer: 'The manager is the dynamic, life giving element in every business. Without his leadership the "resources of production" remain resources and never become production.'[1] Management, then, is not just another job, it is the creative, driving force which makes a business, and effective management is creating conditions in which the business is successful.

With the twentieth-century development of large-scale industry and the divorce of ownership from control, management has become a 'distinct and leading group in industrial society'.[2] And so managers, being the force which creates a business out of resources, have as their first function that of ensuring economic performance. In other and older jargon this means producing the goods and services people want at the price they are prepared to pay. It also means doing this in such a way that the resources controlled by managers are increased.

As distinct from other writers who have claimed that management is a unity, Drucker divides the manager's job into three. The first is 'Managing a business', the second, 'Managing managers', and the third, 'Managing workers and work'. These are developed at length in later parts of the book. For the moment it may be enough to suggest that they correspond more or less, but not entirely, to the three levels of management, top, middle, and junior.

Stress is laid on the obvious but often neglected fact that all management takes place in the dimension of time. It is not simply a matter of here and now. Management must take decisions now whose effects must inevitably be in the future – a future which with the growing complexity of technology and living becomes ever further distant. In doing so the manager must be concerned for the present and the future survival of the business.

A suggestion often made by specialists that technology leading to automation will render managers unnecessary is brusquely brushed aside. Decentralized, flexible, autonomous management will become even more essential.

*Managing a Business*
The first aspect of managing a business brings to the fore the creative function of management. The idea from economic theory that business adapts to events and the market is roundly rejected. Management's job is to decide what the business is, what its objectives should be, and then take active, positive steps to bring them about.

Another economic idea that is given a hammering is that a business exists solely to maximize profit. Profit is important. Profit must be made if a business is to continue to exist (unless it is State-subsidized), but it is the result and proof of business behaviour and good managerial decisions.

A business itself is an 'organ', a part of society and its function, and therefore the purpose of management, is to serve society, or as Drucker succinctly puts it, 'to create a customer'.[3] This function is then divided into two (and only two) sub-functions – marketing and innovation. Marketing is the complete orientation of the whole business towards finding out what the customer really needs (he or she may not know this themselves), creating a market out of these needs, and satisfying the market by production and selling.

Innovation brings in an entirely new concept, that a business as such cannot exist in a static unchanging society. It is necessary, therefore, if business is to survive, for there to be continuous change brought about by innovation in the products (new or better ones), in the market (by the creation of new needs), and in the business itself (by finding new and better ways of running it).

To carry out these functions management must employ resources of men, money, machines and material. Converting these resources into the aims of the business is 'productivity', but existing definitions of productivity are useless. Most concern only labour, but in the complex conditions of modern industry other factors will have tremendous effect. These are the effective use of time, the product mix, the process mix, the organization structure, and the balance between the different kinds of activity which go into the business. We need, says Drucker, a new yardstick to provide objectives and to measure results which takes these factors into account. He states the need but does not satisfy it.

The argument then turns to three interrelated questions which must be asked and correctly answered by management if a business is to succeed and to continue to survive. They are 'What is our business?', 'What will it be?', and 'What should it be?' The answer to 'What is our business?' is found, not in the product or service produced but in the real need which it satisfies. It is determined by the consumer and discovered by effective market research.

Answering 'What will our business be?' shows where the business will go if management simply adapts to outside forces. Probable changes in market trends and structure, new wants which will arise, current ones which will disappear, present wants which are not being satisfied will all influence the shape of things to come.

But management must by definition be creative. It must, therefore, look at these pictures of the present and the future, decide whether or not it likes them, and answer the question 'What should our business be?' The answers to this question will provide objectives decided by management, and broadly the means to be used to achieve them.

The question of objectives leads to a major development in management thinking. Already the idea of maximizing profit as the sole or even main objective of a business has been exploded. In its place we are given, not precise objectives, as these must vary according to the individual business, but areas in which each business must define its own objectives for the future. These areas, eight in number, are:

  (i) Market standing
 (ii) Innovation
(iii) Productivity
(iv) Physical and financial resources
 (v) Profitability
(vi) Manager performance and development
(vii) Worker performance and attitudes
(viii) Public responsibility.

These are explained in considerable detail, and the reader who is interested is strongly recommended to read the original version.

More generally, the first need is to 'balance a variety of needs and goals'.[4] Not all things can be achieved at once, not all are always equally important. Obtaining the correct balance of emphasis at any one time and reviewing it in the light of change are of vital importance. Objectives are needed for all the areas where management decisions will affect the survival and prosperity of the business. They explain the purpose of the business in a few general statements and enable top management to test the statements by experience, to predict managerial behaviour, evaluate decisions as they are made, and evaluate and so improve performance.

Inevitably the question of time comes into objectives. How far ahead should they be set? Again there is no pat answer. It all depends. It depends on the business, its nature, and how far ahead it can reasonably predict, and on the objective area being considered. Some markets may change so quickly that six months is a long time, but a management development programme might well have ten years as its base. In managing a business managers must manage 'in the future', and the only thing certain about the future is its uncertainty.

How, then, should managers cope with this situation? Drucker suggests four methods. The first is to assume that fluctuations are inevitable, and therefore to assess all decisions against the worst possible conditions that might be expected. The second is to discover things that have already happened but whose real impact is still to be felt, and to take these into account. The third one is that of trend analysis, using hindsight to predict what is likely to happen in the future. None of these ways are reliable enough to be used alone, but used together they should produce the 'educated guess'. But even the best decisions for the future are likely to require adaptation when the time comes. So the fourth method is to try to ensure that tomorrow's managers will be sufficiently developed to adapt today's decisions and make them succeed in tomorrow's conditions.

*Managing Managers*

The suggestion frequently made by specialists, who presumably have an axe to grind, that the development of techniques such as operational research and integrated data-processing will render middle and junior managers unnecessary is certainly not supported by Drucker. He maintains that more managers will be required, more money will have to be invested in them, and even greater demands will be made on them.

Fundamental to the success of a business is the managing of managers. At every level except possibly the lowest each manager has under him people who manage other people. And even at the lowest level, where managers might be thought to manage only workers and work, there will be some workers whose work includes some elements of management, so at this level as well, to some extent managers will be managing 'worker-managers'.

The way in which managers are managed determines the level of performance of the management effort, and from this stems the performance of the business and the attitudes of the workers. In a very real sense its influence pervades the business at all levels and in all aspects.

In order to perform this job of managing his subordinate managers a manager at every level must:

  (i) Ensure that the vision, wills and efforts of his subordinates are directed to the goals of the business.

 (ii) Structure his subordinates' jobs so that they are able to perform effectively.

(iii) Create the right spirit in which the team element can develop.

(iv) Take steps to develop his subordinates to provide tomorrow's higher levels.

(v) Provide a sound organization structure.

The question then arises as to what means should be used to achieve these ends effectively. They must meet the overall criterion of directing everyone's effort towards the business objectives.

With specialization and departmental organization, to say nothing of individual and personal aims, this common purpose will not arise of itself. The means suggested for achieving it is management by objectives. Objectives to be reached at every level must be spelled out, agreed and accepted. They must include short- and long-range items. They must show clearly at every level the contribution to be made at that level to the achievement of the objectives of the next level above. This keying-in of one level with the next level is the essential factor in relating to overall objectives.

On the question of the actual determination of objectives Drucker goes along with McGregor (*see* Chapter 16) in implying that managers will make a real effort to attain objectives to which they feel committed. The way, therefore, to set objectives is for each manager to set his own, thereby obtaining commitment. But these 'self-determined' objectives must show the contribution the manager is to make towards the objectives of his 'boss'. The process of determination must include two-way communication between them, and the final agreement of the 'boss' to the objectives set up.

But a knowledge of objectives is only half the battle. Self-determination must be backed up by self-control if it is to be effective. Contrary to the usual practice of feeding back information about results to a superior, who can then 'control' the subordinate responsible for the results, the information, says Drucker, must be fed *direct* to the subordinate. In this way, having become committed to attaining his objectives and getting information on his progress direct, the subordinate manager will exercise self-control rather than, as often happens, finding a dozen 'good' reasons why he cannot reach his objectives.

By these means, says Drucker, the business will get what it needs: '. . . a principle of management that will give full scope to individual strength and responsibility, and at the same time give common direction of vision and effort, establish team work and harmonise the goals of the individual with the common weal'.[5]

Within this framework of management by objectives and self-control, 'managers must manage'. To do this their jobs must be as wide as possible, should involve the maximum challenge, the maximum responsibility and the maximum recognizable contribution. Where, as is happening to an ever greater extent, the job becomes too big for one individual, it must be organized on a team basis, but with definite roles for each individual in the team.

The idea of span of control as the limiting factor is discarded. As managers are self-directing and self-controlling, detailed supervision by a senior manager becomes unnecessary. The content of a manager's job should be determined from the bottom up. The vitally important manager is the one at the lowest level responsible for managing worker and work. His job is to achieve the final results. At each level above this, the job of the manager becomes that of helping his subordinates to do their job effectively and of doing for them the things they cannot do for themselves. This leads to the necessity for vision upwards to see and comprehend overall objectives, and for responsibility downwards as a duty of help, not of control and supervision.

Effectively managing managers, however, needs more than this. It needs what Drucker calls 'the Spirit of the Organization'. Only this can bring forth the necessary effort, the dedication to the job, to achieve the best and not a safe mediocrity. It must be such that it confirms people's strengths, recognizes their achievements and helps their inevitable weaknesses. It must make people, workers as well as managers, grow to the limit of their capacity. It must have a moral basis which shows in actions rather than preaching. Of all aspects of management it is the one which must start right at the top and spread its influence downwards.

But although the spirit shows itself in the practices of management it must be based on a philosophy or what Brech in *The Principles and Practice of Management* called 'the mode of thought'.

Drucker implies that the keystones of this philosophy should be morality and integrity.

So far as the practices themselves are concerned they must include:

(i) Sincere, objective appraisal of performance.

(ii) Financial rewards which are directly related to performance in relation to overall objectives. These should include long-term objectives, which may prejudice the achievement of the short-term ones as usually measured.

(iii) Management jobs which, at any level, can be seen as satisfying in themselves and not just as rungs on a ladder.

(iv) Non-financial rewards related to prestige and pride.

(v) A rational promotion system based on performance, but which is not exclusively internal.

Finally, how does the question of the indefinable 'spirit of the organization' equate with the even more indefinable concept of leadership? Drucker is almost dogmatic about leadership. He says: 'But leadership cannot be created or promoted. It cannot be taught or learned.'[6] He maintains that the position is one where management by its actions and the 'spirit' it creates can provide the conditions and the practices in which potential leaders can grow and develop or in which they can be stifled. An absolutely essential part of managing managers effectively is to see that they are given the opportunity to develop into leaders.

Moving from the development of the next generation of leaders to the one manager who presumably should have arrived – the President or Managing Director – Drucker takes the mightiest of swipes at classical organization theory. Classical theory insists on unity of command, unity of control, on one supreme boss. Drucker will have none of it. Formally there may be only one man who holds the title of Managing Director, but his actual job is so big that it must be performed by a team effort. First the job must be clearly defined, then such parts of it as can be, should be delegated. The rest should be shared by a team of two or three who can consistently act together as equals, although formally and on the organization chart they are not equals.

Although this is admitted to be heresy it is put forward as the only way to manage the modern large business effectively. The alternative is two or three layers of 'top management' between the chief executive and the operating managers. This is too cumbersome and indirect to work properly.

There may be other answers still to be found, but there can be no doubt that here Drucker has put his finger on the biggest sore spot of modern management practice. How does one reconcile the marketing, technological, financial and development requirements for a very large organization with the managerial requirements for a unit which is not too big to manage?

Below the top the need is for more and more managers who can handle a greater range of ever more complex problems, techniques and relationships. To meet this need developing managers becomes an essential activity. This must be more than just a planned promotion scheme. In general it must embrace developing the management team as a whole and preparing for tomorrow's problems instead of today's. It must develop in all managers a view of the business as a whole. It must present a challenge, a chance to grow and to be judged on results, not promise.

But how is this to be achieved? It must be planned as a deliberate activity. Federal decentralization, that is, organization in smaller self-controlling units, will help by providing managerial jobs with greater breadth. This is one aspect of the total problem, which is to provide situations in which managers can *develop themselves*. Essentially this is a job for each level of manager, who must see that those under him are placed in positions where they can make the greatest contribution they are capable of, and that guidance and help is given to them to overcome their weaknesses. Primarily it is a question of knowing, using, and building on the man's strengths. Precise methods suggested are deliberate transfer to another job, project work, and formal training for specific needs.

## The Structure of Management

With the emphasis of the book being on the practice of management it might perhaps seem a little strange to come across a section on structure or organization. However, practice cannot take place in a vacuum; it must be within an organization, and its nature and structure will vitally influence the way in which practice is carried on. Essentially the section deals with this relationship between structure and practice.

The question for any business and therefore for its management is 'What kind of a structure does it need to perform its job effectively?' The answer to this is found by asking three other questions:
  (i) What activities are necessary to achieve the purposes of the business?
  (ii) What decisions will have to be made?
  (iii) What relationships between the people forming the structure are necessary?

When genuine realistic answers, and not theoretical generalizations, have been found to these questions the structure of organization can be built. There are three criteria that the structure should meet. To the greatest extent possible it must design managerial jobs so that they can be judged on business performance and not on the standards of bureaucracy. Perhaps as a necessary corollary to this there must be the minimum number of levels of management. Finally at all levels managerial jobs must be designed to train and test tomorrow's managers.

In contrast to formal organization theory Drucker puts forward only two basic principles for organization structure – federal decentralization and functional decentralization. Either way the emphasis is on achieving the maximum responsibility and accountability at the lowest possible levels.

Federal decentralization organizes the business into separate self-contained product divisions, each virtually complete in itself except perhaps for centralized specialist services, which it can ask for help when required. The two essentials of a federally decentralized unit are that it must have a market of its own, which may be the result of product or geography, and that it must contribute its own directly ascertainable profit to the business as a whole.

If federal decentralization is to function effectively it must follow certain rules:
  (i) Both the decentralized units and the centre must be strong.

(ii) The function of the centre is to set objectives for the business as a whole which will provide clear guidance to the units as to what is required of them.

(iii) The units must be controlled by measurement and reporting of results, not by detailed personal supervision from the centre.

(iv) The units must be large enough to support the management structure they need to perform effectively.

(v) Each unit must have potential for further growth.

(vi) The management job in the unit must provide enough scope and challenge.

(vii) Units must not be dependent on each other.

The limit for federal decentralization is the point at which a unit ceases to 'make a profit' and only 'contributes to the profit'. At that point and below, functional decentralization must take over.

The principle of functional decentralization bears some resemblance to classical theories of organization, although Drucker takes great care to point out the differences between his concept of it and the traditional one. All organizations must come to this eventually when the unit is so sub-divided that it can no longer be regarded as a separate business unit. At this point the unit specializes in some aspect of the total business, whether it be marketing, or production, or development, and so on. Each function will be homogeneous in that it relates to a particular aspect, but within that aspect there will be a very wide variety of skills.

While organization on this principle is necessary it possesses very great disadvantages. First and foremost is the danger of the specialist viewpoint, which regards its own function as all-important and loses sight of the business as a whole. Secondly, its objectives are those of specialist performance, with the tendency to consider professional standards rather than business success as the chief factor. Thirdly, it tends to produce level upon level of management as the unit gets larger.

To cope satisfactorily with these problems the functional unit should deal as nearly as possible with a complete product; practise the maximum of decentralization within itself; co-operate actively with other functions which require joint action, and have at its head a manager who is directly responsible to the general manager of a federal unit.

Finally, the need for a good structure which helps rather than hinders business performance is stressed once more. The signs of a poor structure are clearly spelled out – too many levels of management, poor and confused objectives, pressure for people to 'help' managers to do their job, a need to set up special means of co-ordination and communication, insistence on 'going through the channels', and a lop-sided management age-structure, with staff either all too old or all too young. As Drucker says, a good organization structure, which would show none of these faults, is all too rare.

As if there were not enough problems in getting the structure right at any one time there will be, if the business is developing as it should, the further problem of changing and adapting the organization to meet the needs of changes in size. Drucker finds four sizes of business, each of which presents its own problems, the small, the fair-sized, the large and the too large. And somewhere in between each will be the growing business.

Size is defined not in terms of numbers of employees, but by the amount and quality of management ability required. Two main areas of difficulty arise. The first is where the small business starts to grow into the fair-sized one. Family ownership, the impossibility at that size of affording competent management, the difficulty of finding time to get away from detail to sit back and plan, and a more or less inevitable narrowness of outlook are suggested as the main problems. To them should probably be added another – the very human danger that the man who has built and run a small business single-handed will find it almost impossible to learn to delegate as the business grows.

The large business has its problems, too: chiefly those of adequately defining the top man's job and, as suggested earlier, making it a team effort and keeping managers on their toes so that they do not become smug and self-satisfied. But it is with the very big business that the most difficult, and for today, the most vital problems arise. Very large businesses may be necessary from a

61

technological, marketing, financial or service-facilities point of view, but they are showing every sign of becoming unmanageable. Difficulties of layer upon layer of management make communication to and from the top difficult, if not impossible. Personal identification with the very large business loses its reality. Sectional and group interests and aims interfere with business aims. Functional service staffs become empires in their own right. The very large business is often so diversified that it gets into areas where its technical competence is just not adequate to the type and variety of problems involved, or the objectives of one section compete with those of another. The problems are there in plenty for all who will to see. Drucker perhaps over-simplifies his answer to them: structure the manager's job correctly and use federal decentralization.

## The Management of Worker and Work

The third aspect of the manager's job, that of managing the worker and work, provides a cogent case for a retreat from the blind alley into which 'scientific management' has led us and for striking out on a new path. In fact, the new path is probably more scientific in that it takes into account the total situation including the worker himself instead of assuming as 'scientific management' has tended to do, that the worker is simply a flexible and adaptable tool.

Two main assumptions seem to underlie the whole approach. The first is that the nature of work itself on the shop floor or at the office desk is changing rapidly, from being labour-intensive to being brain-intensive. While many people on the purely routine work of mass production, or the qualified shop-assistant who now works in a self-service store, would challenge this assumption, it is undoubtedly true. The implication of this is obvious. As the trend develops and becomes more widespread workers must increasingly become people with brains which they can use instead of people with brawn and nothing more to offer.

The second assumption is in line with psycho-sociological theories and is one which many managers may find difficult to accept.

No matter what kind of work men do, whether they are skilled

or unskilled production workers or salaried clerks, professionals
or rank and file, they are basically alike. There are, indeed, differences between workers according to kind of work, age, sex,
education – but basically they are always human beings with
human needs and motivations.[7]

The first job in managing workers, then, is to ensure that a
worker is not hired as a pair of hands but that he is fully employed
as a whole man, with all his capacity and talents used to the full and
his potential developed to the limit. In the same way as for developing managers, this is not something that can be thrust upon people;
it can be done only by management providing the situation in
which the worker can and wants to develop himself.

To do this managing work becomes a matter of adapting and
organizing it so that it will best use the resources and limitations of
the worker, including his qualities of being able 'to co-ordinate, to
integrate, to judge and to imagine'.[8] But also work must be adapted
to meet the personal, psychological and sociological needs of the
individual. A machine can be made to work. A human being cannot,
once the fear of the sack and the workhouse has been removed.
Still less can he be made to work well. This he must do willingly.

These aims will not be achieved by a goody-goody soft-footed
approach, nor by welfare schemes, nor by soft-hearted human-
relations approaches. They will be the result of hard-headed
logical approaches to the total situation, including the human
aspects. They result in the firm making demands on the worker,
demands for willing dedication, for loyalty, for *esprit de corps*, for
active responsibility, for willingness to accept change and to accept
profit as the logical necessity for business survival and not as a
'dirty' word.

The bargain, however, is not one-sided. The worker, too, has a
right to make demands on the firm, demands to be treated as an
individual and not as a cog in the machine, for justice and fair
treatment, for a job which is meaningful and a challenge, for status,
and for management which is efficient, knows what it is doing, and
why.

Two aspects of managing the worker come in for somewhat

caustic criticism. Personnel management's claim to be a major function of a business is dismissed out of hand. It has nothing to do with managing personnel, which should be done by line management, and is simply a collection of necessary but routine chores which have to be done. The 'human relations' approach, which probably achieved its highest popularity in the late 1950s, gets almost equally short shrift. By its concentration on aspects which have nothing to do with the work itself and its ignoring of the economic aspect it, too, is considered to miss the point. Both approaches do not appreciate that man, if he is to work effectively, needs positive motivation of as wide and varied a kind as possible.

In a slightly different way the development of the 'scientific management' approach of Taylor and Gilbreth has led us astray. By its insistence that the improvement of work methods must be synonymous with reducing the job to its smallest possible size and variety, and that planning and responsibility must be separated from doing, it has removed two of the major natural incentives to work.

The challenge now lies with line management so to manage worker and work that the worker voluntarily wants to commit himself to the work. To do this management must organize the work. The first approach to this is to organize the worker out of the worst kinds of routine 'one-man one-job' work. This soul-destroying and man-destroying work must be replaced by automatic processes. For work which men must still do the first step is to use scientific method to analyse and improve the method, the parts of the job and the sequence of operations. The second step is to put the parts together to make an integrated meaningful job, which will do a number of things:

   (i) Employ skill and ability to the maximum.

   (ii) Present a challenge.

   (iii) Restore responsibility to the worker.

   (iv) Have a recognizable end-product.

   (v) Depend on the speed and rhythm of the man himself, not on that of a machine, or of the man who precedes or follows him.

The actual practice of this, or rather lack of it when Drucker was writing (1960) led him to suggest that we did not then know very much about management on a large scale. More than ten years later, when this book was being written, apart from a few significant experiments, practice has not progressed very far.

Having correctly 'engineered' or structured the job of the worker, the manager must demand peak performance from the worker. Correct job structure will help to make this demand possible, but more is needed. The worker must be carefully matched to the job and any misfits transferred or removed. High standards of performance must be demanded, with the acceptance of them by the worker and the expectation that they will be met. Information on progress towards these standards must be fed direct to the worker so that he can exercise self-control rather than be controlled 'from above'. The worker must be given the chance to participate in management decisions which affect him – only thus can he develop a managerial viewpoint.

Two other major points remain if management is going to demand and get peak performance from the worker. The first is that a manager cannot demand high standards unless the standards he sets for himself are at least equally high. Materials, tools, organization, leadership, communication and all the other aspects of the management process must leave nothing to be desired in helping the worker to do his job to the limit of his capacity.

Secondly, work, however interesting, however inducing of self-commitment, is for the worker the means of earning a livelihood. More money will only make people work harder if they want to do so, but too little money in absolute or relative terms will make peak performance impossible. A livelihood, too, if it is to mean anything must be reasonably secure. Somehow, and the 'how' seems still to be worked out, management must learn how to maintain wages and employment.

### What it means to be a Manager

In Part V Drucker summarizes and extends what has gone before. The manager's job is to create 'a true whole that is larger than the sum of its parts'.[9] To do this he makes the most of resources and strengths, especially human ones, and neutralizes weaknesses.

He balances the three aspects of managing a business, managing managers and managing worker and work. He balances the present against the immediate and the long-range future. He must see that the business prospers *and* survives.

Analytically the manager's job has five basic operations:

(i) To set objectives and goals for each area of his work. To plan how to reach those goals.

(ii) To organize work. To analyse, divide and allocate work to groups and individuals.

(iii) To motivate and communicate. To create a team, to provide incentives of the right kind and the information which people need.

(iv) To measure results. To check against plans and see that each man knows how he is doing and where he fits in.

(v) To develop people. Or better, to manage them in a way which enables them to develop themselves.


In almost all that he does a manager must make decisions. A number of variations of the decision-making process have been put forward. Drucker has his own version.

(i) Define the problem. Analyse it into symptoms and causes, and locate the 'critical factor'.

(ii) Determine the conditions for its solution, the need to meet objectives and the balance between present and future.

(iii) Analyse the problem; find the facts necessary to a solution and capable of being obtained. Know where facts stop and assumptions begin.

(iv) Develop alternative solutions, as many as possible including 'do nothing'.

(v) Choose between solutions using as criteria for choice, risk, economy of effort, timing, and limitation of resources.

(vi) Make the solution effective.


Looking ahead, the future for managers is one of greater responsibilities and greater demands being made on them, not, as some specialists would have us believe, a diminishing role. Routine, tactical decisions may well be taken away from the manager and computerized, but more and more at all levels he will become involved in the far more important, long-term, strategic decisions.

To meet the challenge the manager of tomorrow must be doubly trained. First he must have training in the principles and techniques of his craft and in scientific method. Later he will need training in the practice of his craft by experience, example, and the use of management methods themselves. Learning for the manager must be a continuous process of adaptation to ever-changing conditions, where he himself must be the prime agent in creating the changes. But above all the manager of the future must learn the ethics of his craft. He must learn and practice integrity as the central core of the managerial job. Finally the manager must develop a multiple sense of responsibility to society in its many aspects.

Managers have power, over people at work, over society as customers, and over society as the general human background. With the size and scope of modern business that power is tremendous, too much so for society to allow it to be used solely for the self-interest of the business and its shareholders. Somehow management must walk the tightrope which meets both the needs of the business and the emerging needs of society. We must end with two quotations which clearly state the problem.

The first responsibility which management owes to the enterprise in respect to public opinion, policy and law is to consider such demands made by society on the enterprise (or likely to be made within the near future) as may affect the attainment of its business objectives. It is management's job to find a way to convert these demands from threats to, or restrictions on, the enterprise's freedom of action into opportunities for sound growth, or at least to satisfy them with the least damage to the enterprise.[10]

But what is most important is that management realise that it must consider the impact of every business policy and every business action upon society. It has to consider whether the action is likely to promote the public good, to advance the basic beliefs of our society, to contribute to its stability, strength and harmony.[11]


## Conclusion

It seems evident that Drucker has produced here a major work with a new approach. If, as is usual, there is more than a ten-year lag between new thinking and its application in practice then these new ideas should now be beginning to make their mark.

In the United States it is probable that this is the case. In other countries the position is more complicated. The book was written by an American, presumably for American businessmen and students in the first place. And here lies the real difficulty. Although the whole of Western industrial civilization is moving rapidly towards internationalism, in each country it must of necessity be based on the traditions, history and folk-lore of that country.

Between other countries and the United States there are significant differences, differences in trade-union practice, in workers' attitudes, even in the position and recognition of the industrial manager in society, to name but a few. The straightforward, unadulterated transfer of management practices and ideas from America to Britain, for example, has over the past decade produced some results which were not entirely happy.

Drucker says that the first two essentials in decision-making are to ask the right questions and to find out the limiting factors in the situation. It is highly probable that he himself would say that the first thing before applying his ideas would be to ask the questions 'How far can these ideas be applied or adapted elsewhere?' and 'What are the limiting factors built into the inheritance from the past?'

Whether other countries should move towards a state where American philosophies and standards in management should be adopted is another question. For the moment generally they are not, and the vital problem is how to adapt and apply his ideas effectively to the current situation. There is always room for improvement in management, and careful thought about and judicious adaptation of Drucker's ideas on practice could do much to bring it about.

*References*

(1) Drucker, Peter F. *The Practice of Management* (Heinemann, London 1955), p. 1.
  (2) ibid., p. 1.
  (3) ibid., p. 29.
  (4) ibid., p. 52.
  (5) ibid., p. 117.
  (6) ibid., p. 137.
  (7) ibid., p. 226.
  (8) ibid., p. 232.
  (9) ibid., p. 301.
(10) ibid., p. 339.
(11) ibid., p. 343.

# 6

## Peter F. Drucker – II
## 1964

*Introduction*

Drucker's book *Managing for Results* is strictly outside the time-span of this book. It is, however, complementary to and an extension of *The Practice of Management*, and, as such, is of sufficiently outstanding importance to be included.

Like the earlier book it is strictly practical. Nowhere are there any 'high-faluting theories', unless we accept that 'theory is the distillation of the best practice'. By substituting the word 'illustration' for 'distillation' we have a perfect description of the book.

In a sense it is narrower in scope than *The Practice of Management* in that it is limited to the top-level overall management of a business. 'It deals with the economic task that any business has to discharge for economic performance and economic results.'[1] On this basis it expands into every corner of the overall direction and control of a business. Modestly Drucker says:

This book lays little claim to originality or profundity. But it is, to my knowledge, the first attempt at an organized presentation of the economic tasks of the business executive and the first halting step towards a discipline of economic performance in business enterprise.[2]

The book deals with the three main aspects of running a business:
 (i) analysis and understanding of results
 (ii) opportunities and decisions
(iii) purposeful performance.

Throughout the method is that of precept and example. The precepts are often short but to the point. The examples are often longer, but they always illustrate and drive home the point that is being made.

For our purposes only the precepts will be dealt with, and this will be done, of necessity, briefly. For a proper and full understanding of the material the reader must go back to the original. If he is, or is likely to be, in the top echelons of management (which includes being the owner of a one-man business) he will find the result many times worth the effort.

## Results – Analysis and Understanding
If there is one thing above all others that can truthfully be said about Drucker it is that he has the courage of his convictions. He is never afraid to throw overboard established conventions and practices when he thinks he has something better to offer. Nowhere is this more true than in this section, where the recognized result areas, and criteria of management and cost-accounting and budgetary control, are discarded one after the other as being at least irrelevant, if not positively misleading.

If managers spend all their time dealing with the crises of today, and that not very effectively because they know the same crises will happen again tomorrow and the next day, it is because they spend their time doing the wrong things. What the right ones may be will depend on the business and the circumstances, so no 'rules' can be laid down. These the manager must find out for himself, but they should be based on generalizations and conclusions which apply to all businesses. These he summarizes as

1. 'Neither results nor resources exist inside the business. Both exist outside.'[3]
2. 'Results are obtained by exploiting opportunities, not by solving problems.'[4]
3. 'Resources, to produce results, must be allocated to opportunities.'[5]
4. 'Economic results are earned only by leadership.'[6]
5. 'Any leadership position is transitory and likely to be short-lived.'[7]

6. 'What exists is getting old.'[8]
7. 'What exists is likely to be misallocated.'[9]
8. 'Concentration is the key to real economic results.'[10]

Accepting these points it then becomes necessary to analyse the current results of the business to see how far, if at all, they are being followed.

First the 'result areas' must be investigated. In the large business these will start with the 'divisions' referred to in *The Practice of Management*. For all business they will include products and product lines, markets and distribution channels. Basically the economic results will depend on factors outside the business – the impact of the products and distribution methods on the market and the market's response to that impact. These three essential factors of product, market and distribution must be analysed in as much detail as possible to find the *real* answers. These may often take the form of doubts, uncertainties and differences. In fact, Drucker would have it that if they are not they are probably the wrong answers.

Going into detail, the analysis of a product range is used to illustrate what are called 'Revenues, Resources and Products'. This uses the figures of accounting, often divided up in non-traditional ways, and a new concept of 'transactions'.

Four basic assumptions are used to underpin the analysis.

Revenue money and cost money are not necessarily one stream. Business phenonema follow the normal distribution of social events in which 90% of effects follow from the first 10% of the causes and vice versa.

Revenues are therefore proportionate to volume, with the bulk of the volume and of the corresponding revenues produced by a small fraction of the product numbers (markets, customers etc.)

Costs are therefore proportionate to transactions with the bulk of the costs attributable to the large number – 90% perhaps – of the transactions that produce only a small fraction of revenues.[11]

With these assumptions in mind, normal cost-accounting is ruled out as a guide because its methods do not show clearly the difference between the relatively small number of transactions that produce large revenue (and profits) and the relatively large number that produce small revenues, large costs (and losses). A further point is that fixed costs which bear no relation to volume of work and production must be left out of the calculations. A new analysis which bases costs and revenues on transactions, whatever the appropriate unit for a transaction may be, is therefore required.

But to have a product is not enough. In some form, not necessarily or even advisedly in all, the product must have leadership qualities in the market. This, too, needs analysis to find out in what way, if any, it does possess the edge over competitors, and whether it is the right way. And leadership arises when the product better fits some real need of the customer and the customer accepts this as a fact. It has nothing to do with the manufacturer's own opinion of the product, but it has a great deal to do with differentiation of the product in some way which gives it a specific appeal to customers.

The one thing which makes Drucker's analysis different from the ordinary concept of market researching a product is that it must be done for all the products of the business at the same time, so that we get not only facts but also a comparison of facts. This will show up the leaders, the also-rans, the marginal products, and the losers. Once the manager knows the real answers to the enquiries given so far he will at least be on the right road, provided he uses what he knows.

The first step in using this information is the correct allocation of the vital, key resources of the business. The key resources are given as knowledge and money. Knowledge is held by trained people, in sales, buying, technology and management. These resources, which are the ones capable of being moved and re-allocated from one result area to another, are the ones which must be 'managed' and whose management will determine results. Again the formula crops up – the 10 per cent of resources which are the key ones produce 90 per cent of the results.

The determination of the vital areas on which to concentrate key resources depends on the classification of products. Drucker's version[12] is:

1. Today's breadwinners
2. Tomorrow's breadwinners
3. Productive specialities
4. Development products
5. Failures
6. Yesterday's breadwinners
7. Repair jobs
8. Unnecessary specialities
9. Unjustified specialities
10. Investments in managerial ego
11. Cinderellas (or sleepers).

The allocation of key resources should be mainly to those products in the above list which will show worthwhile results. These are tomorrow's breadwinners; development products; repair jobs for one try only, and then only provided they really qualify as repair jobs; unnecessary specialities if they have the potential to be combined into a new major product, perhaps with a new market; and cinderellas which, given a chance, can develop into something worth-while.

Today's breadwinners are at or close to their peak, and any excessive allocation of resources to them should be cut back. At most their cost burden should be no greater than their share in revenues. Productive specialities should have a low cost burden, and failures should be eliminated, as should unjustified specialities and investments in managerial ego. Yesterday's breadwinners should be allowed to die, and the sooner the better. Any attempt to keep them going is only a waste of resources.

But change is inevitable and products move from one category to another, so a once-for-all analysis is not enough. A periodic review is required to assess changes in the situation and to re-direct resources to match the developing pattern. Inherent in all this is the fairly new and unfamiliar concept of the life-cycle of a product.

The use of resources necessarily involves the incurring of costs, so they, too, must be identified and controlled. Drucker is unhappy about the traditional accounting and costing methods and even more so about the traditional 'across the board' cost-cutting exercise by which companies try to keep costs under control. Again he produces the formula that 90 per cent of the costs are incurred by 10 per cent of the activities. Costs, like products, require different treatment according to their nature. Simply cutting back costs is seldom effective; the real answer is to find unnecessary activities and to cut them and their costs out altogether. A further very important point to watch is the effect on the business as a whole. It is worse than useless to save £5,000 in one department if the result is only to increase costs by £5,000 or more somewhere else. Cost reviews must go outside the business to find the total cost of what the customer buys, so they must include the analysis of distribution channel costs. Finally, costs must be analysed not as isolated items but in terms of cost centres, which create meaningful wholes and relate together those costs that logically belong together, whatever the accounting system may say. Again, within a cost centre a few major items will account for the bulk of the costs, and it is those items which need attention so that worthwhile savings can be made.

Cost categories are productive costs, support costs, policing costs, and waste. Productive costs relate to activities directed to supplying customers' needs. Support costs are indirectly necessary, as the activities enable productive activities to carry on. Policing costs come from preventing the wrong things from happening. This leaves waste as all forms of unnecessary activity. Support costs should be kept to the minimum required to get by; policing costs should always be checked to see that they are not more than the risks of not policing; waste must be ruthlessly cut out.

The book then returns to a major theme of *The Practice of Management* under the heading 'The Customer is the Business'. In essence it restates the theory of the marketing approach, that who the customer is and what the customer really wants constitutes the business, and that this information is not known until it is deliberately searched for.

Knowledge has already been referred to as a key resource, and

*The Work Approach*

the idea is expanded around the statement that 'Knowledge is the Business'. In business, knowledge by itself and for its own sake is useless. It is only when it is applied to produce results which meet specific customer needs better than other businesses can do that it becomes valuable. According to the differing needs which businesses meet, so do they require differing forms of knowledge. Or, to put it the other way round, according to the business's strength in knowledge areas so should it see that the markets supplied make the greatest use of that strength. This means that the business must analyse its available knowledge and acquire that which it needs and does not possess.

In summary, then, if top-line management is to manage effectively it must know what its business is by analysing
  (i) Results, revenues and resources
 (ii) Cost centres and cost structure
(iii) The market
(iv) Its knowledge areas.

The analyses of the first two should be tentative, and should be reviewed in the light of the analyses of the last two when these have been made. From there the next step is to decide what the business should be doing, which leads into Part II of the book.

*Focus on Opportunity*
For Drucker it seems to be a foregone conclusion that if management really carries out the analysis given above it 'always shows it [the business] to be in a worse disrepair than anyone expected'.[13] In other words everyone's preconceived notions about the business will be proved to be wrong.

Assuming that a decision is made to improve matters, there are three possible alternatives:
  (i) Start with an idea of the 'ideal' business.
 (ii) Concentrate available resources on the most likely opportunities.
(iii) Maximize resources so that they have the greatest impact.

The common factors in all three are that they build on strength and search for opportunities. Ideally all three will be merged into a common multi-pronged approach. Difficulties and problems must, of course, be overcome (policing activities must go on), but they must use the minimum of resources, while the maximum is applied to exploiting or creating opportunity.

From consideration of ideals comes the direction which the business must take and the targets it must reach. Targets are only useful if they are linked to time, and management must decide what, in its business, is the 'present', the 'short-term future' and the 'long-term future'.

Using the analysis of the previous section gives three areas for targets: the great opportunity; the line or lines which must be quickly and deliberately abandoned; and the rest – the 'also rans'. The opportunities are tomorrow's breadwinners, development work for the breadwinners of the day after tomorrow, new know-ledge, new channels of distribution and their application, and support costs, policing costs and waste which can be cut out or cut back with significant results. The 'also rans' should be kept going, but with the minimum necessary resources.

Opportunities for development may be of two kinds. The first is replacement of, or minor alterations to, existing products or methods which improve their prospects considerably. The second is innova-tion, or the relatively rare completely new development which, when it happens, provides the greatest of all opportunities. Some-what paradoxically, after the point has been made of 'building on strength' we are told that 'Dangers and weaknesses indicate where to look for business potential.'[14] Restraints, imbalances, and fears are the dangers and weaknesses, and if these can be tackled properly and turned into strengths they will provide opportunities.

Too often managers assume that the trouble is inherent, that they have had it so long that there is nothing that can be done about it except to live with it. This is, of course, completely the wrong attitude. Something – the right thing – must be done about it, but it needs a very open and enquiring mind, which is prepared to challenge its most cherished illusions. The most typical troubles lie in the productive process and in the economics of the industry and of the market. But even if it were possible to grasp all opportunities, to convert all problems and weaknesses to strengths, the business could never be in a perfect state of balance. It is itself a dynamic, changing organism in a dynamic, changing world. It must, therefore, be constantly in a state of transition, moving from one imperfect equilibrium to another, better one hopes, but still imperfect. This is not to say that much imbalance cannot and should not be avoided. Wherever it can be dealt with and put right it should be.

One major difficulty which gets special mention is the business which is wrong in size. Perhaps it is too small as a whole to support the necessary volume of resources needed for some important aspect of its work. Or perhaps it is too big and too 'mixed up' to be properly manageable. Normal growth for the too-small business may be too slow, so merger or acquisition is the answer. If it is too big the parts that do not 'fit' should be hived off and sold.

However, in spite of all the targets, objectives, and planning, the one certain thing is the uncertainty of the future. One ray of hope lies in spotting the things which have *already happened* and whose future effects can be anticipated, for example changes in population or in scientific ideas. The second is that '. . . precisely because the future is going to be different and cannot be predicted, it is possible to make the unexpected and the unpredicted come to pass'.[15]

Making the future happen involves having the new idea today on which it may be possible to build a real business tomorrow. As Drucker says in *The Practice of Management*, managers take decisions today for tomorrow's results, but it will be up to tomorrow's managers to make those decisions work. And the longer the time-span of business becomes the truer this statement becomes. But if an idea today is to make a business tomorrow, it must be economically valid, that is, it must be directed at a market; it must attract and hold personal commitment by the management; it must be reviewed as it develops.

Many businesses can survive for some time even if they do nothing about the future. But the future always comes, and the most important task of management is to accept the responsibility for making the future happen. It involves risks, but it is better than the risk of being overtaken by a future for which one is unprepared.

*A Programme for Performance*

This, the last part of the book, is by far the shortest, but the most crucial and the most concentrated. It converts the ideas of the first two parts into precepts for practice. It is a blueprint for the title of the book, for managing for results – for successful results.

Performance depends first and foremost on the correct decisions being taken by management. The decisions required result from the analysis of the business, and they lead to tasks and work assignments for individuals. These tasks and assignments must be designed to show measurable results. Separate piecemeal decisions are not enough, and may even lead to a worse situation. They must create and at the same time be geared to a 'unified *programme for performance*'.[16] This programme must take into account not only the needs of the present but also those of the future. Unless care is taken to integrate the two they may conflict, and, as there is only one set of resources to deal with both aspects, one may be achieved at the expense of the other.

To do this means taking key decisions in certain areas so as to make the integration. The first of the key decisions is on 'The idea of the business'.[17] This is a definition of the business, what it is, and what it exists for. It must be based on the performance of the business, the customer needs it must satisfy, or the specific knowledge it must use to do so. It must be broad enough to allow for growth and change, but not so broad as to lead to lack of definition and inability to concentrate. It must be precise enough to lead to action, which woolly generalities will not. It must show clearly where excellence is required and where the business is to be a leader and not an also-ran.

The second key decision follows from the first. In what areas must excellence be attained, must the efforts of the business be concentrated ? Again, while the standards laid down must allow for change, they must also be precise enough to give concentration, to lead to action and to show who is to be promoted where.

The third is not one but a series of decisions. It consists of those decisions which set up priorities and, equally important, which say what must be left out. No business ever has enough resources to do everything which might be possible, and the rejection of those things which the business will not do is vital if sufficient concentration is to be given to the things which it does do.

Every business must make decisions in these three key areas. The question is whether they are made at random, by accident or default and without a coherent pattern, or whether they are taken deliberately to produce a consistent pattern as a guide to the operation of the business. Long-term success can only come from the second way. The key decisions give a base, a series of objectives, a policy as guides to operation. In themselves they do not say specifically what has to be done or how. A further series of decisions is needed to define the strategy of the business – the broad lines of approach by which it is hoped the objectives will be reached.

Inevitably there will be different, alternative ways of achieving the same ends. Management must therefore decide on

  ' (i) Opportunities and risks
  (ii) Scope, structure and specialization
  (iii) Building or buying increased resources
  (iv) Organization structure.

Between them these decisions set the strategy, the broad plan of how the business will work. Again, these decisions should be taken deliberately so as to ensure conformity between them.

Opportunities are graded as additive, complementary, and breakthrough. Additive opportunities merely use existing resources more effectively. If they are to be taken they must not involve either much risk or the use of resources which could be used for the other two. Complementary opportunities provide something new which should increase the size and scope of the business. They involve some new knowledge area and considerable change in the business. They carry a good deal of risk. To avail itself of them management must be sure that it can face the dislocation of acquiring and incorporating considerable new resources. The breakthrough opportunity, if accepted, will fundamentally change the entire business. The risks, if it is a genuine breakthrough, will be very great and the potential returns must be very great also if it is to be followed up. When the genuine breakthrough presents itself it must be grasped if the business is to survive.

Decision-making in a state of uncertainty involves risks, and these are classified according to degree. First there are those which are built into the nature of the business, and must be accepted. Then there are risks which one can afford to take, which implies that the possible gains are worth the risk and if things go wrong the losses are expected to be no greater than the business can afford. Where the possible loss is such that it would cripple the business the risk is one that the business cannot afford to take. Finally, and the most important when it arises, there is the risk one cannot afford *not* to take. This will often relate to the breakthrough opportunity. If the business takes it and makes good the rewards will be very high. If it does not take it, or if it does and fails, then it must lose either way.

What is needed, then, is a careful appraisal of opportunities and risks, reviewing them all at once, to select those which suit the business and its objectives and which provide a balance between immediate and long-term goals.

On the face of it Drucker then states the paradox that the business must both specialize and diversify. The contradiction is more apparent than real because he is using 'diversify' in a somewhat restricted sense. As a base from which to work the business must have specialized knowledge, a product line unique in some way, and a specific market. But, while not going outside this field, it must have enough scope to manoeuvre and find sufficient opportunities to employ its resources to the full.

Still within the field of strategy, there is the question of growth. Growth in a business takes time, and time may be the one thing the business cannot afford. Strategic decisions must therefore be taken as to whether to grow slowly and naturally or whether to achieve growth by takeover or merger. Another reason for combining with other businesses is to obtain resources which are needed but the business does not adequately possess.

Finally, decisions on organization structure must ensure that it is suitable to the objectives and strategies and that it highlights the really important areas (the 10 per cent) which determine results. As with other decisions, these must be reviewed regularly in the light of the changing situation.

It is a common experience of life that 'The best laid schemes o' mice an' men gang aft a-gley.' Business objectives and strategies are no exception. For effective results they must be converted into effective action by many people. To do this three things are essential. The programme must be converted into work or tasks which can be assigned to individuals, so creating personal responsibility for results. Realistic time-limits must be set in which results are to be achieved. Also new objectives and new tasks must be reviewed in the light of the overall situation and probable results. Unless new resources have been obtained, new tasks must mean the abandoning of old ones. Finally, management must create the right attitudes within its own ranks and among the workers, with the emphasis on the achievement of economic performance.

In his concluding chapter Drucker emphasizes that in most businesses today the management team have taken the place of the earlier economic entrepreneur and that they, therefore, must take the economic decisions. The individual manager must take on the commitment to contribute to economic results, to concentrate, and to systematically carry out his own job. He must also do his share of making sure that people outside the business world know what business really is and what part it plays in modern society.

## Conclusion

Where does *Managing for Results* fit into the pattern of development of management thought? In all fields of knowledge, as more and more has become known so the individual exponent or the single book has become narrower and more specialized in scope. The same tendency has become apparent in our knowledge of management. Fayol could write a whole theory of management in 150-odd pages. Drucker writes a whole book on two aspects – analysing situations and making economic decisions. It is indicative of the phenomenal mushrooming of thought about management in the last sixty years. Is it also indicative of a real peril? Is there a real danger that in future the manager who, above all, should have an all round overall view, will get sidetracked into a few narrow specialized fields?

To sum up, *Managing for Results* puts the emphasis on the fact that management's job is economic performance, and it spells out in more detail than has been done before two aspects of how to achieve it.

*References*

(1) Drucker, Peter F. *Managing for Results* (Heinemann, London 1964), p. ix.
(2) ibid., p. x.
(3) ibid., p. 4.
(4) ibid., p. 5.
(5) ibid., p. 5.
(6) ibid., p. 5.
(7) ibid., p. 7.
(8) ibid., p. 7.
(9) ibid., p. 8.
(10) ibid., p. 10.
(11) ibid., p. 26.
(12) ibid., p. 48.
(13) ibid., p. 123.
(14) ibid., p. 141.
(15) ibid., p. 162.
(16) ibid., p. 183.
(17) ibid., p. 183.

*Bibliography*

BOOKS BY PETER F. DRUCKER

*The End of Economic Man* (The John Day Co., New York 1939; Heinemann, London 1939).
*The Future of Industrial Man* (The John Day Co., New York 1942; Heinemann, London 1943).
*The Concept of the Corporation* (The John Day Co., New York 1946); published in Britain as *Big Business* (Heinemann, London 1947).
*The New Society* (Harper, New York 1950; Heinemann, London 1951).
*The Practice of Management* (Harper, New York 1954; Heinemann, London 1955; Mercury Books, London 1961).
*America's Next Twenty Years* (Harper, New York 1957).
*Landmarks of Tomorrow* (Harper, New York 1959; Heinemann, London 1959).
*Managing for Results* (Harper and Row, New York 1964; Heinemann, London 1964; Pan Books, London 1967).
*The Effective Executive* (Harper and Row, New York 1967; Heinemann, London 1967).
*The Age of Discontinuity* (Heinemann, London 1969; Pan Books, London 1971).
*Drucker on Management* (Management Publications, London 1970).

*Technology, Management, and Society* (Harper and Row, New York 1970; Heinemann, London 1970).

*The New Markets . . . and Other Essays* (Heinemann, London 1971); a similar book was published in the U.S. as *Men, Ideas, and Politics* (Harper and Row, New York 1971).

# PART II

*The Experience Approach*

# 7

# Henri Fayol
# 1916

*Introduction*

The earliest manager to systematically examine his own personal experience and to try to draw from it a theory of management was Henri Fayol. A qualified mining engineer, he was made manager of a coal-mine at the early age of 25. At 31 he became general manager of a group of mines, and at 47 Managing Director of the whole combine, a post which he held for thirty years. Throughout his career he showed all the signs of a successful manager. This became most obvious, though, when he took over the top job of the combine, which was almost bankrupt. By the time he retired the business was more than twice its original size and one of the most successful coal and steel combines in Europe.

He showed he could manage successfully and, with the assurance that was typical of the Victorian era, he was certain he could distil from his experience a universal theory. For trying to do it, for his intellectual capacity, for his ability to produce a generalized theory from a lifetime of experience, he deserves all credit.

His book *Administration, industrielle et générale*, to give it its original French title, was first published as a bulletin of the Société de l'Industrie Minérale in 1916. It is better known, at any rate in the United Kingdom, as *General and Industrial Management*, in the translation by Constance Storrs, published by Pitman in 1949. An earlier limited English edition translated by J. A. Coubrough had been published in 1929. Miss Storrs' translation has been used as the basis for this chapter.

Fayol in the Preface to his book says,

Management plays a very important part in the government of undertakings: of all undertakings, large or small, industrial, commercial, political, religious or other. I intend to set forth my ideas here on the way in which that part should be played. My work will be divided into four parts:

Part I.   Necessity and possibility of teaching management.
Part II.   Principles and elements of Management.
Part III.   Personal observations and experience.
Part IV.   Lessons of the war.

The first two parts which are to be the subject of the present volume are the development of the lecture which I delivered at the fiftieth anniversary of the Association of Mining Industry of Saint Étienne in 1908. The third and fourth parts will be the subject of a second volume to appear shortly.[1]

Unfortunately the third and fourth parts were never written, so all that we have is Fayol's case for teaching management, and the principles or theory of management which are to be taught.

*Management Teaching*
Having developed from successful experience a body of principles, a 'Theory of Administration', as soon as he retired from active business Fayol set about the task of insisting that management could and should be taught, and took active steps to see that this happened. Under his guidance a Centre of Administrative Studies was set up to hold weekly meetings and to publish many pamphlets and articles on the subject of administration or management.

To set the stage for the teaching of management Fayol analyses the activities of an industrial undertaking. The analysis is into six aspects:

(i) Technical – manufacture, etc.
(ii) Commercial – buying and selling.
(iii) Financial – provision of capital.
(iv) Security – protection.
(v) Accounting – including costing.
(vi) Managerial.

Rather curiously, while management is separated out as a sixth aspect the activities which it consists of are necessarily carried out by managers who are directly concerned with one of the other five aspects. Only at the top of the business does the job seem to become one of pure management. So a factory superintendent will be concerned with technical functions for part of his time and managerial functions for the rest. A managing director will be concerned almost entirely with managerial functions.

Why, then, separate it out as a function on its own? The answer lies in Fayol's definition of management, which is 'to forecast and plan, to organize, to command, to co-ordinate and to control'.[2] These are activities quite different in kind from the technical ones of the other five functions.

Each group of activities or aspects of the business requires a basis of abilities in the people who carry them out. These are:
  (i) Physical qualities.
 (ii) Mental qualities.
(iii) Moral qualities.
 (iv) General education.
  (v) Special knowledge of the function concerned.
 (vi) Experience.

Having set out in this way the various 'abilities' required and added that they are difficult if not impossible to measure, Fayol then confuses the issue by using the term 'ability' for knowledge of the different functions. He gives tables of the percentage of each function required at levels from workman to Head of State, and again from the head of a one-man business to the head of a State enterprise. One may, perhaps, now, be allowed a smile at the naïveté of trying to quantify such attributes when considering the reality of working at different levels and in many different types of business, but full credit must be given for a really serious attempt to show for the first time what qualities really are involved.

From this analysis, Fayol draws the conclusion that the major ability required is the managerial function. However good technical or other ability may be, if the managerial function is weak the business will not succeed. He makes the point that when considering a man for a new job, whether foreman or manager, it is managerial ability which usually determines the choice, provided reasonable technical ability is also there.

This leads, somewhat dogmatically, to the conclusion that managerial ability 'can and should be acquired in the same way as technical ability, first a school, later in the workshop'.[3] But management is not being taught along with technical subjects, because there is no theory of it to teach. An adequate theory is essential, and Fayol devotes the rest of his book to providing his version of it.

*Principles of Management*

Before setting out the 'principles' which he says he has found he has had to use most often, Fayol makes a very important and not-to-be-forgotten proviso. Management is the one function which operates only on people, and in a very wide variety of circumstances. The principles, therefore, are only guidelines, and great skill is required in using and adapting them to particular circumstances. There are fourteen principles given and elaborated to a greater or lesser extent, but again he is cautious in saying that there is no limit to the possible number of principles.

(i) Division of work. Specialization, whether by workers or manager, is necessary to provide the required knowledge and expertise. Without elaborating this point he says there are limits beyond which this principle should not go.

(ii) Authority and Responsibility. Authority may be formal, conferred as a result of position in the organizational hierarchy, or personal, the result of personal characteristics. Ideally it should be both. Responsibility must go with and match authority. The purpose of authority is to direct activity in the right direction, and sanctions or punishments must be available to be applied to those who won't conform.

(iii) Discipline. The obverse of the exercise of authority, and in Fayol's view it is essential. It may arise from formal or unwritten agreements between management and worker as to what is proper conduct, or it may be imposed one-sidedly by management. There is the interesting hint, foreshadowing much later thought, that 'discipline depends on the worthiness of the leaders'.

(iv) Unity of Command. Each man must have only one boss from whom he can receive orders; departmental responsibility must be very carefully set out so that there are no clashes; departments should not link up so that their work becomes intermeshed.

(v) Unity of Direction. There can only be one head of the organization, whose job it is to see that all efforts are directed to the same overall goals.

(vi) Subordination of Individual interest to General Interest. In common with authority and discipline, this is typical of the way of thinking of the nineteenth and very early twentieth century. At the individual level the employee or manager must submerge his personal interests or leave them behind at the workplace door. In the case of sections and departments, group interests and aims must be subordinated or suppressed for the common good.

(vii) Remuneration of Personnel. It must be fair and satisfy the employer as a reasonable cost for services rendered and the employee as a means of livelihood and return for effort. Time rates, job rates, piece-work and bonus schemes are all admissible as appropriate. Profit-sharing Fayol regards as attractive and a possible means of achieving harmony between Capital and Labour, although he admits the difficulties involved.

(viii) Centralization. This is not something which can be used or not at will, but a natural order of things such that 'sensations converge towards the brain or directive part, and from the brain or directive part, orders are sent out which set all parts of the organism in movement'.[4] He does agree, however, that the degree of centralization would vary according to circumstances and the abilities of the people concerned.

(ix) The Scalar Chain. This is the line of authority from superior to subordinate, from the very top to the bottom of the business. In each aspect of the business the chain must be unbroken, i.e.

at each level a man must have an immediate boss, who himself has a boss, and so on up to the managing director.
Nobody must be out on a limb. The scalar chain is the
channel for authority, for communication up and down, and
for decision-making. The one exception to its use is when,
with the consent of their respective bosses, two men on
different chains can make direct contact across 'the gang
plank', reach a decision, and inform their bosses of the
decision reached. The latter, of course, have a right of veto.

(x) Order. A place for everything and everything in its place.
This applies to materials, layout, and human or social order.
Social order needs a careful balance of requirements and
resources.

(xi) Equity. Fairness, kindliness and justice to all must not only
be done but be seen to be done.

(xii) Stability of Tenure of Personnel. So far as possible a firm
should provide a career structure so that its managers stay
and progress within the firm. Outsiders may at times have
to be brought in, but there must be good reasons for doing so.

(xiii) Initiative. After the principles of authority, discipline, unity
of command, and centralization, it is rather surprising to
find initiative mentioned as something which should be
encouraged at all levels. It is said that it must be within the
limits of respect for authority and discipline, but the
encouragement of its use promotes zeal and energy.

(xiv) *Esprit de corps*. The last of the principles and the one which
must permeate all others. It is described as harmony among
all members of the organization. The all too frequent
management practice of 'divide and rule' is roundly condemned, and verbal rather than written communication is
preferred.

As is only to be expected with precepts formulated sixty years ago,
changing conditions and ideas have made some of them look
decidedly old-fashioned. But many are as true today as when they
were written, and if more managers observed them it could do
nothing but good.

## The Elements of Management

The elements of management involve a more radical approach. Fayol admits that the principles were a distillation of personal experience, a basis for discussion. The elements represent a basic attempt to analyse the nature of management jobs.

Although there is a tremendous lack of balance in his treatment of them, management in Fayol's view consists of five essential elements or functions:

(i) Prévoir. (a) To foresee.
           (b) To plan.
(ii) To organize.
(iii) To command.
(iv) To co-ordinate.
(v) To control.

This constitutes an analysis of what a manager does when he is actually managing, as distinct from many other non-managerial duties which he will necessarily carry out. The analysis was the first of its kind. Since then other writers have modified it, e.g. substituting motivation or direction for command, which is now somewhat dated, or have added other items to it, for instance developing people (Drucker), or communication and decision-making (Dale and Michelon), but one can argue whether the additions are really functions or elements or whether they are 'tools' which a manager uses in performing his functions. Fundamentally Fayol's list still stands.

Planning, as has been shown, has to be split to translate accurately the original French 'prévoir'. First the manager must look ahead and try as best he can to forecast the future. It has been well said that management may be based in the past and present, but it takes place in the future. Little is said about how to forecast. In fact, of course, at the time the relevant tools and techniques had not been invented and flair, hunch and judgement were the manager's only aids. But on the basis of the forecast, however reached, both broad and detailed planning is essential. What constitutes a good plan? Plans can be simple or complex, short- or long-term, good, bad and indifferent. A good plan whatever else it is will have certain characteristics. These are unity, continuity, flexibility and precision according to Fayol.

Using his own experience in mining as an example he suggests 'yearly forecasts, ten-yearly forecasts, monthly, weekly, daily forecasts, long term forecasts, special forecasts and all merge into a single programme which operates as a guide for the whole concern.'[25] Leaving on one side the somewhat illogical order of the forecasts, it seems very doubtful that they could all be built into one *single* programme, as he calls it here. Later he does say that the yearly, ten-yearly and special forecasts constitute the basis of the general plan, and one can assume from this that short-term plans are derived from and dovetail into a general plan. General planning should be carried out by using the knowledge and enterprise of all departmental heads, each contributing in his own sphere. When first tried general planning will seem exceptionally difficult, but with experience and by learning from mistakes it will become easier.

Finally, planning calls for high qualities in managers themselves. They must possess energy and moral courage and the art of handling men to carry through the plan. They must have experience, competence and reasonable safety of tenure in their job if they are to plan at all. They must be able to see the best possible results while being prudent enough not to be too optimistic and raise false hopes.

The next element is that of organization. One of the troubles that always beset writers and speakers on management is the difficulty of using ordinary, everyday words and trying to apply to them rather specialized meanings. Fayol, who takes nearly half his book to write about organization, gets round the problems easily, if not neatly. He follows the example of Humpty Dumpty in *Through the Looking-Glass*: when he uses a word it means just what he chooses it to mean!

To be fair, he does start with a definition which at a stretch might be wide enough to cover all that follows: 'To organize a business is to provide it with everything useful for its functioning: raw materials, tools, capital, personnel. All this may be divided into two main sections, the material organization and the human organization.'⁶ He is concerned only with the human organization.

Seemingly out of place, sixteen 'Managerial duties of an Organiz-ation' follow the definition. If one is prepared to accept that in the tremendously varied situations in which management can and does take place, there can be such things as universal rules or guidelines then, perhaps, Fayol has a point. In any case, useful or not, they have become so much a traditional part of management thought that they must be quoted in full here:⁷

1. Ensure that the plan is judiciously prepared and strictly carried out.
2. See that the human and material organization is consistent with the objective, resources, and requirements of the concern.
3. Set up a single, competent energetic guiding authority.
4. Harmonize activities and co-ordinate efforts.
5. Formulate clear, distinct, precise decisions.
6. Arrange for efficient selection – each department must be headed by a competent, energetic man, each employee must be in that place where he can render greatest service.
7. Define duties clearly.
8. Encourage a liking for initiative and responsibility.
9. Have fair and suitable recompense for services rendered.
10. Make use of sanctions against faults and errors.
11. See to the maintenance of discipline.
12. Ensure that individual interests are subordinated to the general interest.
13. Pay special attention to the unity of command.
14. Supervise both material and human order.
15. Have everything under control.
16. Fight against excess of regulations, red tape and paper control.

Obviously most of these are only the imperative version of the Principles given earlier. Equally, by no means all of them would be recognized as valid today.

Organization structure is dealt with next, and it may be as well to remind the reader that at the time Fayol was working on this (say

1900–16), specialists were few and organizations, however big, were much simpler than today. A delightful exercise in simple arithmetic shows that if one foreman can control fifteen workers and one manager can control four junior managers, then step by step as the layers of management increase even the largest firms would only require eight or nine layers of management (nearly a million and four million employees respectively)! This calculation and a diagrammatic representation of the development of layers shows that Fayol was thinking mainly of what is known as line management. Each function has its scalar chain from the one man at the very top, to each individual at the lowest level. While all businesses should have the same basic form of structure the size and importance of each 'line' will vary according to the nature of the business. Also similar organization structures will not necessarily be equally effective. This depends on the competence of the people making up the structure. Having defined the structure, Fayol goes on to consider the different 'organs or members' within the structure. This surely must be an unfortunate translation. First they are 'organs of the six essential functions',[8] i.e. technical, commercial, financial etc. In the one-man business they are all represented in the owner-manager. In the large business they are individuals or groups representing the different levels in the hierarchy.

At the very top are the shareholders whose job is to appoint the Board of Directors and consider their recommendations, usually annually. The Board of Directors' function is given as exercising legal, statutory powers, assessing proposals of general management, and exercising overall control.

The most important level comes next – general management. This may consist of one or more general managers with the responsibility of directing the enterprise towards its objective, drawing up plans of action, selecting personnel, and directing and controlling performance.

Earlier it was suggested that basically the organization given was the 'line' variety. At this point, however, staff are mentioned for the first time. Their function is to support general management with specialized knowledge and to help him or them to carry out his or their duties by dealing with detail. They have no executive responsibility for lower levels in the organization. One of their main jobs should be to look out for and work on ideas for developing and improving the enterprise.

Rather as an aside, Taylor's system of functional foremen is quoted in detail. As might be imagined, Fayol supports the idea of technical and specialist assistance to the foreman but is horrified by the idea of betraying the principle of Unity of Command.

For lower levels in the organization the managerial function in the job, which predominates at the higher levels, gradually diminishes and gives way to the technical or other function.

Following these rather sketchy descriptions of the different levels of management, Fayol goes back to the qualities which a good manager should possess. The list is slightly different from his earlier one, and as it still has real validity it is worth quoting in full:[9]

1. Health and physical fitness.
2. Intelligence and mental vigour.
3. Moral qualities: steady persistent thoughtful determination, energy, dash if need be, courage to accept responsibility, sense of duty, care for the common good.
4. Sound general education.
5. Managerial ability, embracing foresight, the ability to draw up and have drawn up the plan of action; organization and, in particular, knowledge of how to build up an organization; command, the art of handling men; co-ordination, the harmonizing of all activities and focussing of all efforts; and finally, control.
6. General knowledge of all the essential functions.
7. The widest possible competence in the specialized activity characterizing the concern.

And so back from these qualities, especially the fifth one, to a restatement of his case for the training of managers.

The next element is that of command. The purpose of command is to set the human organization in motion towards its objective. Its object is to get optimum return from all employees. To command effectively the manager must know his employees, get rid of the incompetent, know the employer-employee agreements, set a good example, periodically review his organization and use conferences with his subordinates to ensure unity of direction, delegate the detail, and establish *esprit de corps*.

Co-ordination. This was, and still is, a difficult aspect to separate out. Where does command end, co-ordination begin and end, and control begin ? Fayol collects together something of a hotch-potch under this heading. To co-ordinate a manager must:

(i) Harmonize all activities.
(ii) Keep a proper balance between material, social and functional aspects.
(iii) Watch the effects of one function on the performance of another.
(iv) Maintain a balance between expenditure and resources, tools and equipment and requirements, stocks and consumption and sales and production.
(v) Accord to all things their rightful proportion and adapt means to ends.

Signs of poor co-ordination of the business as a whole are self-contained watertight compartments, sectional and departmental interests overriding the interests of the whole firm, and the practice of taking cover from personal responsibility behind 'pieces of paper'.

'Control' is the last and shortest of the sections. In effect control is checking the results against the plan, pointing out weaknesses and failures, so as to prevent them from happening again. The need to have information on results early is stressed, as is the use of sanctions when things go wrong. Information which does not result in corrective action is wasted and cannot be called control. All this sounds very familiar to modern ears although not, perhaps, appropriate to very modern ears backed by ideas on self-control. But on the next-to-last page of the book there is an innocent-looking sentence which explodes like a bomb. 'A further danger to avoid is *infiltration of control into management and departmental running*.'[10] It seems that 'control' is the fifth management function, but that management does not exercise it. It is carried out by 'an inspector' or, presumably, inspectors. 'Control is a precious auxiliary to management.'[11] Examples of control and how it works are promised for Part III of the work. What a pity Part III was never written.

## Conclusion

Inevitably the debt we owe to Fayol diminishes as time and greater complexity make his day and age seem more and more remote. At the time his attempt, the only one of its kind, to build a basic theory of management was invaluable. It was incomplete, of course, it was too narrow, being based solely on his own personal experience, but there was a great deal of value in it.

While no serious management writer today would produce some such dictum as, 'Here are ninety-nine rules of management: follow these to the letter and you will be a good manager', there are, for those who can separate the wheat from the chaff, principles and guidelines in Fayol's work which we would do well to remember today.

## References

(1) Fayol, H. *General and Industrial Management* translated by Constance Storrs (Pitman, London 1949), p. xxi.

(2) ibid., p. 6.

(3) ibid., p. 14.

(4) ibid., p. 33.

(5) ibid., p. 46.

(6) ibid., p. 53.

(7) ibid., pp. 53–54.

(8) ibid., p. 60.

(9) ibid., p. 73.

(10) ibid., p. 109.

(11) ibid., p. 109.

## Bibliography

BOOKS BY H. FAYOL

*Administration, industrielle et générale* (Société de l'Industrie Minérale, Paris 1916); translated by J. A. Coubrough as *Industrial and General Administration* (Pitman, London 1929).

*General and Industrial Management* translated by Constance Storrs (Pitman, London 1949).

# 8

## Oliver Sheldon
### 1923

*Introduction*

Oliver Sheldon was, for much of his life, a senior manager at Rowntree's in York and a contemporary of Seebohm Rowntree. It was inevitable that they shared the same ideas and ideals. In this case there may be some doubt in the reader's mind as to the necessity of including both of them in this book.

There are, in fact, two very good reasons for doing so. The first is that the writings of the two men are complementary. By and large Rowntree wrote of the philosophy, the morality, the ethic behind his method of managing a business. Sheldon wrote of the application of these ideas in detailed practice. In fact the title of his book, *The Philosophy of Management*, is somewhat misleading. It would be better entitled *The Practice of Management*. The second reason is that in the early 'twenties, when this book was written, there were only a very few British books on management available, and this was one of the best. It is a pioneering book in that although it represented management practice at Rowntree's it was probably well ahead of its time so far as much of British industry was concerned.

*Background*

Surveying the background in which British management was developing in the 1920s, Sheldon picks out four elements for special consideration:

    (i) Publicity – the increasing knowledge in the community at large about industrial affairs.

    (ii) Self-development – the need felt by workers to express and develop themselves generally through increased leisure pursuits, resulting in a lack of interest in work and incentives.

(iii) Association – the overgrowth of associations of all kinds, and in particular trade unions, leading to concentration of power at the centre and a loss of influence by the individual. This might lead to the factory as the unit of association, with labour and management combining in a common interest.

(iv) Science – the growth of a scientific management of analysis and synthesis in the management of the firm. This is only a part of a change in general approach in all aspects of living.

Management by now, it is claimed, has become a separate function in industry, different from both capital and labour and critical of both. Labour, too, is critical of the existing set-up, but at two levels. The theorists and extremists demand a Utopia, a revolution, a complete change by violent means. The inarticulate mass, divorced from the extreme centre, are critical of the balance of power and influence in industry and the existing balance of social opportunity. As Sheldon puts it, 'Fundamentally, however, the claim of the mass of Labour is not for material equality, not for wealth irrespective of the means whereby it is gained, but for its own moral right to be given an open road to self-realization.'[1] It is stressed that if management misjudges these feelings or does not take them into account in its managerial practices the results could be disastrous. Industry is moving into an era when ethical values and not just material ones must be taken into account.

Management is being presented with a new series of problems. How much control should workers have? What status should they have based on their social contribution? What is the social value of the individual? What are reasonable or good working conditions? What is desirable is not the issue, not even what is possible, but what is right. 'The interpretation of that mentality [of labour as represented by these questions] is the preliminary task of management.'[2] The need is for new methods of and approaches to management to meet a new social conscience and existing social problems.

On the other hand capital is becoming much less of an active partner in business. Its place is being taken by the most senior level of management, the Board of Directors. Sheldon seems not to accept that this should be so and puts the point that shareholders should 'accept a direct burden of industrial service'. How this might happen is not explained.

The essence of this background is best summarized in two quotations: 'Industry cannot be rendered efficient while the basic fact remains unrecognized that it is primarily *human*. It is not a mass of machines and technical processes; *it is a body of men*.'[3] And 'The progress of any section of a community is governed by the progress of the whole. It is impossible to carry out a great scheme of industrial development, founded upon the common humanity of those engaged in industry, unless it is supported by a vivid public feeling, an informed public opinion, and a resolute public will.'[4]

### The Fundamentals of Management

Management as a generic term is divided into three aspects, all of which are essential to the running of a business.

  (i) Administration: the determination of a top-level policy, the co-ordination of the major aspects of the business, and the control of management proper.
 (ii) Management in its narrower sense: the function of carrying out the policy, and through the organization reaching the objectives set.
(iii) Organization: combining the work of groups or individuals with the required faculties so that the duties, so formed, provide the best channels for the efficient reaching of objectives.

At this stage management is still regarded as functioning within a framework of objectives and policies set by a higher level of authority and towards which it contributes nothing except performance.

An important distinction made is the emphasis that while there is a science of management, management itself is an art. A knowledge of the science is required, but the practice is the art of applying the science, or rather it is more, because the science is admitted to be fragmentary and incomplete.

It would seem that Sheldon accepts that the ideas of Taylor, in so far as they had been developed, constitute the 'science' of management, but that 'Into every branch of industry the human factor enters, and where that factor exists, there must always remain a field outside the province of science.'[5] To say, as he does, 'There may be a science of costing, of planning, of manufacturing, of dispatching, but there can be no science of cooperation'[6] shows how very limited were the knowledge and the ideas of the 1920s.

At the same time as management is said to be developing slowly into a science it is also said to be rapidly taking over as the controlling factor in industry, usurping and extending the power formerly exercised by the employer and owner. This is ascribed as being due largely to the particular circumstances of Great Britain in the early 1920s. These are given as:

(i) The progress of industrial science, by which he apparently means applied research.

(ii) The post-war economic situation of increased costs and demand for increased production.

(iii) The stirring of social conscience.

(iv) The American emphasis on efficiency.

(v) The need to meet rapidly rising costs.

(vi) The increased use of conferences at all levels and for all purposes.

(vii) The increased scale of invention for production and clerical work.

Not very conclusively Sheldon argues that management is also becoming a profession in its own right. His criteria for a profession are not as wide as Mary Follett's (*see* Chapter 12), and he seems more optimistic that the near future would see the emergence of a professional, qualified élitist group of managers engaged in the practice of a 'science of management'.

The task of management is divided and analysed in two different ways, one based on a functional or departmental division of a hypothetical business, the other on faculties required or levels of management. Both divisions are illustrated diagramatically (Figures 2 and 3).

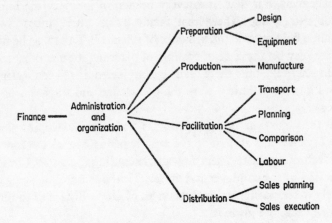

*Figure 2.* The functions of management[7]

One or two comments of particular significance are called for. Finance is really a split function, one half being the provision of the necessary capital – a function of the owners or shareholders and not management – the other half being the application and conservation of the available money – a management function. Administration and organization, too, is sub-divided into policy determination by the directors or owners, and implementation, or organizing the business and control of execution, which are management functions.

For the rest the emphasis is on production as the prime purpose of the business, with the preparation and facilitation functions as subsidiary to and aiding production. Distribution is added to complete the picture, but seems to be regarded as of little importance and is not referred to again in the book. This contrasts very sharply with, for instance, the ideas of Drucker, forty years later (*see* Chapter 5), and shows clearly that at this time the function of marketing was completely unknown. The clerical function of organizing and distributing information is not shown separately, but is regarded as a part of each of the separate functions shown.

The faculties of management are really levels in the hierarchy of a business, and are shown in Figure 3.

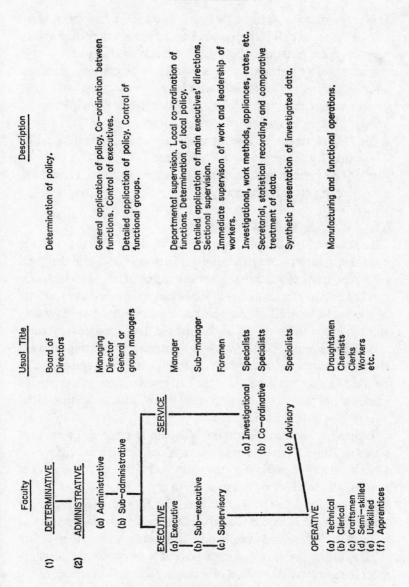

| Faculty | Usual Title | Description |
|---|---|---|
| (1) DETERMINATIVE | Board of Directors | Determination of policy. |
| (2) ADMINISTRATIVE | | |
| (a) Administrative | Managing Director | General application of policy. Co-ordination between functions. Control of executives. |
| (b) Sub-administrative | General or group managers | Detailed application of policy. Control of functional groups. |
| EXECUTIVE | | |
| (a) Executive | Manager | Departmental supervision. Local co-ordination of functions. Determination of local policy. |
| (b) Sub-executive | Sub-manager | Detailed application of main executives' directions, Sectional supervision. |
| (c) Supervisory | Foremen | Immediate supervison of work and leadership of workers. |
| SERVICE | | |
| (a) Investigational | Specialists | Investigational, work methods, appliances, rates, etc. |
| (b) Co-ordinative | Specialists | Secretarial, statistical recording, and comparative treatment of data. |
| (c) Advisory | Specialists | Synthetic presentation of investigated data. |
| OPERATIVE | Draughtsmen Chemists Clerks Workers etc. | Manufacturing and functional operations. |
| (a) Technical | | |
| (b) Clerical | | |
| (c) Craftsmen | | |
| (d) Semi-skilled | | |
| (e) Unskilled | | |
| (f) Apprentices | | |

*Figure 3*. The faculties of management[8]

It is emphasized that, while these are, as we should say now, levels in a hierarchy, at all levels below Sub-administration they appear in each of the functions shown in Figure 2, so that to get even a semblance of organization chart it would be necessary to combine and expand both. This is dealt with later.

This section concludes with three fundamental principles:[9]

   (i) 'There exists a scientific basis to management.'

   (ii) 'Management can be operated by scientific means rather than by the autocracy of the "boss".'

   (iii) 'The practice of management can no longer be entrusted to incompetent individuals.'

## The Social Responsibility of Management

There can be little doubt that the First World War of 1914–18 was a shattering catastrophe to all who were involved in it, and that it set off a new train of thinking, a revulsion from the past which was typified by the phrase 'a land fit for heroes to live in'. The thinkers of the 1920s were all of one opinion, that society must move forward to better things and that the bad old days must never return.

Sheldon seems to take a mid-way position. In putting forward the social responsibilities which he felt management must assume he was as idealistic as anyone in the early part of the decade, but his idealism was tempered every so often by the realization that social change is a very slow business.

In dealing with social responsibility he is using the term in a meaning which today would be misleading. He is concerned mainly with proposals for the responsibilities of management towards the workers in so far as these are affected by changes in society itself and in social structure. The broader question of the responsibility of industry and therefore management to society as a whole is dealt with virtually only in its economic context.

He starts by insisting that management is 'primarily the management of men', with the object of satisfying the material needs of the community but also of satisfying and developing the material requirements and moral and mental faculties of the workers themselves. The worker is no longer to be regarded as an adjunct to the machine, but as a person in his own right with needs and desires which management should satisfy through the working situation. There must be no return to the 'hands philosophy' of pre-war industry, nor must the development of systems and science in management be allowed to obscure the humanity of industry. Management must become 'the art of combining human and material factors into a single harmonious enterprise'.[10]

The point is made that in order to be able to afford to give the individual a better working life industry itself must be as efficient as possible. Social responsibility rests, therefore, not only on ideals and standards but on economic performance, and for this management has the prime responsibility, but labour must also show responsibility. It is possible too that improving working conditions may in itself eventually improve economic performance.

More specifically, management is charged with responsibility for doing the following:

(i) Providing for all at least a minimum basic wage on which a man can live decently and bring up a family.

(ii) Providing adequate leisure hours away from work in which the individual can develop himself and contribute to the life of the wider society.

(iii) Providing work wherever possible which is interesting and which enables a man to make the fullest use of his capabilities.

(iv) Reducing unrewarding, exhausting toil to a minimum.

(v) Regarding the worker as an individual.

(vi) Setting up a fellowship between management and worker which will be 'the flower of a truly profound sense of common humanity, bound together in the pursuit of a common purpose'.[11]

(vii) Accepting the ideals of society as those of industry.

(viii) Taking the lead to bring these things about although, in fact, workers are not yet completely ready for them.

On the question of the so-called social responsibility of management to the community at large Sheldon is much less original. He does say that as capital withdraws as the ruling factor in industry and salaried management takes over 'the motive of profit alone becomes increasingly remote and archaic'.[12] Management must control not simply the production of goods, but the production of goods which have value to the community, at a price the community can afford to pay, and of a quality which reasonably satisfies the needs for which they are designed. In a broader sense he gives ' "service to the community" as the primary motive and fundamental basis of industry',[13] and such service 'may be economic in character, but must be ethical in motive'.[14]

## The Organization of the Factory

Generally in management thinking it has happened that practice has preceded theory and that when theory does appear it tends to be crude and ill-developed. Nowhere does this seem to be more true than in this attempt to put forward a theory of organization, though even today the theory of organization is probably the least satisfactory aspect of management studies.

After a major effort to clear away the fog of popular and erroneous meanings of the term, Sheldon comes up with a good definition. Organization is the division of work into jobs, and the pattern of relationships between these jobs that results from division. This is then elaborated into the five 'fundamental ingredients':[15]

a. Function – or, work to be done.
b. Objective – or, the ideal and object.
c. Faculty – or, the human capacity for work.
d. Relations – or, the relationships, administrative, and physical, between the faculties employed.
e. Method – or, the way in which work is done.

The basis of organization is the division of work which has become too much for one man to do, and/or too specialized in its various aspects for one man to cope with it. But the nature of the work depends on the aims and objectives for which the business exists. When the work has been determined and divided the jobs so produced must be matched with individuals who have the right faculties (presumably skills and abilities) to be able to do them. Organization then goes into action through the operation of the relationships between individuals in jobs. The specific reason for including the fifth ingredient, method, is a little obscure.

Although few firms get the opportunity to set up an organization scientifically from scratch and it is much more likely that the majority are faced with the task of re-shaping on scientific lines an organization which has grown haphazardly, specific advantages are claimed for a scientific structure as compared with an unscientific one. These are:

(i) Permanence, the capacity to survive changes in personnel and periods of growth
(ii) Concentration on effective work arising from real knowledge of the scope of the job, its responsibilities and related sphere of authority
(iii) Individuality, or job satisfaction among managers arising from status and self-confidence
(iv) Combination, or effective working relationships
(v) Human standards, or effective matching of job and individual.

Specific forms or patterns of organization are given, but with several qualifications. The form of organization must depend on the extent to which functions have been developed, the size of the business, and the degree of delegation and specialization. In any case, apart from in the simplest business, the structure is likely to be a combination of different forms arranged to match the needs of the individual firm.

The different structures are claimed to be based on principles, of which there are four:

(i) The principle of function
(ii) The principle of decentralization
(iii) The principle of specialization
(iv) The principle of conference.

Functional organization has as its basis the separating out of particular functions or aspects of work which are common to several or many parts of the business and placing them under separate control and responsibility. This pattern is based exactly on the diagram shown on p. 104 except that manufacture is sub-divided into the different processes. Except for the rather curious separation of Finance it is obviously an early instance of the way in which larger businesses have tended to develop ever since.

Departmental organization would appear to be a 'left-over' from earlier and much more primitive forms of organization which no doubt still existed in the 1920s. Each process of manufacture is shown as being self-contained under its own departmental head, who is directly responsible to a General Manager. Each departmental manager is assumed to be fully responsible for everything which goes on in his department, which includes not only actual production but also all the 'functions' relating to his own work, such as planning, hire of staff, purchasing, transport, and so on.

Staff and line organization, from the principle of specialization, adds another dimension to the first two principles. The organization of the work of production may be on either functional or departmental lines, but parallel with this is an advisory structure based on 'bureaux' to give specialist advice to functional or departmental heads. The heads of the bureaux have no operating authority at all (except presumably in managing their own staff), their functions being those of investigation, analysis, and advice on problems which it is assumed the line managers have neither the time nor the specialist expertise to deal with. It is suggested, however, that because functional managers have a narrower field to control they might be sufficiently specialist either to do their own 'staff work' or to control the staff who do it.

Committee organization is thought to be a necessary adjunct to the other forms in order to co-ordinate the efforts and ideas of different departments or functions. A proper committee structure might include ones which are executive (decision-making), advisory, co-ordinative, and educative (information dissemination).

*Labour Management*

Largely as a result of Rowntree's work and the interest which was aroused in the effect of hours and working conditions on output during the 1914–18 war there was a considerable upsurge of concern over these ideas in the 1920s. This is clearly shown in

Sheldon's book, which devotes a whole chapter to 'Labour Management'.

In a sense it justifies Drucker's quip about Personnel Management, that 'it puts together and calls "personnel management" all those things that do not deal with the work of people and that are not management'.[16] For 'personnel management' substitute 'labour management', its original name, and the comment is still applicable.

The whole idea, which no doubt seemed right at the time and indeed has not altered much in practice up to today, was to tack on to the working situation a number of practices which were external to the actual job of work and the functioning of line managers. To put it this way is, perhaps, to put the cart before the horse so far as Sheldon is concerned. This is what he sees happening, and he protests long and loudly against it. To him labour management is fundamentally an attitude of mind, a view of the relationships between management and worker, which must have the right motivation behind them so that they permeate the whole of management in practice; and not just a collection of gimmicks which are introduced with the idea that they might pay off in increased output and profit.

He calls this 'the new spirit in industry'; 'It betokens a change, not in structure, methods, objects, environment or conditions, but in mentality.'[17] This requires new attitudes not only on the part of management but also on the part of the workers; so that the new spirit in industry would be 'fellowship'. This is to be the goal. How easy to say; how difficult to achieve. The General Strike was but two years away when his book was published, the Great Depression of the 1930s with its millions of unemployed less than a decade. The blizzards of bitterness which they produced froze the tender plant to its very roots.

The first area to which Sheldon applies this new spirit is that of wages. Industry must raise production to meet a minimum wage which removes poverty from the industrial scene. Such a minimum is socially and ethically essential, but its realization is economic in that it must be based on productivity adequate to pay it. Ineffective workers must be eliminated and treated as a social, not an industrial problem. Equally if not more important is the elimination of inefficient management.

Above the minimum, wages should be linked to output backed by assurances of continuous employment and adequate social security for unemployment. This would remove the worker's objection to working to his maximum capacity. Also, above the minimum the rates for different jobs should be co-ordinated centrally so that they are not only fair but are seen to be fair. The machinery for this is negotiation between management and unions.

Turning to employment, the Employment Department must be a specialist agency concerned with the engagement, transfer and discharge of workers, but it must also be closely connected with welfare work and be concerned as the 'conscience' of the factory, which watches the way that line managers manage and keeps them informed of the effects of their management methods and practices. The first two have developed apace. The third is one which few Personnel Managers, let alone Employment Departments, have dared to do even if they were competent to do it.

The need to put people into the right jobs and to avoid square pegs in round holes is emphasized. Psychology should be used to determine the characteristics required for each job and to provide tests for selection.

Labour turnover, the ratio of leavers to work-force, must be watched and reasons found for any excessive turnover. The causes must be remedied. Here the Labour Manager is to be 'Lord High Everything Else', dispensing wisdom and advice in all directions.

Discharge for disciplinary reasons should only be after 'trial' by a court of management and workers. Discharge for lack of work, or redundancy as it would be called today, must be based on efficiency, the least efficient to go first, with social reasons coming in if efficiency is equal. Unions must be consulted.

To add to the problems of management, Sheldon would make it responsible for alleviating general unemployment. To do so it must ensure efficient production, reduce costs and prices, even cut the flow of production, and use short-time working rather than dismissal, and so constantly employ more people.

Welfare is to be an affair of the spirit, not simply one of profit or of duty. Welfare work must now be concentrated under a welfare officer because of the separation which has taken place between employer and worker, and while it is the employer's job to appoint a welfare worker to co-ordinate the work it should largely be a matter of welfare projects run by the workers themselves.

Sheldon quotes with apparent approval a definition by a Miss Proud in 1916 that 'Welfare work consists of voluntary efforts on the part of employers to improve within the existing industrial system conditions of employment in their own factories.' By itself this seems to be a limited definition of welfare work, and would not appear to include tackling problems outside actual working hours. He does, however, go on to add to this definition not only decisions on the colour of work rooms and the provision of canteens, but also such things as sports and social clubs, and other matters outside work.

Still appealing for a partnership between management and workers, he says, 'Welfare is essentially a corporate enterprise. Though the responsibility for it must rest with the management, it is one part of management in which the workers are immediately concerned and for which their claim for control may first find application.'[18] In order to achieve this workers must be convinced that it is being done not just for the profit of the employer nor for advertising him as a 'good' employer, but with the real interests of the workers at heart. Then he takes it beyond the bounds that we would perhaps accept today and says that it must concern workers in their mental and moral as well as physical aspects. It should not be limited only to working hours but should extend out into the private life of the employee. In so far as this relates to social and sports clubs this might be admissible, but it is open to question whether further extension might not be going too far into what must be the employee's private concern.

Sheldon appears at first to quote with approval Taylor's idea from *Scientific Management* that one of the essential parts of management is the training of the worker in the correct way of doing the job. Later, however, this seems to be qualified by what was a very British attitude to scientific management when he says that 'because a way of performing an operation is discovered which, if adopted, will produce treble the previous output, there is no valid reason for supposing either that the average worker will adopt it, even under the highest monetary incentive, or that the methods of setting or performing the task are universally or socially desirable'.[19] He would appear to anticipate modern thinking in suggesting that there are grave psychological objections to the idea that there is only one best way of doing a job. He suggests that it is probable that most tasks may be performed with equal efficiency in different ways by different persons.

Once more we have the idea of a sharing of responsibility, and that the question of improving methods and timings should be one which is decided not solely by management but by management working together with the employees. There must be mutual agreement after combined research. He suggests that without such co-operation the whole success of work-study and training may be in jeopardy.

In so far as education in the broader sense is concerned he suggests that while management should not do this in the work situation it should at least provide a work situation which is not antipathetic to it, and it must also accept a wider social responsibility in seeing that education is, in fact, provided outside.

In writing of trade unions the shining optimism, the almost naïve simplicity of Sheldon shows itself at its height. He admits that unions have done great things for workers in the past in redressing things which were wrong, but in doing so against the opposition which arose from employers in earlier days the state has now been reached where the union stands in opposition to management instead of, as he maintains it should, working with it. This leads to conflicts within the worker as his loyalty is not to the firm for which he works but to the union to which he belongs. Somehow a way out of this dilemma must be found.

In order to reach the stage where co-operation is substituted for conflict he suggests three steps which management must take, and management must be the initiator of these steps. The first is to recognize the union fully and completely not only as the representative of the workers but as a party which has the right to help in practical management and to contribute to the formulation of policy. Secondly, management must honestly try to appreciate the attitudes of the union and to understand its aims and its methods. This should lead to understanding rather than condemnation, to co-operation rather than opposition. In more practical terms he suggests the appointment in each section of the factory of a union representative as the man who can consult the management on the part of the workers and with whom the management itself can confer. It will be management's job not only to deal with questions raised by this representative but also to keep him informed of management's intentions and policies. This, of course, is an anticipation of the shop-steward of twenty years later.

He concludes with this: 'We must aim at forging some strong link between the interests of the workers as members of Unions and their interests as members of individual factories.'[20]

Finally, on labour relations there is an impassioned plea for an end to the conflict, the differences, the self-seeking in industry. Elsewhere in human life man lives by co-operating in groups; in future the people in the firm, from managing director to the lowest labourer, must learn to co-operate for the good of the firm. But such co-operation must have a motive and someone to give the lead. So far the motives for work have been the pay packet, profits, and security; the results, distrust and antagonism, the inevitable division into conflicting groups with conflicting aims.

Just what the motive is to be is not made clear. It must embrace self-interest and go beyond it. It must be an ideal to which all can subscribe. It is vaguely described as 'service'. The pattern is to be set and the lead given by the new management imbued with new ideas and willing to undertake the difficult, if not well-nigh impossible, task of overcoming suspicion and hatred, of instilling confidence and, by setting the example, of infusing the new spirit into industry. To do this management must bring workers in to share in the task of managing.

## Production Management

More and more production but at less and less cost, so increasing consumption, is Sheldon's statement of the essential point to which management must turn its attention. This is to be done not by more physical or mental effort but by a greater use of what he calls 'the impersonal means of production'. Today these would be called the techniques of production. He seems to be peculiarly ambivalent about Taylor's *Scientific Management*. At one point he is insisting on the service it had rendered to industry by emphasizing the necessity for the scientific treatment of manufacturing problems. Later on he is not so sure, in fact he goes so far as to suggest that Taylor's ideas on production, on the organization of the individual would be completely unacceptable, not only to the worker in Britain but also to the average manager.

The way forward for management, then, is to be the elimination of waste by the use of research, by planning, by costing and by time study. All of these are to be used to get the facts rather than to rely on opinion – an echo, albeit a rather faint one, of Taylor in 1900. Following this he says that the procedures for management should be standardized as well as the actual processes of production themselves. This he suggests is the foundation of Scientific Management, and a state towards which the science of management is striving. One is left wondering whether he had in mind a standardized form of management, a standardized form of practice which could be universally applied and which would guarantee efficiency. Was he hoping for the alchemist's dream, a method which would turn all managerial action into gold, not the gold of excess profits but the gold of a perfect managerial/worker partnership in industry? It looks rather like it when he says, 'When management can be said to be 100 per cent efficient, it will be found that the workers have achieved approximately the same efficiency.'[21]

It has perhaps been obvious so far that his concern has been almost entirely with production, and he goes on to emphasize the point that the production function *is* the business. The other functions are ancillary to it, whether they be work-study, costing, selling, or whatever. The whole purpose is to make the goods. Once they are made it is someone else's job to go out and get rid of them. The concept of marketing is still a very long way away. But manufacturing itself has now become such a complex business of separate processes, perhaps consecutive, perhaps parallel, of separate specialist functions which are there to serve manufacturing, that the main function of higher management has become the co-ordination of these separate functions. This must, says Sheldon, be by a single individual. A single managing director at the top, or a Chairman if the Board members are full-time executives, is essential. It is his job first and foremost to co-ordinate the separate functions and to see that the business as a whole runs smoothly towards its objectives.

While production management as seen by Sheldon is now moving far away from the do-it-yourself, bowler hatted foreman, it still has a long way to go to reach either the sophistication of its American opposite number or the ideas which were to be current in Britain in 1960. It is perhaps a masterpiece of British compromise: taking some of the ideas of the Americans, and adapting them to make them fit the British character and British ideas. As a matter of politics, which, after all, is the art of the possible, perhaps this was as much as could be done at the time. Perhaps if Sheldon's scheme had been generally followed, it would have been quite a large step forward.

*Training*

Sheldon insists, somewhat paradoxically, that, as management is developing into a science, the training of managers, foremen and clerks has become essential. Experience itself is no longer enough. But in spite of this he says, 'The science of management has at present none of the definite features of Medicine or Law. It is chaotic; it has no accepted text-books or principles. It has no accepted ideals, no proven methods.'[22] Training managers must be by a patient study of the writings which are available, of the best of others' performances, and by comparison of results. He suggests lectures, talks and discussion groups. For all managers the widest possible general education is needed.

Foremen, too, need training to fit them for the new situation. The first thing is for management to incorporate the foremen into the ranks of managers. Management must then reconsider the real nature of the foreman's job and see it as one in which training in leadership, in the 'spirit' of the firm, and in the objectives of the business are first priorities.

Although he suggests that clerks should be trained because they are becoming much more specialized and engaged in functional duties, and are likely therefore to become the functional managers of the future, he is decidedly vague as to what sort of training they actually need.

*Conclusion*

In the doubtful political and economic conditions of the early 1920s it must have seemed difficult to forecast ahead. Sheldon is prepared, however to conclude that whatever happens to the structure of industry, to its ownership, to political intervention, 'In management we have the one stable element in our process of evolution.'[23] Whatever happened management would remain as the controlling force in industry.

He suggests that management has two main problems to cope with: the idealism, as he sees it, of the labour movement, and how to learn to use the scientific method in management on an ever-increasing scale.

He concludes with a 'Philosophy', setting out ten points which may be summarized as follows:

   (i) Production to meet the highest ends of the community
  (ii) An ethical basis for business
 (iii) Management divided into Administration, Management proper and Organization
  (iv) The development of efficiency
   (v) The use of analysis, standards and the development of people and co-operation
  (vi) Correct organization
 (vii) The division of management itself into functions, with manufacturing as the main one
(viii) The use of scientific method
  (ix) Correct policies with regard to employees
   (x) The evolution of a science of industrial management.

It is a thoroughly detailed book for its time, and on both its practical and ethical side it is probably a good guide to the very best thinking and practice of the day, almost certainly as developed in

Rowntree's of York. But with its almost extreme ethical flavour, its high ideals and almost religious fervour it was probably too idealistic and its philosophy too remote from average realism to appeal to the majority of managers. Admittedly Sheldon was arguing that this is what should be, this is the ideal towards which management must move, but the question seems to hang over this book more than any other: Is this the source of the practising manager's complaint 'That's all right in theory, but . . .'?

## References

(1) Sheldon, O. *The Philosophy of Management* (Pitman, London 1923), p. 19.
(2) ibid., p. 23.
(3) ibid., p. 27 (italics are the author's).
(4) ibid., p. 29.
(5) ibid., p. 35.
(6) ibid., p. 35.
(7) ibid., p. 53.
(8) ibid., p. 66.
(9) ibid., pp. 68–69.
(10) ibid., p. 72.
(11) ibid., p. 85.
(12) ibid., p. 76.
(13) ibid., p. 74.
(14) ibid., p. 75.
(15) ibid., p. 104.
(16) Drucker, P. F. *The Practice of Management* (Heinemann, London 1955), p. 243.
(17) Sheldon, O. *The Philosophy of Management*, op. cit., p. 146.
(18) ibid., p. 177.
(19) ibid., p. 182.
(20) ibid., p. 192.
(21) ibid., p. 233.
(22) ibid., p. 253.
(23) ibid., p. 281.

## Bibliography

BOOKS BY O. SHELDON

*The Philosophy of Management* (Pitman, London 1923).
(Jointly)
*Factory Organization* by C. H. Northcott, O. Sheldon, J. W. Wardropper and L. F. Urwick (Pitman, London 1928).

# 9

## B. Seebohm Rowntree
## 1938

*Introduction*

If the development of management thought includes not only written and published work but also the effect of precept and example on the thinking and practice of industrial managers, then Seebohm Rowntree must rank in the forefront of developers. It is doubtful whether many people exerted more influence on British management in the 1920s and 1930s.

Born in 1871 into the Quaker family who had founded and were still running the cocoa industry at York, he inherited and was brought up in the high practical, ethical, and humanitarian standards of the Society of Friends. As such he was inevitably an idealist, but with a difference. He was a very practical idealist, quiet and purposeful, far from the Victorian image of the domineering entrepreneur, but nevertheless a keen business-man.

He was the able industrial executive concerned to improve the whole working conditions of industry, but recognizing clearly that the better conditions he sought could only be realized in practise on a basis of efficiency. He was, therefore, at one and the same time, interested in industrial welfare, and in all the best developments of scientific management.[1]

His life and work are of more than usual interest to this book because to a greater extent than most, except perhaps Taylor and Gilbreth, they were his contribution to development, and his written work is simply an account of what he and his colleagues on the Board at Rowntree's did in practice.

From an early age he was interested in and carried out practical field research on the problem of poverty. At an early age that is in 1901, he published his first findings in *Poverty – a Study of Town Life*. The interest remained with him all his life, as he wrote *The Human Needs of Labour* in 1918, with a second edition in 1938, and *Poverty and Progress – a second Social Survey of York* in 1941. From the point of view of this book, this aspect of his work formed the basis of his argument for a minimum wage below which no one should be paid. This, if industry was to meet it, would require a great increase in the efficiency of many firms.

He started work at York in 1889 and was made Labour Director in 1897. In 1923 he succeeded his father as Chairman of the Board, a post which he held until 1936. He remained on the Board until his final retirement at the age of 70 in 1941.

### Outside Work

In 1916 he was appointed Director of the newly established Industrial Welfare Department of the Ministry of Munitions. Under his guidance much was done to change the ideas of industry for getting greater production from more overtime and Sunday work to providing conditions where people were able to work better during normal hours. The upsurge of welfare work in the 1920s was largely the result of his efforts. Still concerned primarily with the welfare side of business, he was very influential in the setting up of the Boys' Welfare Association in 1918. A year later it widened its scope and became the Industrial Welfare Society.

But welfare and minimum wages can only be paid for out of efficiency, and the spread of scientific management (in the British rather than the 'Taylor' sense) was another major aspect of his work. One way in which this was done was by setting up the first week-end Lecture Conference for managers at Oxford in 1918. Seventeen such conferences were held between then and 1922, when they became known as the Oxford Management Conferences, and from then on they were held twice a year. L. F. Urwick and E. F. L. Brech suggest at p. 61 of Vol. I of *The Making of Scientific Management* (Pitman, London 1957) that 'They [the Conferences] have exercised a powerful influence towards improved standards of business organization.' The same book also refers to the Management Research Groups set up in 1927. These appear to have consisted of groups of firms whose senior managers met regularly and exchanged information and ideas on their management practices and problems.

Briefly, then, this was Rowntree's outside life in so far as it was concerned with the development and encouragement of sound and, at the time, modern management thinking and practice. It is, of course, one thing to preach to the unconverted, it is another to put the preaching into practice. Rowntree was in a position to do both, and he did both.

## Management Development

His own account of what was done at York appears in three editions of *The Human Factor in Business: Experiments in Industrial Democracy*. The first appeared in 1921 while he was still Labour Director, the second in 1925, two years after he had become Chairman, and the last in 1938, two years after he had retired from the chairmanship of the company. What follows has been taken from the 1938 edition, because this shows the full story of the developments and is, therefore, a more complete version of his work.

While he is careful to disclaim all credit for himself and to insist that the responsibility for the policies followed was that of the full Board of Directors, it may well be fair to assume that this was his natural modesty showing through and that, while it was strictly true in that policy was the Board's concern, he was probably the main instigator of change and reform.

Again, modestly, he says in the concluding chapter of the book 'Of course, I am not labouring under the illusion that working conditions at the Cocoa Works represent the best that is being done under the capitalist system, and still less the best that the capitalist system is capable of doing.'[2]

Right at the start it should be stated that his view of the situation was that management should manage in such a way that workers could and would become co-operators with management. There would appear to be two reasons for this. One was his innate and natural humanitarian outlook, which rebelled against the way workers had been treated as 'hands' or as an impersonal economic factor of production in Victorian industry. The other was a reaction to the growing view of many workers and thinkers at the time that the only solution to the workers' problems was the overthrow of the capitalist system.

He maintains that, one way or the other, workers desire two things from industry: better material conditions and improved status. The company's labour policy was framed deliberately 'to introduce into the management of the business, *in all matters directly affecting the workers*, as great a measure of democracy as possible *without lowering efficiency*'.[3] Two fundamental points are raised here. Democracy would improve status and self-respect for the worker, but it was not to interfere with the prerogative of management to manage the business; it was limited to aspects affecting the workers, and here control would be shared between management and workers. Secondly, it must not interfere with the efficient running of the business. Indeed only if the business was efficiently run could it afford to carry out such policies.

Behind the policy lay the question 'Could capitalist industry do these things for workers at least as well as socialist or communist systems?' Rowntree thought that it could.

Before enlarging on the ways in which this policy was put into effect he lays down four conditions[4] on which efficiency, whether under capitalism or any other system, must rest:

1. Under any system of industry, every enterprise must be conducted efficiently. This involves that, so far as possible, every employed person, whether an executive or a manual worker, shall work at the task and under the conditions which will enable him to make his greatest contribution to the enterprise.
2. No business can be efficiently managed by mass meetings of the workers. The workers must be divided into those whose duty it is to give orders and those whose duty it is to obey them. Orders must be given by individuals, not by committees.
3. The "order givers" should be selected by those best qualified to do so and they should be chosen because among all the available candidates for the posts they are those who can make

the greatest contribution to the success of the enterprise.
4. Managerial policy should be devised by those best qualified
to do so . . .

How, then, were these policies and principles put into effect? First
and foremost was the question of status.

While the Trade Board insisted that the industry should lay down
minimum wages and working conditions, Rowntree's went a step
further and belonged to the Interim Industrial Reconstruction
Committee, a voluntary body which imposed on its members
conditions better than those required by the Trade Board.

On the question of trade unions the Company by open and
honest dealings maintained permanently satisfactory relations with
the unions and encouraged its workers to join them, while still
leaving the final decision on joining to the individual. But negotiations with trade unions were only the start and could only lay the
'foundations on which the structure of co-operation may be built'.[5]

Democracy and co-operation were developed within the factory,
and the first step was the setting up of formal Works Councils
before 1917. Informal consultations had existed long before this.
To begin with it was a three-tier system with Section Councils,
Departmental Councils and the Central Council. Sectional Councils
were found to be of little practical use and were scrapped in favour
of official shop-stewards who could deal direct with management
on behalf of any worker in their section.

Departmental Councils consisted of roughly equal numbers of
workers (shop-stewards *ex officio* and elected members) and
management representatives appointed by senior management.
Originally Departmental Councils met every month, but as shop-
stewards gradually took over direct negotiation the regular meetings
were dropped and Councils only met when matters concerning a
whole department came up.

The Central Council consisted of twenty-six management
members, some elected by managers, others nominated by the
Board, and thirty workers' representatives elected by the members
of the Departmental Councils. The chairman was selected alter-
nately from the management and the workers' side. The only

matters which the Central Council were not allowed to consider were departmental questions and conditions laid down by the Interim Industrial Reconstruction Committee. All decisions of any Council were subject to veto either by the Board or by the trade unions. Rowntree says that he could only recall two occasions in twenty-odd years when either side used the veto.

Departmental Councils dealt largely with matters concerning the individual department, but also with the report from the Central Council representative, and with a periodic statement from the departmental manager on the state of trade and in particular the way it affected the department. Suggestions from members on production difficulties and improvements were a regular part of the proceedings.

The scope of the Central Council was much wider, dealing with questions affecting the works as a whole. These tended to be less routine and more fundamental in character and showed the essential aspects of democracy in practice. They included the approval of the complete revision of works rules, decisions on reallocation of hours from $5\frac{1}{2}$ to the 5-day week, a recommendation that workers should share in the appointment of foremen, consideration of the appointment of a works psychologist, profit-sharing and unemployment benefit schemes. But, equally importantly, the works side of the Committee could and did raise questions of productivity, improvements in methods and designs, reducing costs, and general welfare matters.

Although production and technical matters had to be referred to the appropriate manager for approval, these arrangements must surely have gone as far in the direction of industrial democracy as any before or since in large-scale industry. For the individual worker the right to vote for his or her representative and to approach him at any time with any problem, criticism or suggestion must consciously or otherwise have given feelings of status and belonging. A further step in democracy was the detailed revision of the works rules by a sub-committee of the Central Council consisting of four workers' representatives and four management representatives. Their draft was, as stated above, discussed and agreed by the Central Council.

An even more 'revolutionary' system was instituted for the appointment of foremen and forewomen. While it was felt that the workers were not really concerned with the appointment of higher managers, whose qualifications for the post would be more technical, the appointment of first-line supervisors was a very different matter. Workers were in daily contact with their supervisor, and a bad or disliked supervisor could create havoc. The ensuing drop in morale (and in efficiency) would be bad for the workers and the firm. The Central Council ruled that before appointing a foreman the manager must submit his name to a small committee of the workers on the Departmental Council concerned. If they approved, all well and good. If they objected they could put up other names, which would be considered by the manager and the committee together. It was provided that if no mutual agreement could be reached then the Directors should have the final word, but this apparently was never necessary. Later the shop-steward had to be consulted in place of the small committee. It is interesting to note that the original suggestion for this procedure came from a works representative on a Departmental Council.

Discipline was another matter in which Rowntree's took the lead very early on. In this case the initiative came from the Directors as a suggestion to the Central Council. Instead of the management being prosecution, witness and judge and there being no right of appeal except to higher levels of management it was proposed that a joint 'court of appeal' should be set up. The proposal was agreed and an Appeal Committee consisting of two elected workers' representatives and two nominated management representatives was set up. The Committee appointed a fifth member as independent chairman. Any worker feeling that disciplinary action taken against him for a breach of works rules was unfair could appeal to this Committee for a 'proper trial'. The Committee could alter the sentence in any way and its decision was final. Once it upset a Directors' decision! On average up to 1938 it had heard about two cases a year.

Still on the question of justice, Mr Rowntree drily points out that where you are making a commodity as desirable as chocolate, theft can be something of a problem. A Theft Committee of six members, three workers and three management, with an independent Chairman, was set up to try all cases of theft. They were directly referred to the Committee by the manager concerned who, possibly apart from giving evidence, took no further part in the proceedings. The idea was to create a 'public opinion' against theft in addition to the basic concept of independent trial, and it appeared to succeed to a considerable extent.

Turning to another aspect of democracy and the freedom of the individual brings us to the question of freedom of speech. The attitude of the company is probably best summed up by the following quotation: 'You cannot expect to develop a spirit of true co-operation if the workers are refused the right to ask questions as to why certain things are done, and if they are not allowed to bring before the management criticism of any managerial policy with which they disagree.'[6]

Through the Departmental and Central Councils workers were able to raise almost any question they liked. Once a year the Chairman addressed three meetings after the Annual General Meeting: these were a meeting of managers, the Central Council, and an open meeting of workers. At these he explained in more detail and at more appropriate levels the report given to the shareholders. The real purpose of these meetings was, however, not so much the Chairman's report but an open opportunity for anyone to ask whatever questions he wished on the running and future of the company, or to make whatever criticism he felt appropriate. Yet another meeting was the annual meeting of shop-stewards, with the chief shop-steward in the chair and the Chairman of the Board there to answer 'any questions that any shop-steward likes to ask'.

Add to these the deliberate policy actively carried out by Directors and managers of making every possible scrap of information available, whether it was to trade unions in negotiations, the Councils, to shop-stewards and to the workers generally, and it can be seen that two-way communication was a reality and not a pious hope.

One final point on this broad aspect of status is the question of shop-stewards. At some early date, probably about 1916–17, shop-stewards elected for each department by the union members were recognized and incorporated into the Council system. In 1920 the management suggested to the union that the chief shop-steward should become a full-time employee in the Labour Department and devote his whole time to shop-steward activities. After some hesitation due to doubts about 'management influence' the union accepted and the system appears to have worked very well. Six years later a similar set-up was put in by Sir Charles Bartlett at Vauxhall Motors. The absence of strikes at both factories in the years that followed amply justified the policy.

The space given so far to these aspects of democracy at work may seem disproportionate compared with the somewhat cavalier treatment of what is to follow. On the other hand what has been dealt with so far constitutes the most original and, if it is the right word, the most 'revolutionary' aspects of the work at York. It was on these aspects that Rowntree's led the field and carried out the most significant developments in management as examples to the rest of the world of what could be done. They anticipated in a practical way much of the 'theory' of the psycho-sociologists of half a century later.

Regrettably, although many changes have taken place in management practice which, directly or indirectly, can be ascribed to the influence of Rowntree's, it is still true to say that fifty years and more later most managers have still not yet got the full message.

## Wages

Wages were another topic on which Rowntree held very decided and, for his time, revolutionary views. As stated earlier, these arose in connection with his interest in poverty. Human dignity for him meant that no-one should be required to work for a wage on which he could not bring up a family of three children in at least reasonable conditions.

The answer to this was a form of two-tier wage system. At the lowest levels economics should be ignored and wages determined by the minimum amount required to bring up a family, or, for women, the minimum to meet her own living costs and essential extras. Above this level the wage should vary according to the economic value of the services performed.

## B. Seebohm Rowntree

These, of course, were to be minimum conditions. Where they did not exist, while he was prepared to admit that a single employer could not easily go against a whole industry, he pressed for fair-minded employers to get together to persuade the Employers' Federation to set up a Trade Board which would then establish the minimum wage levels for different trades. Within his own factory the employer should try to be efficient enough to pay reasonable wages, subject to economic conditions, whatever others were doing. With this as a starting point, the employer should take steps to ensure that wages are administered properly, and in particular that:

   (i) comparative rates are kept in line.
   (ii) workers are encouraged to earn as much as possible.
   (iii) day workers' rates are adjusted as and when necessary.
   (iv) payment-by-results systems are just and equitable.
   (v) proper organization exists to deal with questions on individual or group problems.

In the Cocoa Works itself precept was turned into practice, by the company belonging to the Interim Industrial Reconstruction Committee (*see* page 124) and in 1919 by the transfer of all questions of wages from the separate work departments to a specially set up Wages Section, which was made responsible for wage policy throughout the factory.

In particular the function of the Wages Section can be summarized as follows:

   (i) To co-ordinate methods of dealing with wages.
   (ii) To survey constantly all individual wages and to advise departments when anomalies were noticed.
   (iii) To ensure the conditions laid down by the Trade Board and the Interim Industrial Reconstruction Committee were scrupulously observed.
   (iv) To advise departments on payment-by-results systems.
   (v) To obtain and keep up to date comparative information on wages throughout the country.
   (vi) To obtain information on wage systems.
   (vii) To negotiate with trade unions on wages.

Payment by results based on time study were used wherever possible. The appropriate shop-steward had to be notified before a time study was made of the workers to be studied, and on completion of the study signed joint statements with the manager and the time-study officer on the conditions and the piece-rate to be paid. If through conditions beyond the workers' control their earnings dropped, compensation was paid to make them up. Rate-cutting because of high earnings was forbidden and rates could only be altered once set if the machines, material, process or conditions were altered or if *both* sides agreed that a mistake had been made. Day rates of wages were subject to upward variation for merit awards.

Profit-sharing was investigated in 1919–20 and a scheme adopted. While the scheme was probably as good as could be devised and allowed for equal control of the distribution by representatives of the workers, it was not really a success. The economic conditions of the 1920s and 1930s were probably chiefly to blame.

*Security*

While as a matter of policy the company tried wherever possible to avoid creating unemployment, the depressions of the 1920s and 1930s and a seasonal trade together with the overriding requirement of business efficiency forced it at times to dismiss workers or to work short time.

To dismissed workers the company paid a supplement based on the size of the family and the time he or she had been with the firm. This was over and above the unemployment benefit paid by the State. It was a requirement that the employee should have been contributing to the union's unemployment benefit scheme. Short-time working entitled the worker to proportionate benefits. The scheme was financed entirely by the company, first by a capital sum, followed by the self-imposed obligation to contribute 1 per cent of the annual wage bill to the fund. In practice this contribution was seldom required.

Further steps to help with dismissals were for the company to try to place people with other companies, to persuade other employers to come to York to provide further employment, and even to set up new companies themselves under independent management to provide work. Somewhat ruefully Rowntree admits that these last schemes generally did not work well.

Sickness is inevitably a risk for any worker, but it was regarded by Rowntree's as one against which they could reasonably be expected to insure provided it was short-term. Long-term sickness or becoming an invalid was, however, another matter and was covered by an Invalidity Insurance Fund, again set up by the company and run jointly by trustees from management and workers. Pensions for manual workers on retirement were instituted as early as 1906, and for the families of those not entitled to pension in 1911.

In justifying provisions for employees on such a scale Rowntree says that the cost of the pension schemes was about 4 per cent of the total wages and salaries bill plus certain capital sums used to set up the schemes. He admits that it might be argued that industry as a whole might say it could not afford this, but:

> many employers are now paying 'hidden pensions' which I imagine are often much more costly than they ever realized. However, apart from this, I suggest that in one way or another, either with or without further state aid, a measure of security not less adequate than that described above is the least that should be regarded as satisfactory.[7]

This illustrates an interesting balance of economic and humanitarian argument.

### Working Conditions
For the time the working conditions were no doubt excellent. The most interesting part of the system is the way in which decisions were shared between management and workers; for instance, the decision to reduce working hours from 56 to 44 a week was referred to the Central Council for decision and the Council decided on a plebiscite of all workers.

### The Labour Department
The Labour Department, or as it would be called today the

Personnel Department, was yet another aspect in which Rowntree's showed the way to development. How well it was showed is demonstrated by the fact that their Labour Manager for many years, Dr C. H. Northcott, wrote what became the standard British textbook on Personnel Management for almost thirty years.

## Welfare Conditions

Welfare work, organized both by the company and by the workers themselves with management encouragement, would today be regarded as exceptional only in that it occurred so early. It consisted of brighter conditions, paintwork, lighting, corridors; adequate cloakrooms and lavatory facilities and clubs to cater for all tastes and most activities; and medical, dental and optical services on a full-time basis.

## Education and Training

There is an interesting sidelight on the state of management when Rowntree starts his argument to justify training and education. He says, 'In addition to the older sciences of engineering and chemistry, we now have costing and planning systems, scientific organization and psychology at our service.'[8] Even allowing for the fact that from his own experience in the company he could have added economics, statistics, and sales-forecasting at least, it is enlightening to see how few management techniques are mentioned.

Experiments in general education for juniors and for adult workers, in training for clerical staff, in apprenticeship schemes for the relatively few tradesmen employed, and conferences for managers, technical staff, and foremen were all carried on under the guidance of a full-time education officer. For juniors the schemes started as early as 1905 and 1906 and continued until transferred to York Education Committee classes. For adults 1920 was the date of inauguration.

## Conclusion

How far did Seebohm Rowntree influence the development of management thought? The question is almost like asking how far do the ripples go when you drop a stone into a lake. His influence at

the Cocoa Works, first as Labour Director, and then for thirteen
years as Chairman, must have been enormous, although he modestly
disclaimed responsibility when Urwick and Brech persuaded him
to let them write about him in Vol. I of *The Making of Scientific
Management*. He apparently asked them 'to make it clear that all
the experiments at the Cocoa Works were the responsibility of the
Board of Directors as a whole' (footnote to p. 58). The example of
the Cocoa Works must have done much to influence other firms
and managers. His work for outside bodies such as the Industrial
Welfare Society and the Oxford Management Conferences made
his own and other 'modern' ideas better known.

While he himself again and again insisted on efficiency and
scientific management as the basic aim of management if it was to
be able to afford to manage workers properly, he is, perhaps, best
known for his humanitarian ideas. Can he also be held partly
responsible for the books on efficient management and techniques
which came from other managers at the Cocoa Works? To mention
the more important, C. H. Northcott's *Personnel Management;
Principles and Practice* (Pitman, London 1945), Sheldon's *The
Philosophy of Management* (*see* Chapter 8), and W. Wallace's *Sales
Forecasting and its Practical Application* (Pitman, London 1932) all
came from York. All were pioneers in their respective fields.

*References*

(1) *B. Seebohm Rowntree. In Memoriam*: obituary by William Wallace,
Chairman of Rowntree and Co. Ltd, York (Rowntree, York 1954).

(2) Rowntree, B. S. *The Human Factor in Business: Experiments in
Industrial Democracy*, Third Edition (Longmans, London 1938), p. 186.

(3) ibid., p. 1 (the italics are the author's).

(4) ibid., p. 2.

(5) ibid., p. 8.

(6) ibid., p. 28.

(7) ibid., p. 86.

(8) ibid., p. 154.

*Bibliography*

BOOKS BY B. SEEBOHM ROWNTREE

*Poverty. A Study of Town Life* (Macmillan, London 1901; The
Macmillan Co., New York 1902). New Edition (Longmans, London
1922).

## The Experience Approach

*The Way to Industrial Peace and the Problem of Unemployment* (T. Fisher Unwin, London 1914).

*The Human Factor in Business: Experiments in Industrial Democracy* (Longmans, London 1921; Second Edition 1925; Third Edition 1938).

*Industrial Unrest: a way out* (Longmans, London 1922; G. H. Doran Co., New York 1922).

*Poverty and Progress* (Longmans, London 1941).

# 10

# Chester I. Barnard
## 1938

*Introduction*

Chester Barnard says of his book *The Functions of the Executive*, 'It is not the work of a scientist or a scholar, but rather of an interested student of affairs.'[1] As the statement of a practising manager who rose to the top in his career as President of the New Jersey Bell Telephone Company, it is correct, but it is an understatement.

In 1937 he gave a series of eight lectures under the same title as the book. These lectures created a sufficiently strong impression for half a dozen of the top professors of Harvard to press him to give them more permanent form as a book. The book which resulted is the subject of this chapter. It is an 'experience' book in that it is based on an analysis of Barnard's own experience as a manager. But it seems to go further. The analysis is so deep, so profound, that it is more than a statement of the functions of the executive. It is a comprehensive and scholarly statement of a theory of management, whatever Barnard's modest disclaimers may be.

There are two parts to the book. The first half analyses the then existing knowledge from the social sciences as the background within which management operates. The second half deals in very general terms with the process of management itself and the problems which it faces.

*The Social Sciences Background*

While human society is, in fact, made up of individual persons the individual by himself can achieve little, in fact his physical, biological and psychological powers are such as to be a limitation on achievement. The universal answer to this is organization, the coming together of people into large or small groups to achieve ends which would be impossible for them as individuals. This raises major problems of social factors and social relationships.

Organization itself is the result of and operates in conditions of opposing forces. At the personal level there will be conflict of emotions and of motives. Between the aims of the individual and those of the organization there will again be differences. Aims themselves will always be opposed by limitations, of resources, of powers, of abilities. Over all hangs the insoluble and final conflict: is any action or decision the result of free will, or are all determined by forces beyond the control of the individual? Barnard considers that to explain what *is*, both must be accepted as viable explanations of conduct.

Co-operation, which is organization in action, inevitably suffers from and must, as far as possible, overcome limitations. But a limitation only exists in so far as it is related to a particular aim. Some different combination of resources must then be found to overcome the limitation or make it irrelevant, or the aim must be modified.

Further, although the aim of co-operation is the achievement of ends, it can only take place in a social and psychological framework. If they are to co-operate effectively, or even at all, the individuals concerned must receive in return satisfactions from doing so which are at least as great as the efforts and sacrifices which they make. Co-operation, therefore, has two criteria to meet: effectiveness, i.e. the achieving of the aim set, and efficiency, i.e. the provision of satisfactions sufficient to ensure that co-operative efforts are forthcoming.

Failure to achieve and maintain co-operation is claimed to be more frequent than success, and this failure is due to unawareness of or inability to realize the importance of these background factors.

## Theory and Structure of Formal Organizations

Co-operation takes place within the framework of an organization. Attention now turns to the study of organization itself. The definition of organization presents difficulties in deciding what shall be included and what excluded. The total situation in which organization exists is made up of a complex of many different systems. In the end the definition is 'a system of consciously co-ordinated personal activities or forces'.[2] This leaves outside the physical environment, the social environment and much of the human environment. It places the emphasis on organization as a system of co-operative action to which the individual contributes some, but by no means all, of his efforts and acts. The system exists within other physical, social and human systems which impinge on and influence it without being part of it.

A further point which receives great emphasis is that an organization must be greater than the sum of its parts. The individuals who come together as an organization, or co-operative co-ordinated system, must 'produce' more in quality and quantity as a result than they could do by their own individual efforts. An analysis of organization shows that the large, complex organization consists of a combination of smaller organizational units and that the principles governing the smaller apply also to the larger, although there may be modifications in quality and in form.

The existence of organization pre-supposes three things:

(i) Willingness to co-operate, although for the majority this will not be spontaneous or constant. It therefore requires incentives to co-operation.

(ii) Purpose or objective to provide direction for effort. This must be acceptable to the people involved if co-operation is to be forthcoming.

(iii) Communication to provide the link between purpose and people.

The difficulties of communication are the main factor in causing differences between small and large organization structures. In the small structure, face-to-face communication is easy and straightforward. In the large structure this is impossible, and so a pattern of 'points' which can receive and transmit information throughout the structure has to be built up. These 'points' are the executive or managerial positions organized as a hierarchy from top to bottom of the structure.

Quite apart from the formal organization structure there will inevitably be an informal one alongside it. This deals with relationships and communication which the formal structure is not designed to handle. In marked contrast to later thinking, which maintains that a chief function of informal organization is to achieve sub-group aims not met by the formal organization, Barnard says specifically 'The characteristics of these contacts or interactions is that they occur and continue or are repeated without any specific *joint* purpose.'[3]

While the informal organization is claimed to be unconscious, which apparently here means not deliberate, it is regarded as an essential part of the total situation because it 'establishes certain attitudes, understandings, customs, habits, institutions'.[4] It also provides the condition in which formal organization can arise. Conversely it is claimed that formal organizations 'create and require informal organizations'.[5]

At least the fact of informal organization is recognized and the need for taking it into account is stressed, although a fuller understanding of its real nature and purpose is still a long way off. Rather as an aside Barnard gives its functions as communication, providing cohesion and enabling the individual to protect his integrity.

## The Elements of Formal Organizations
The first element of organization is specialization in terms of place, materials, kind of work, skill and so on. To put it in another, more general way, it is the sub-division of the main purpose of the organization into sub-purposes, which can be assigned to individuals or groups. This involves firstly the existence of people willing to submit to the restrictions involved, and secondly, adequate communication between them. Barnard maintains that with specialization the individual and the sub-group must know and accept the *immediate* purpose which he or it must attain, but need not know or understand the overall purpose of the whole organization. If, however, this is known, understood and accepted it makes a detailed purpose more acceptable. The voice of the 'practical' manager is heard here when he suggests that while this is desirable, in most complex organizations it does not happen.

Certainly in industrial organizations co-operation between

individuals is not something which will happen of itself. The second element of organization is, therefore, incentives. These are an essential pre-requisite of co-operation. It is equally essential that the satisfactions derived by the individual from the incentives must at least equal and preferably exceed the efforts, discomforts and losses involved in co-operating. On the question of incentives Barnard moves a long way beyond the idea that people only 'work for the money'. He lists the following as some possible incentives:

 (i) Material or financial inducements.
 (ii) Personal opportunities, e.g. status, power.
 (iii) Good physical conditions.
 (iv) Attractiveness of social conditions.
 (v) General conditions adapted or suitable to the individual's ideas and attitudes.
 (vi) Opportunities for participation.
 (vii) Good communication.
 (viii) Opportunities for satisfying personal motivation, e.g. pride in work, sense of adequacy, and so on.

Taking perhaps a very realistic point of view in the late 1930s, Barnard says that if an organization is unable to provide sufficient incentives to call forth adequate co-operation then its executives must be able to exercise sufficient persuasion to get the people involved to accept less and still co-operate. The alternative is to rationalize material aims into a 'sense of duty'.

The next element in organization is authority. The theory of authority put forward is, at the least, novel for its time. Rather as an aside the first comment is that in almost all forms of organization authority is very frequently flouted. The definition of authority is quite different from most that were current at the time. It is: 'Authority is the character of a communication (order) in a formal organization by virtue of which it is accepted by a contributor to or "member" of the organization as governing the action he contributes.'[6] Two vital points about this definition are that it makes authority an inherent part of organization structure and not something conferred from above, and it emphasizes the point of acceptance as being essential. It foreshadows very exactly later concepts of 'valid' authority. While management must accept that it can effectively only issue orders which are acceptable, this does not mean that it is subject to the whim and caprice of every individual in the organization. Acceptance depends on understanding, belief that the order is not inconsistent with the aims of the organization or the general aims of the individual, and physical and mental ability to comply. To make things easier, orders in industry generally meet these conditions. In addition the general atmosphere is usually one which creates and maintains a 'zone of indifference' in which individuals accept orders without question.

Authority is exercised through communication and certain conditions are necessary for it to be effective. They are:

(i) Channels of communication (lines of authority) must be definitely known by all.

(ii) These channels must be formally laid down.

(iii) Each channel should be as short as possible.

(iv) Normally communication should go through all stages in the channel from source to destination.

(v) People acting as communication centres (managers) should be adequate to their tasks.

(vi) Channels of communication should not be interrupted while the organization is functioning.

(vii) Communications (orders) must come from points where the necessary authority is known to exist.

The final element in organization is the decision-making process. The point is made that decision-making within an organization must be a much more logical process than for an individual making personal decisions. This applies both to ends and objectives, which must be logically defined, and the means or organizational acts required to attain them. This does not prevent non-logical behaviour within the organization, particularly within the informal structure.

Organizational decision-making involves two major aspects. The first is the objective which, it is claimed, is always a modification of some previous objective. The second is the environment. Parts of this will be irrelevant to the purpose, parts will be relevant. The relevant parts may be favourable or hostile. If hostile they must be capable of being changed by some action brought about by sub-decisions, or the objective itself must be abandoned or modified. Decision-making requires analysis of situations, primarily to determine the strategic factors. These are the elements in the total situation which if properly controlled will enable the objective to be achieved. There may be some existing element which requires modification or some missing element which must be supplied. Within an organization decision-making is seldom, if ever, a one-off process. Each decision when taken will necessitate a whole series of ever more detailed sub-decisions, taken probably by other people.

Again, this theory of decision-making, although incomplete, seems to be the forerunner of later theories.

## The Functions of Organizations

Finally, in the last quarter of the book Barnard comes to the functions of the executive. In very marked contrast to, say, Fayol, he gives these in very general terms under three headings – functions, process, and responsibility.

The functions can be described very briefly. They are:
  (i) Maintaining organization communication
      (*a*) determining the scheme of organization
      (*b*) fostering loyalty in subordinates
      (*c*) maintaining the informal system
 (ii) Obtaining essential services from individuals
      (*a*) correct selection of individuals
      (*b*) provision of the necessary inducements, maintaining morale, providing incentives and sanctions, supervision, training.
(iii) Formulating purposes and objectives at all levels.

These functions are, of course, only elements in the total executive process. While the process does largely consist of logical, specific acts, it is also 'the sensing of the organization as a whole and the total situation relevant to it'.[7] This reverts attention to two terms mentioned much earlier – effectiveness and efficiency. As previously defined effectiveness means the attainment of organizational objectives. But the overall objectives are only reached by a continuous process of reaching the sub-objectives involved. So the executive process includes attaining sub-objectives *and* co-ordinating them towards general objectives.

Efficiency means maintaining the balance between necessary activities and efforts by satisfying the motives of the individuals concerned. In order to be able to do this management must see that sufficient utilities are created by the efforts of the organization to be distributed in exchange for the individual efforts and sacrifices involved. A detailed balance in this exchange is impossible because four different 'economies' are involved.

  (i) the physical energies and materials
 (ii) the individual economy
(iii) the social economy
(iv) the complex economy of the organization itself.

The only effective measures of success are the survival and growth of the organization. In money terms the individual contributing to the organization should be paid up to the point where for the organization further money would be worth more than the contribution received and for the individual further money is worth less than extra effort. Beyond that further effort must be obtained by non-financial incentives.

So far the structure and functioning of organizations have been regarded as objective facts from the point of view of analysis. But ultimately they have a moral aspect. This leads directly to executive responsibility '... responsibility is the property of an individual by which whatever morality exists in him becomes effective in conduct'.[8]

For the manager he is in a situation which implies a complex morality, requires a high standard of responsibility, involves activity, requires abilities 'as a moral factor' and requires the faculty of creating moral standards for his subordinates. Ultimately the test of the executive or manager is leadership, and leadership can only survive if it involves responsibility based on an adequate and satisfactory moral code.

## Conclusion

There can be little doubt of the value of Barnard's book as a contribution to the development of management thought, or of its influence on the management world in general. First published in 1938, its sales were such that 1966 saw the seventeenth printing. Not many management books can have had such a wide and continuous market. In terms of content it is a masterly, detailed analysis of management which, on the whole, is as valid today as on the day it was first published. Again there are not many books of which this could truthfully be said. The summary in this chapter does not, of course, do it justice. Too much has had to be left out. Of all the earlier works perhaps this is the one where it is most necessary to read the original.

## References

(1) Barnard, C. I. *The Functions of the Executive* (Harvard University Press, Cambridge, Mass., 1938), p. 292.

(2) ibid., p. 72.

(3) ibid., p. 114.

(4) ibid., p. 116.

(5) ibid., p. 120.

(6) ibid., p. 163.

(7) ibid., p. 235.

(8) ibid., p. 267.

## Bibliography

BOOKS BY C. I. BARNARD

*The Functions of the Executive* (Harvard University Press, Cambridge, Mass., 1938).

*The Nature of Leadership* (Harvard University Press, Cambridge, Mass., 1940).

*Organization and Management* (Harvard University Press, Cambridge, Mass., 1948).

# 11

# Lord Wilfred Brown
## 1960

### Introduction

It is appropriate that the last work we deal with in the 'Experience' section of this book should come at the end of our allowed time-span. It was at the time of publication the most up-to-date, and also the most personal and original statement of management practice to have been written.

Like all books based on personal experience, it is a statement of a personal 'credo', but it is, in fact, much more than that. Wilfred Brown was fortunate, or unfortunate according to one's point of view, in being pushed into the Managing Director's chair at Glacier Metal at an early age. However much worry and anxiety it may have caused him it is fortunate for posterity that he was that rather unusual combination – a practical and, dare one say, a born manager with innate ability, combined with a mental capacity to think and to analyse as a scholar. Although he himself would probably be the last to claim that he has put forward a new 'theory of management', in the sense that a 'theory' is a statement and a rational explanation of good practice this seems to be just what he has done. By rigorously thinking through the situations which he faced as a Managing Director, by applying the results of this thinking, adopting it where it worked and thinking again where it did not he has produced a framework of management based fundamentally on the ideas of sociology. In doing so he was considerably helped by Elliott Jaques of the National Institute of Industrial Psychology, who in one capacity or another was also at Glacier during most of the time on which this book was based.

From our point of view *Exploration in Management* is a difficult book to handle. Much of it is, of course, an account, often detailed, of what was done at Glacier Metal. Now we need from it the basic principles and ideas which seem to emerge. The separation will be difficult. Brown himself argues that he is not putting forward a new theory or even recommending anything new. To such suggestions he says he has always replied:

> No – I am recommending nothing except that you absorb these ideas, and then see if in your actual experience they are not a description of your own practice – I am not recommending new organizational practices or ideas to you, but I am giving you, in general terms, a description of what I believe goes on in your own company.[1]

He is too modest. It may be 'what goes on', but to use his own term he has 'taken it to a higher level of abstraction' by thinking about and by analysing 'what goes on', and so has produced new ideas about management which work at least at Glacier Metal.

The question then becomes: 'Have they a wider, general application or are we forced back to the "total complex" situation?' This concept would suggest that the ideas worked because they were suited to a particular *total* situation comprising Wilfred Brown, the nature of the company, its previous history, the particular people of all levels who worked with him, the modes of thought which were current, and so on. Remove any one of these factors, for example Wilfred Brown himself, and there is a different situation which calls for different measures and action. Basically, of course, this is true. No two situations are identical, but it would seem equally true that he has produced new insights into management which, adapted somewhat to meet another particular situation, would be of enormous general usefulness and would do much to improve managerial performance.

Broadly the book can be divided into four parts. First comes a detailed analysis of organization and the Executive System, and secondly a review of the nature and purpose in the business of the Representative System. This is followed by discussion of a new concept, the Legislative System, for the clarification of policy, and finally Brown describes the Appeals System, which he now regards as being a part of the Executive System. The Company Policy Document is omitted from this book as being too detailed and concerned solely with the particular conditions at Glacier Metal.

## The Organization

Before the analysis of the Executive System there are a number of comments on organization. The basic point of view is declared early on as being based on sociology. 'The study of administrative methods is the study of people at work, their behaviour, their relationships, the way work is split up between different roles, and the often unrecognized social institutions which companies have established and are using.'[2] But it is sociology and the consideration of human groups, not as entities in their own right, but in relation to the job, which the business has to do with. It is, as Eric L. Trist calls it in the Foreword to the book, 'the task approach', neither just the work to be done considered in isolation, nor the people who have to do it in isolation, but the two considered as aspects of one phenomenon – the task – the job *and* the person to do it. From a study over twelve years within Glacier Metal has emerged the different systems, Executive, Representative and Legislative, mentioned above. An important corollary derived from this is that people, whether they be managers or workers, can and do move from a role in one system to a role in another and back again, and that this change in roles calls for different forms of behaviour and different types of relationship.

Basic to carrying out the tasks is the Executive System within the organization. This should be a logical pattern of roles and relationships based on an authority structure, roles of superior and subordinate to which specific tasks, responsibilities and relationships can be assigned. In this sense the organization is 'a function of the work to be done and the resources and techniques available to do it'.[3] By implication the term 'resources' must include the people, their aptitudes, their abilities – what Drucker would call 'the whole man'. Any change, whether of market or product, of technique or process, should involve explicit and deliberate change in the system.

One aspect which comes out of this study of work is the lack of definitive knowledge about what it is, at least once the shop-floor manual work is left behind. A distinction is drawn between the 'prescribed' content of a job, which is defined by someone in higher authority as 'things which the man or manager must do' and the 'discretionary' content, which consists of the decisions and choices he must make for himself.

Most people have known for a long time that like many other things organization is not what it seems. Brown differentiates four aspects:

(i) The manifest organization. The formal description, perhaps by organization charts and job descriptions.

(ii) The assumed organization. What the people who work in it assume it to be. This is an individual subjective view which may agree with or differ from (i) and (iii).

(iii) The extant organization. The structure as it actually is. For many reasons, such as unplanned growth, development and changes, 'empire-building', or opting out, it may be very different from (i).

(iv) The requisite organization. The pattern required to meet the real needs of the situation.

Ideally, of course, the four should coincide. In a situation where things, of necessity, are always changing they are unlikely to do so. The only answer is a regular review of the extant situation so as to bring it and the manifest situation into line with the requisite.

Leading on from this is the idea, which is not new, that effective organization depends on placing any item of work at the correct point in the organization. What is perhaps new is the insight obtained that not enough is yet known about the 'discretionary' element of work to be sure as to just where an element of this kind should go.

*The Executive System*

One of the social systems, this depends for its functioning on two concepts. The first is that of policy, which however else it may be defined is treated here as decisions which limit the discretionary element in the subordinate's job. By setting out objectives and principles it shows the area of discretion allowed to the subordinate, and by implication rules out discretion in other areas. These may be prescribed areas where the subordinate is told precisely what to do, or they must be referred upwards to a higher level where discretionary power does exist.

The other concept involved in the executive system is delegation, the process whereby the superior transfers to his subordinate(s) the prescribed work which they must do and the discretionary powers within the limits of the policies he has laid down.

Primarily, then, the executive system is a pattern of roles or jobs with superior–subordinate relationships. The content of a role depends partly on its definition by the superior and partly on changes in the work content brought about by external or internal forces. This pattern of roles should be thought of objectively and as distinct from the people who at any time happen to fill them. Not to do this is to cause confusion between tasks and personalities.

The problem of the true position in the hierarchy of a particular role has always been a difficult one. Here at least an attempt has been made to get a more realistic answer than the usual one of the number of levels between the particular role and the top role in the company. The answer given is based on the time-span of the decisions allowed in the discretionary element of the job.

A role in the organization, then, has three dimensions by which it can be more or less accurately described:

   (i) Its position in the system.

  (ii) Its relationship with other roles.

 (iii) Its work content (prescribed and discretionary).

Having analysed the nature of the structure of the Executive System, Brown then turns to the relationships which are necessarily set up by the pattern. The first is, of course, the manager–subordinate relationship.

Rightly or wrongly all communications between a manager and his subordinate, whether phrased as orders, requests or advice, are stated to be instructions provided they occur within the executive relationship of superior–subordinate. Within the sphere of his command a manager is regarded as having total responsibility. This means that he is responsible for all the acts of his subordinates, and if he is to carry this responsibility he must (subject to the Appeals Procedure: *see* p. 157) have the right to appoint people to and to discharge them from the area of his command. In addition he must have the authority and responsibility for assessing, training, promoting and criticizing his subordinates.

Difficulties arise here, frequently from a failure on the part of the manager to realize precisely what his own role is. In assessing a subordinate's performance, for instance, he must not only assess his actions and his decisions but also these in relation to higher management and company policies over which he himself has no control and which may influence his subordinate's results. Neither must he take into account any actions by the subordinate in a representative role as distinct from his executive role.

Difficulties arise, too, in deciding what are or should be the different work contents and work loads of his subordinates and the salaries which are fair, and also in determining promotions. Brown admits that at Glacier they have done little more than start work on these problems, that there is a great deal more to be learnt, and that even when it is known line managers will need specialist advice and help in this part of their work.

Another inevitable aspect of the system of roles is that disagreement and conflict between the holders of different roles is inevitable. By implication he agrees with Follett that conflict is a good thing provided it is brought into the open, correctly handled and used to improve the situation. Generally it seems that although adequate machinery and guidance are given for dealing with them disagreements are frequently not brought out into the open. From the firm's point of view it is most desirable that they should be because they so often indicate something which should be put right, for example an out-of-date, confused or missing bit of policy, or because they are not brought out the managers concerned may make private agreements which run counter to the good of the firm.

## Policy

In writing and thinking about policy Brown makes a radical change from all earlier 'classical' views on the subject. Prior to this policy was assumed to consist only of objectives, and decisions on the broad methods of achieving them, as determined by the Board of Directors. In one sense this earlier view is specifically excluded in the careful definition given in Glacier's Policy Document. This reads: 'Policy – any statement adopted by a Council [see Legislative System, p. 156] or laid down by a manager, or any established practice or custom, which specifies the behaviour required of members in given situations.'[4] According to this a manager or a Council exercises discretionary power to issue instructions, which then become prescribed behaviour for subordinates. In a way this seems too narrow and to exclude too much, but it must be accepted within the context as being what is meant. What is vitally new is that policy is not just something 'at the top' but a whole series of more and more detailed decisions being taken all the way down the hierarchy to control the actions of those still further down.

Centralization is said to occur when a high-ranking manager sets policies which prescribe action for roles several ranks below him. Decentralization occurs when the higher manager sets policies only relating to his immediate subordinates and leaves them to re-interpret and promulgate them as their own policies for the next rank below, and so on, to the point where a manager must prescribe for all below him. The essential question is not whether to centralize or decentralize, but the position of the correct and appropriate point at which to prescribe for *all* ranks below.

One very important inference from this idea of different levels of policy is that they are described in 'different levels of abstraction'. Brown says that it is difficult to define a level of abstraction but easy to realize when one is moving from one to another.

Once custom and precedent are accepted as policy or rules for conduct then the very important conclusion follows that managers do not necessarily have to give written or spoken versions of policy. Their own conduct and example may be enough. Under these circumstances the formation of policy, if it is to be complete and watertight, must be an explicit and deliberate activity undertaken after due thought.

If policy and his job description show a manager what he must and must not do they must also show him where and to what extent he has freedom to make changes. It is maintained that where the job is clearly defined the freedom to change and the willingness to do so is greater than in the ill-defined or undefined situation, where the superior can at any time come down on his subordinate with 'You should not have done that', and the latter has no clear means of knowing where he stands.

## Communication

One major difficulty with communication is and always has been transmitting it accurately up and down the managerial line. Sometimes to do this the normal means must be by-passed, but this often has other disastrous results. Following the pattern on other things a useful and workable policy has been laid down for all to follow. When he feels it necessary any manager may contact anyone in his 'extended command' in his executive capacity (i.e. all people under him, not just his immediate subordinates). When he does so he must also do two other things as soon as possible – inform all intermediate subordinates of his action and take steps to restore the situation to normal where his action has, for example, overridden the authority of an intermediate manager. This takes care of the 'by-pass' and ensures that people in between are not left out of the picture.

A second difficulty can arise when a senior manager (A) wishes to give an order to apply not to his immediate subordinates but either to their subordinates or even to lower levels. In this case he must give it to his subordinates in the form 'This is *my* order to X, Y and Z.' His subordinates must then pass it on not as their own order but as manager A's order. Many orders can be issued either way, for example from A to his subordinate B, for the latter to interpret and pass on in his own way as his own order, or as a direct order from A through B to a lower level. The effects of these two methods can be very different, and A must be careful to choose the appropriate one when issuing orders.

A senior manager may also feel it necessary to speak to some or all of his 'extended command' at once. So long as all ranks in between are present no other action is necessary except for the senior manager to realize that he is, in effect, temporarily taking over his subordinate managers' jobs and that there should be some very good reason for it.

Confusion can sometimes arise between communication in the executive/managerial sense up or down and in the representative sense (*see* p. 154). Representative communication must be through and with elected representatives, but this may lead to executive communication, for example when a manager as a result of a representation realizes that an explanation of policy, a new policy or an instruction is required. This must be given direct in his *executive* capacity and not be passed back through the representative.

A very strong case is made out for all policy to be in written form once it has been finally decided. It will require very careful writing if it is not to be ambiguous, and should be published for all to read. It is then available for permanent reference, and interpretation will be more reliable than it would be from memory. Short-term instructions on the other hand should be verbal.

Formal meetings between a manager and his subordinates should always be minuted, and the minutes published in the form of the decisions the manager has taken. The case is made that in these meetings, if the superior–subordinate relationship is to be maintained, only the manager has the authority to take decisions. It is not a committee meeting, where the meeting itself must decide. In fact committee meetings, whatever other functions they may have, are regarded as completely out of place in the Executive System.

*Specialist Work*
One of the most difficult practical questions in organization is where and how to fit the specialist into the hierarchical structure. The other is whether he does or does not have authority over 'line' people. Brown distinguishes between 'operational work', consisting directly of the development, making and selling of the product, and 'specialist work', which is not directly concerned with these three functions but which is based on specialist knowledge of some aspect of the work. This specialist work is divided into three broad groups – personnel, technical and programming.

Any specialist function can be regarded as part of the line or executive manager's job, which he would do if he had sufficient knowledge and sufficient time. The solution to the problem is on the face of it complex but is, in fact, remarkably simple and logical. At any stage in the hierarchy of operational managers there will be attached to the manager such specialists as he needs to carry out his executive role effectively. In rank these specialists will be equivalent to the manager's immediate subordinates. But they are performing part of the manager's own job so that, within the policy laid down by the manager, they can issue orders to his subordinates on his behalf. The manager determines the content of the specialist's work in relation to his whole command. Instructions on how the specialist function is to be carried out are given by higher-ranking specialists in the same function. Thus the specialists in each of the three groups form a Division with a specialist chief at its head who is responsible for the jobs being properly carried out. At all levels the specialists are attached to operational managers, who determine what they should do.

The accounting function is seen as something quite different. It has two functions – to supply independent information in financial or cost terms to managers, and to maintain on behalf of the Board of Directors the necessary financial records. It should be organized independently of the rest of the firm.

### The Supervisor

Another area of great difficulty is the position and role of the supervisor, foreman, or charge-hand. Is he part of the management team or not? Brown seems to come down quite heavily against his being part of management. The organization he envisages has a Section Manager who carries full managerial responsibility, with one or more Supervisors under him but outside the line of authority. Their job is to do all those things which enable the worker to get on with the job without interruption. At least it is a unique answer to a very thorny problem, but one which raises doubts which Brown himself seems to share.

### The Representative System

Early in this chapter it was stated that within the firm there were three parallel systems. So far all that has been written relates to the Executive System. Now we turn to the Representative System.

The first suggestion is that it is not open to a firm to decide whether or not it will have a Representative System – the only real question is whether it will officially recognize and encourage it. From this follows the suggestion that for the effective running of the firm an efficient, properly organized system is essential.

It is necessary to differentiate very clearly between the two systems and their functions. The Executive System consists of managers in a hierarchy whose job it is to form policy, issue orders and direct the workers to see that the purposes for which the firm exists are carried out. The hierarchy also exists for information relating to the specific carrying out of the work to be passed upwards to the appropriate level. But items of information, for example on feelings and attitudes of individuals, and more particularly groups, grievances, problems and so on arise at all levels: these should be communicated to management but are not appropriate to the Executive channels. To cope with these there must be the Representative System, under which groups of people elect a representative whom they can approach as a group or individually and who is authorized to take their complaint or whatever to management on their behalf.

However, if the Representative System is to work effectively and cause the minimum of confusion with the Executive System, it is essential that the representatives fully understand their position. As with other matters which should not depend on memory, Glacier Metal have reduced the terms for a representative to writing, and it is worth while quoting them in full:[5]

*Responsibilities of Elected Representatives*

A representative is accountable to that constituent group or electoral unit which elects him; and it is his responsibility (F.4):

To make himself aware of the main interests of all his constituency (F.4.1).

To represent the point of view of his constituents in committees and Councils, even where this may mean presenting a point of view contrary to his own personal opinion or his view in his executive role (F.4.2).

To allow Councils or committees to work with the greatest possible realism by judging when to state any views held by minorities within his constituency or committee (F.4.3).

To judge when reference to constituents is necessary, and when to accept responsibility for acting without such reference (F.4.4).

To initiate proposals for change which would be in the best interests of his constituents (F.4.5).

To take appropriate steps when in his judgement executive actions or the actions of his constituents are inconsistent with policy (F.4.6).

To assist his constituents to understand the executive implications of the agreements he has accepted on their behalf (F.4.7).

To familiarize himself with the Constitution and Standing Orders of those bodies of which he is a member and with established rules of procedure (F.4.8).

To know policy, and in particular to understand those aspects of policy which are of most immediate concern to his constituents (F.4.9).

To ensure, before taking up an appeal with and on behalf of a constituent, that the constituent has in the first instance taken the matter up with the manager concerned (F.4.10).

To act as adviser to any of his constituents in cases of appeal when requested to do so (F.4.11).

The main function of the Representative System is to act as a safety valve. It makes possible communication from groups of people, it covers breakdowns in the communication of the Executive System, it enables subordinates to speak more frankly than they might feel inclined to do in their executive roles, and it enables small grievances to be dealt with quickly instead of building up as feelings of discontent and aggression which finally explode in major trouble.

Inevitably if the system is to work managers have their role to play. They must understand absolutely that a representative is not speaking as an individual but on behalf of an anonymous group, and never under any circumstances hold what he rightly says as a representative against him as a person in his Executive role. They must at all times be prepared to listen and to judge fairly even when the item under consideration may seem almost too trivial to bother about. They must accept at face value all representations made to them. If they feel certain that the representative is not putting forward the views of his constituents they must not argue with him but must go back to the constituents in their Executive role as manager to find out in a command meeting what the real situation is. Finally a manager must never try to use the Representative System to do his managerial job, for instance to issue policy, to explain what he wants doing, or to criticize his subordinates.

### The Legislative System

All through his work at Glacier Metal and in his exposition of it in his book Brown seems, above all, to have been trying to do one thing – to make explicit the real implications behind confused and complex situations where vague and woolly generalities are the usual order of the day. Nowhere is this more noticeable than in the Legislative System which he has set up.

It is usually the manager's job to set the policy within which he will work. Behind this lies the fact that he cannot validly set policy which the people concerned are not prepared to accept. The explicit situation then is that he must get the consent of the governed (or the customers) before he makes his decision. If he does not and that consent is not forthcoming he is wasting his time and creating a situation which can only lead to trouble.

To recognize and deal with this situation Glacier Metal have set up a series of 'councils . . . in which the Executive and Representative Systems meet and by means of which every member can participate in formulating policy and in assessing the results of the implementation of that policy'.[6]

The function of councils is not to sanction every decision which a manager makes: it is his job to make decisions in his executive role. But where a manager is considering making a change in policy and he feels unsure of what the reaction to it is likely to be then he uses the council as a 'sounding board' to canvass opinions, to discover and work through the difficulties and opposition *before* he makes up his mind. The council is not executive, because it does not decide. But it can stop the manager deciding. After discussion and possible amendment the suggested change must be unanimously supported, even if grudgingly, by all members of the council, otherwise the manager must go back and think again. It must be clearly understood that the council helps to establish principles; the interpretation of principles into action lies in the executive role of the manager.

In addition the council is a two-way channel in that representatives can ask the manager for a meeting where, provided they are appropriate to that particular council, questions of change can be brought up from the other side to the manager. As a council consists of a manager and representatives of his extended command, which will include his subordinate managers, two types of question cannot be discussed by a council – questions affecting a part of the command which should be dealt with by the subordinate manager concerned, and, on the other hand, questions which go outside the jurisdiction of the manager whose council it is.

*The Appeals Procedure*
While the Appeals Procedure as first set up was regarded as a sort of fourth system it was subsequently realized to be a part of the Executive System. In effect it gives to any member of the firm or to representatives the right to appeal against a decision of a manager, if necessary, up to the Managing Director himself. The person making the appeal has the right to the help of his chosen representative, and once the appeal has got beyond the immediate manager concerned all managers involved must be present at the hearing. The manager hearing the appeal must base his decision on existing policy, standing orders and precedent. If he feels that he has no policy applicable he must refer the case up to the next level.

*Conclusion*
It is very difficult indeed to do justice to Lord Brown's book in the

space available. A great deal of detail and explanation has had to be left out. It can only be hoped that he does not feel he has been the victim of injustice.

The validity of his ideas for general application has been challenged on the grounds given in the Introduction, that they apply to a particular man in a particular situation. If one takes the full detail of the book there is some truth in this, but to argue in this way is to reject all hope of ever getting a theory of management. The value of the book lies in the particular qualities and gifts of the brain behind it, and the pattern that it sets for a rigorous analysis of practice over as wide an area as possible to see what common principles do emerge. If it is not asking too much, what is needed now is a score of Lord Browns.

## References

(1) Brown, Wilfred. *Exploration in Management* (Heinemann, London 1960), p. 12.
(2) ibid., p. 5.
(3) ibid., p. 18.
(4) ibid., p. 79.
(5) ibid., pp. 206–207.
(6) ibid., p. 225.

## Bibliography

BOOKS BY WILFRED BROWN

(With W. Raphael) *Managers, Men and Morale* (Macdonald and Evans, London 1948).

*Some Problems of a Factory* (Institute of Personnel Management, London 1953).

*Exploration in Management* (Heinemann, London 1960; Wiley, New York 1960; Penguin Books, Harmondsworth 1965).

*Piecework Abandoned* (Heinemann Educational Books, London 1962).

*Product Analysis Pricing* (Heinemann Educational Books, London 1964).

(With E. Jaques) *Glacier Project Papers* (Heinemann Educational Books, London 1965).

*Organization* (Heinemann Educational Books, London 1971).

# PART III

*The Psycho-Sociological Approach*

## 12

# Mary Parker Follett
## 1924-33

Every so often there appears some particular person to whom the term 'prophet' must be applied. In the field of management thought there can be no one more deserving of this title than Mary Parker Follett. Almost everything she said and wrote in the 1920s and early 1930s has been 'rediscovered' and amplified by the psycho-sociologists of the 1950s and 1960s. But in her day and age she was almost a lone voice crying in the wilderness.

Born in 1868 in Boston, U.S.A., she spent five years at Radcliffe College, Boston, and one year in England at Newnham College, Cambridge. Her university studies were centred around philosophy, government and economics. A real interest in people and their problems, particularly those of the under-privileged, led her into social work on leaving university. Starting with what would now be called a Youth Club, she progressed into other community activities and from this work into vocational guidance.

It was at this point that she first met and talked with business-men and managers and found what she called 'the greatest vitality of thinking today'.[1] Admittedly she was talking of 'not all, but a few',[2] but this, surely, was her great contribution, that she was able to read the smallest signs of a new approach to management and to expand them into a whole philosophy.

The basis of this philosophy is the idea that one cannot separate work from human beings, their hopes, fears and aspirations, nor can one look on work and business as a series of isolated causes and effects but only as a continuous process of interrelationships between people.

Mary Follett's main ideas on management were set out in a series of papers read either in America or England, and these have been gathered together and published in the book *Dynamic Administration* edited by Metcalf and Urwick.

Probably the main areas covered are included in the papers with the following headings:

Constructive Conflict

The Giving of Orders

Power

The Psychology of Control

The Psychology of Consent and Participation

Leadership Theory and Practice

How must Business Management develop to become a Profession

## *Constructive Conflict*

While it may be usual, if not almost inevitable, for the natural reaction to conflict to be to consider it a bad thing, she starts by insisting that this is the one thing we must *not* do. Conflict is 'the appearance of difference, difference of opinions, of interests'.[3] As such it is neither good not bad, but provides the opportunity for a good or bad result. Using it constructively will make it good. Using it destructively will make it bad. It is inevitable in life and at work, therefore managers must learn to use it constructively.

In dealing with conflict she gives three ways for resolving it:

Domination   –  victory by one side

Compromise –  both sides surrendering some part of what they want

Integration   –  finding a new solution which satisfies the *real needs* of both sides.

Domination is unquestionably bad. Simply put, it leaves one side defeated and waiting to 'have another go', i.e. to resume the conflict at the earliest possible moment. Compromise, while better, still leaves much to be desired. In order to reach it there must be some mid-point between the needs and desires of both parties on which they can agree, even if unwillingly. It means that both sides surrender some part of what they are demanding. How much depends on the relative strengths of both sides. In order to gain extra bargaining power both sides are likely to state their first demands at a level higher than their real needs. While compromise was then, and usually still is, the most common form of settling conflict, it is clearly inadequate compared with integration.

Integration is Mary Follett's third and best way of resolving conflict. Here she gives a few examples or near-examples of the process, and develops a full new method. The first step is for each side to recognize for itself what its *real* needs are, to state these needs clearly and to 'bring the whole thing into the open'.[4] This may well lead to what she calls revaluation:

(i) breaking down whole demands into their constituent parts
(ii) examining the real meaning of symbols
(iii) preparation for the response of the other side.

Such actions by both sides may bring about unity out of conflict in that both sides see a way out which will satisfy their real needs. This way lies progress because it develops a new situation and resolves once for all the original conflict.

Integration, then, is the best but not the easiest way. It requires 'a high order of intelligence, keen perception and discrimination, more than all, a brilliant inventiveness'.[5] It is, perhaps, easier to fight: we enjoy domination, we theorize instead of suggesting active steps, we are not trained in making integrations. But in spite of the difficulties managers should attempt integration. It resolves conflict, it puts it to use constructively to develop a new and better situation. And, as conflict will always be with us, the best thing is to learn to use it this way.

### The Giving of Orders

This paper was presented in 1925 when the 'carrot' of incentive schemes and the 'stick' of the sack were, perhaps, the only motivating forces known to almost all managers. Its insight into the problems which most managers have faced in the post-Second World War period is remarkable. Admittedly its ideas have been modernized and brought up to date by post-war psycho-sociologists (as we see later), but if all practising managers got no further than applying Mary Follett's ideas the industrial and commercial scene would be revolutionized.

If managers were asked today what their job was the answer, in part at least, would be in most cases 'to get others to work'. Few would add 'efficiently', fewer still 'to optimum capacity'. Yet optimum capacity is what is needed, and the way in which orders are put over will have a very considerable bearing on how far it is achieved. On the face of it the title of the paper 'The Giving of Orders' would appear to imply, as does Fayol's use of the word 'Command', that the manager's job is simply to *give* orders, but nothing could be further from the truth. The paper anticipates by almost forty years Argyris's idea that the giving of orders by one person to another demeans the latter or, at least, that it can do so. It all depends on how and why the orders are given.

A brief excursion into pure psychology shows that:

  (i) Mere ordering will not necessarily produce satisfactory results.

 (ii) Mere intellectual agreement to an order will not of itself guarantee good performance.

(iii) Action depends more on habit-patterns formed from a lifetime of previous experience.

 (iv) Managers should build up in their workers habit patterns and mental attitudes.

  (v) These patterns and attitudes are developed by training.

 (vi) Managers should anticipate and prepare for the possible responses to their actions.

(vii) People may have conflicts within themselves.

(viii) Orders should resolve rather than create conflicts.

This excursion could be used to develop an argument that it is the manager's job to learn so to manipulate workers that they will accept orders without question. There is no doubt that this could be done and has been done, for instance in the armed services, but it is certainly not Mary Follett's intention that this practice should be followed. She attacks order-giving both in method and in substance. As a start she attacks the disagreeable way in which many orders are given: 'What happens to a man, *in* a man, when an order is given in a disagreeable manner? ... He loses his temper or becomes sullen or is on the defensive; he begins thinking of his "rights".'[6] This is no way to get people to behave as well or as efficiently as possible. At the other end of the scale is the manager or supervisor who is so close to his workers that he cannot give orders. This too leads to poor performance.

The way out of the difficulty looks deceptively simple. It is to depersonalize orders by a joint study of the situation to find the *law of the situation*, and for all, managers and managed, to obey that. This way nobody *gives* orders to anybody. The *situation* provides a course of action which all must follow. But the study of the situation must be of the *total* situation, not just a part of it, and this study must be a joint one by managers *and* managed. Here lies a truth which, even in the 1970s, is not sufficiently realized or, if it is, is not sufficiently stressed in either the theory or the practice of management. We can never effectively manage a part of a situation. It must always be the total situation, all the factors, the influences, the personalities and the attitudes, the past, the present and the future.

Once this is stated it should be so obvious as to be self-evident truth. But it is perhaps an idealistic truth. The down-to-earth questions remain: How many managers are capable of sharing or willing to share their power in this way? How many workers are intelligent enough, far-sighted enough, unsuspicious enough of management to accept, let alone to look for, the law of the situation? Mary Follett says that managers must create 'the attitude required for cooperative study and decision'.[7] But how far are we away from that? The pessimist would say 'As far as ever'; the optimist might say 'Two generations of managers'. Some theorists and many practising managers would argue that the best we can hope for is a balance of power based on fundamentally opposing interests. At this stage time alone will tell who, if anybody, is right.

Moving on from a general theory Mary Follett quotes some specific instances of difficulties in the giving of orders:

(i) Many people will willingly *work with* other people but dislike intensely having the feeling of people being *over them*.

(ii) Many workmen, particularly skilled ones, have a knowledge of and pride in their work which makes them resent others telling them how to do it or even what to do in detail.

(iii) The giving of orders, especially detailed ones, removes responsibility from the person to whom the order is given. If anything goes wrong the answer 'I did exactly as I was told' is the perfect alibi and the negation of responsibility. This contrasts very sharply with Taylor's view that responsibility must be removed from the shop floor as completely as possible and be placed in management's hands. Mary Follett would have responsibility spread as widely as possible and as low as possible.

(iv) Orders in the generally accepted sense raise conflicts between obedience and liberty.

(v) An order which is a response to the law of the situation must take into account the evolving situation and management's part in making it evolve.

In a way this paper seems to have a number of built-in contradictions. At the beginning Mary Follett says managers must find out the principles underlying the different ways of giving orders, then adopt a responsible attitude by deciding which principles to follow, and, finally, experiment and note results. The middle of the paper in effect gives her view of the 'one best method' or, as she suggests, 'the only effective method'. At the end she comes back to saying:

We students of social and industrial research are often lamentably vague. We sometimes do not even know what we know and what we do not know. We can avoid this vagueness only (1) by becoming conscious of what we believe in, (2) of what we do not believe in, and (3) by recognising the large debatable ground in between those two fields and trying our experiments there.[8]

Perhaps it would be fair comment to extend this and to suggest that managers should deliberately take the same three steps and, in particular, take them in relation to the giving of orders.

*Power*

This talk can probably be more easily summarized than some of the others. As a starting point there is the indisputable fact that so long as differences between 'sides' in industry are resolved by bargaining then power is essential on both sides to be able to drive the best bargain.

In more general terms most people have an urge or need to possess power of some sort. Whether it is an instinctive urge to be satisfied for its own sake or whether it is needed only as a means to an end is perhaps, but by no means certainly, immaterial. The simple fact is that people want power. The real issue is how they use it when they have it. This leads to an intriguing distinction between 'power over' and 'power with'.

'Power over' is condemned out of hand, whoever has it. It means forcing another to do your will. It means resentment. It means reaction. It means the demand for and action to get more power by the vanquished to renew the struggle and to turn the tables. And yet, she says, most of us are trying to get 'power over': salesmen, advertisers, propagandists, managers, trade unions and even, one supposes, the demonstrators of the late 'sixties and 'seventies with their passive resistance. Ways of reducing 'power over' are given briefly. They are the use of integration (the solution that meets the real needs of both sides), the correct use of circular behaviour, and the use of the 'law of the situation'.

'Power with' really gets very little mention although one might have expected it to be central to the purpose of the talk. One hint seems to be given in the sentence 'Every demand for power should be analysed to see if the object is "independent" power or joint power.'[9] Does this pinpoint the difference? 'Power over' is independent power to be used solely for the benefit of the individual or group using it. 'Joint power' arises when two individuals or groups pool their power to arrive at a settlement satisfactory to both. If so, then 'power with' seems to be working together to achieve an integration.

Again she says 'In a store or factory I do not think the management should have power *over* the workmen, or the workmen over the management.'[10] This would appear to eliminate management's right to give orders, and bring us back to the 'law of the situation' when both workers and management take *orders* from the facts. It is interesting to speculate on how she would have reacted to the situation of the nineteen-sixties and early 'seventies. During this time some workers and unions used their 'power over' to create the wage spiral, to dictate overtime as an essential part of employment, or to insist on the re-instatement of sacked and suspended workers. Judging by her comment that 'It is right for the employers to resist any effort of the unions to get power over'[11] one can only imagine that her reaction would have been one of stupefied horror that management had allowed it to happen.

We are not told, however, how to achieve 'power with'. Perhaps it would be unfair to expect a newly born idea to arrive fully fledged and ready to be put into practice. Perhaps, too, it demands a perfect world of perfect individuals and groups. If so, to dream of its complete achievement is baying for the moon. But still the responsibility must rest on management to try to set up conditions such that it is possible to move towards it.

The next section of the paper is devoted to a consideration of the trade unions' demand for power. While undoubtedly related specifically to the situation in America in the mid-1920s there are parts of it which seem to be of more permanent significance. First Mary Follett questions the possible reasons behind the demand, and gives eleven possible answers, varying from the instinctive urge to power, a means to higher wages, through the frustration set up by modern industrial conditions to the urge for self-expression and self-determination. Then follows a lengthy and somewhat abstruse discussion on the delegation of power. Summarizing it briefly gives the following propositions:

(i) Real power cannot be delegated.
(ii) Power without responsibility cannot [?should not] be allowed.
(iii) Power for the workers is really a question of how much they are *able* to assume.
(iv) It is management's responsibility to give the workers the chance to grow capacity for power themselves.
(v) Power and authority are not the same thing.

(vi) Power is legitimate when it is integral to and grows out of the situation.

This is, perhaps, the least satisfactory of her papers. It appears vague, it seems to leave too many unanswered questions. Perhaps, after all, it is just the one which was furthest ahead of its time so that its development had to wait for a later generation of psycho-sociologists.

*The Psychology of Control*

Starting from the proposition that 'the aim of organisation engineering is control through effective unity',[12] Mary Follett contends that we cannot understand control until we understand the nature of unities. She quotes parallels from the medical science of the time to show that doctors were beginning to think of patients not as a single complaint or disease which needed attention but as a whole person of which the complaint or disease was but one aspect. The implication is that in management we cannot, or should not, separate the economic, the psychological and the ethical aspects and consider each separately. They are all part of the total situation and, as such, must all be given due weight and further considered in relation to each other.

This brings us back to a further consideration of circular behaviour. If there are two activities, A and B, A does not just influence B while B influences A. 'Reciprocal influencing [circular behaviour] ... means that A influences B, and that B, made different by A's influence, influences A, which means that A's own activity enters into the stimulus which is causing his activity.'[13] All of which sounds very abstruse and needs an illustration to clarify it.

Let us assume we have a man, A, an awkward cuss, who everybody knows to be awkward. B, who wants some action out of A, knows this fact. B could approach A as if he knew that A was awkward, which confirms A's awkwardness and produces a negative response. This reacts on B's further behaviour and he tries to drive A. The result is failure. But let us make another assumption, that B approaches A in a friendly manner and implies or says that A is a friendly chap who will be willing to help. A's reaction to this must, of necessity, be different. He may niggle a bit still, but he won't dig his toes in so hard. So B, still friendly, meets the objections in a way that will satisfy A, and achieves his objective. B's final behaviour in the two cases and the end results are in part caused by his own behaviour in making the first approaches. They are different because A's reaction was different, and this difference was caused by the variation in B's approach. This may be over-simplified but it works, as any good salesman will know.

But back to Mary Follett and her understanding of unity. Any whole, whether it be a business, a major policy or a group of people, is made up of parts. Not only does the whole influence the parts, but the parts individually and collectively influence the whole, as do the relationships between the parts. In real life we cannot separate these influences. They are working all the time towards a developing whole or unity. The same activity develops the whole and the parts at the same time. The result of this interaction and unifying of parts is the emergence of a new situation, and a change in the individual factors or activities which are doing the interacting. These are all aspects of the same process and go on simultaneously. To quote her own words, 'Functional relating is the continuing process of self-creating coherence.'[14] Which seems to mean that in a business which is being properly managed the different policies, departments, functions, personalities should interact continuously to develop a new and better situation for the business as a whole *and* for the individual parts of it.

The need to understand unity arises because unity is the basis of control. We cannot have control in any effective sense without it. In physics, medicine and psychology there are integrative unities which are self-regulating, self-directing organisms. Business, if it is to be effective, must develop the same processes where the interaction between the parts is the control. Social control must develop from the process of integration. Admittedly this is still, as it was then, in the future, but it is the goal for management to aim for.

## Psychology of Consent and Participation

In starting off this paper Mary Follett fires a full broadside at the basic concepts of 'scientific management'. The mere consent of the workers to do as they are told is not enough. It uses only the ideas of managers who give the orders to which the workers consent. It does not give us what the others, the workers, are capable of contributing.

And what a broadside! It assumes that workers have something to contribute and that it will be worth while having it contributed. What a contradiction of Taylor, with his ideas of separating planning and doing, and his outright condemnation of what the workers had been contributing before he developed 'scientific management'. What a contradiction of Gilbreth and his 'one best way' which all must follow. She agrees that it is better to have consent than not to have it, but beyond that, she says, we must have participation – a working unit with all contributing their ideas and knowledge.

How then does she propose that we attain this end? Here, perhaps, she is more specific than usual. She gives three courses which must be followed consciously and deliberately by management:

(i) Setting up an organization which provides for it, i.e. which provides clear two-way channels of communication and consultation.

(ii) Daily management practices which recognize and act on the principle of participation by constantly allowing for, expecting and using the contribution of ideas which the workers can make.

(iii) A method of settling differences, of dealing with the 'diverse contributions of men very different in temperament, training and attitudes'. And this method is, of course, integration, as explained in the paper on conflict.

So we are back again in the difficult but not impossible field of using conflict to produce a better and more satisfactory result. But this time she goes further. She deplores the lack of confidence in each other existing between employers and workers, and goes on 'I do not believe that confidence will ever be attained except by making the aims of employers and employees the same.'[15]

This raises two interesting points. First there is still the school of thought, both in the academic and the practical management field, that these aims are so diametrically opposed that reconciliation can never take place, and the best one can hope for is a balance of power and an armed truce. Secondly, that the differences now, in large-scale industry at any rate, are not between employers and employees but between two groups of employees, the managers and the workers.

Then there follows some detailed guidance on how to achieve integration. Never let an either-or situation develop; search for as many alternatives as possible. Encourage, in fact insist, on openness and explicitness – all cards on the table. Both sides should find out what they *really* want. Start co-ordination at the bottom, not at the top. Use joint investigation from the very beginning, not after separate investigations when opinions and attitudes will have developed and possibly hardened.

To draw the ideas together and to put the stress in the right place she concludes: ' "the will to integrate", as it has been called, is not enough . . . To draw out the capacities of all and then to fit them together is our problem.'[16]

*Leadership*
Mary Follett wrote two papers on leadership, one on 'Leader and Expert' and the other on 'Some Discrepancies in Leadership Theory and Practice'. From the concept of business as an integrative unity it follows that the leader not only influences his group but is also influenced by them. He must, therefore, be influenced by the experts within the group, taking the group as the whole firm. Power is the combined capacities of the group, and the function of the leader is to draw out these different wills and capacities, to give them driving force and to create group power rather than to exercise personal power.

She suggests that there are signs that businessmen are beginning to develop a new kind of structure 'which is not democratic in our old understanding of the word, but something better than that. It is a system based neither on equality nor on arbitrary authority, but on functional unity.'[17] Within this pattern the knowledge of the expert is becoming an integral part of the decision-making machinery. The 'advice' of the expert becomes something which must be taken into account, not accepted or rejected at the whim of the leader. The function of the leader, or top man, then becomes to set the pattern and objectives, to co-ordinate the different parts and weld them into effective unity, and in doing these things to take the opinions and advice of his experts and to build them into the total structure.

She goes on to anticipate Drucker by more than forty years when she says, 'In defining anticipation in an earlier paper, I said it meant far more than *meeting* the next situation, that it meant *making* the next situation.'[18]

On the theory of leadership she suggests that the accepted *theory* was and still is (1930) that the leader has a compelling personality, wields personal power and constrains others to do his will. But, she suggests, in fact ascendancy is not the real characteristic of leadership. Orders do not always or even often arise directly from the leader's wishes, they arise from the work situation itself, and subordinates may contribute to their making.

The real function of the leader is to heighten individuality, to draw out others' capacities, to increase their freedom. In this way obedience, self-expression or even self-direction are reciprocally involved. So that while the current theory is that the leader is one who can by personality get orders obeyed, the real and best leader is the one who can show that 'The order is integral to the situation.'[19] It follows from this that, while leadership based on personality may continue to exist, in what she would call the best-organized firms leadership is based on function, and by implication it may move from one person in the group to another as circumstances change and one function or another becomes the vital one at the moment. This means that for a particular situation, control or leadership will go 'to the man with the largest knowledge of that situation, to him who can grasp and organize its essential elements, who understands its total significance, who can see it through . . .'[20]

There are two essential corollaries to this situation. One is that all should share in the knowledge of, and perhaps even the creation of, the objectives of the group. The other is that those who are led must know how to lead, and be encouraged to take their share in control. They should take an active part in helping to keep the leader in control of the situation. These points imply an essentially new pattern of relationships between leader and led.

The details of this thesis may have been worked out more thoroughly in the 1960s, especially by Likert (Chapter 17) and Argyris (Chapter 15), but the principles were clearly laid out here in 1930.

## Management as a profession

The emergence of management as the 'third power in the land', as the power between the workers and the employers had, in the larger businesses, already occurred long before Mary Follett's day. One of her chief wishes was to see it develop into a profession on a par with those of doctors, solicitors, architects and all the other occupations to which the term profession can be strictly applied. That it was a dream in the 1920s, that it is still a dream fifty years later, cannot be disputed. That it was and still is desirable is beyond doubt.

The full title of her paper on this subject was 'How must business management develop in order to become a profession', thus confirming that at the time it was not recognized as such. Her criteria for a profession are two in number. It must be regarded as a function of or service to the community and not be exercised solely for private gain. And it must be based on the application of an accepted and proven body of knowledge and principles.

If one takes the wider view of all people as producers and consumers then all work can be regarded as service to the community, but somehow a distinction is drawn between this idea of service and professional service. Further, in the non-Communist world, at least, the idea of business and therefore of management is still overlaid with the Victorian economic maxim that the sole purpose of business is to maximize profit. If this were true – Drucker argues that it is not – then management does not qualify as professional service.

Mary Follett says of professional men that they go into this work and go through a long and arduous training because they love the work and get real satisfaction out of doing it. Of men in business she says that many just drift into it, but that once a man reaches managerial status he may often work longer hours than the shop-floor workers and the clerks from a sense of satisfaction arising from his work. One basis for a profession of management may be there already in this sense of satisfaction from work.

Each profession, however, has its own association of members which sets group codes of conduct, which sets and tries to improve standards, which keeps members up to standard and may even banish them to the wilderness if they fall below par, which educates and protects the public and protects members from each other. She suggests, perhaps a little naïvely, that trade associations and the newly emergent association of managers might in time do the same for a profession of management.

Expanding on three of the points, she says that members of a profession 'feel a greater loyalty to their profession than to the company'.[21] Ignoring what must have been a slip, because the majority of professional men are self-employed, the implication that managers can only be loyal to their company, having no other standards, must be accepted. Even by 1971 in Britain only one managerial body, the Institution of Works Managers, has developed and published a code of conduct which its members are supposed to follow. But it is a code which lacks effective sanctions.

On the second point she says that it is a profession's job to inform the public as to what are good practice and standards. She quotes Sheldon as saying that 'Management acknowledges as master the public will of the community alone',[22] and then violently disagrees with him. If management is going to become a profession it must learn to educate the public to higher standards of business (and presumably practise them).

Thirdly, a professional man must try to extend the boundaries of knowledge in his profession and then pass on his extra knowledge for the benefit of all. Managers may be doing this when they try a new method, a new way of getting things done. They do not realize the importance to management as a whole of what they are doing. Often they do not even try, they 'get by' with an old but familiar method.

Perhaps because her experience was mostly in America where Harvard and the other Business Schools were beginning to flourish in the 'twenties and 'thirties, she does not mention the need for a body of scientific knowledge on which a profession of management could be based. A hint of this shows in her comment '. . . business management needs . . . as thorough a training as any of the "learned" professions'.[23] If she could have realized how little they really knew at that time, how much more would be learnt in the next forty years and, in spite of that, how far away management would still be from a recognized and organized body of knowledge which would guide managers in the day-to-day conduct of their affairs, she might have despaired.

Management is not yet a profession. Maybe it can never become one, not at least in a capitalist society where the conflicts of loyalty to the firm and loyalty to an outside code may be too great. But some day someone will need to organize the theory of the craft. After all, medicine in 1870 was pretty much where management was in 1970.

## Conclusion

To summarize Mary Follett's work in a few words is virtually impossible – the range of its ideas is too wide. Is it enough to say that, like the Delphic oracle, she foretold the shape of things to come ? Perhaps it would be nearer to say that she seized upon the signs of early significant changes which were going on around her and used her basic training to project these. That she was an idealist there can be no doubt. That she was always talking of management from the sidelines with no practical personal experience of her theories is true comment, if something short of fair comment. Her ideas have stood the test of time and change. Again and again when reading the psycho-sociologists of the 1960s one is bound to say 'But Mary Follett said that forty years ago.' In the development of management thought she provided a main stepping stone between the practical work/experience approach of earlier times and the psycho-sociological approach of forty years later.

*References*

(1) *Dynamic Administration* ed. Metcalf, H. C. and Urwick, L. (Pitman, London 1957), p. 17.

(2) ibid., p. 17.
(3) ibid., p. 30.
(4) ibid., p. 38.
(5) ibid., p. 45.
(6) ibid., p. 57.
(7) ibid., p. 61.
(8) ibid., p. 69.
(9) ibid., p. 101.
(10) ibid., p. 101.
(11) ibid., p. 101.
(12) ibid., p. 184.
(13) ibid., p. 194.
(14) ibid., p. 200.
(15) ibid., p. 219.
(16) ibid., p. 229.
(17) ibid., p. 249.
(18) ibid., p. 263 (Mary Follett's italics).
(19) ibid., p. 275.
(20) ibid., p. 281.
(21) ibid., p. 137.
(22) ibid., p. 138.
(23) ibid., p. 143.

## Bibliography

*Creative Experience*, Follett, M. P. (Longmans, London and New York 1924).

*Dynamic Administration: The Collected Papers of Mary Parker Follett* ed. Metcalf, H. C. and Urwick, L. (Management Publications Trust, London 1949; Pitman, London 1957).

*Freedom and Coordination* ed. Urwick, L. (Management Publications Trust, London 1949).

# 13

# Elton Mayo
## 1933-49

*Introduction*

Any manager or student of management, if asked 'What do you know about Nero?' would be likely to reply 'Nothing', or, more probably, 'That he fiddled while Rome burned'. A few might add that he had Christians thrown to the lions. Given the same question about Mayo the likely answers are again 'Nothing', or 'The Hawthorne Investigations'. Very few could go beyond this.

This is nothing less than tragic, because, although the work on Hawthorne is now under attack, the work of Mayo as set out in his two books, *The Human Problems of Industrial Civilization* (1933) and *The Social Problems of Industrial Civilization* (1949), is probably the most significant contribution to management thought of the late 'thirties and 'forties.

Its significance lies not in that it provides the right answers, but that it asks the right questions. Answers there are, but they are tentative and little more than hints of possibilities. The real quest for solutions starts with the writers of a decade or more later – with Argyris (*see* Chapter 15), Likert (Chapter 17), and McGregor (Chapter 16), but even they are not prepared to claim finality for their answers.

It is beyond doubt that the growth of scientific knowledge, of technology, of business-organization structure and of management techniques in the twentieth century has been such that the increase in industrial and commercial efficiency should have been phenomenal. Yet the simple facts are that while there has been growth it has been pedestrian compared with the growth of knowledge (politicians in the 'seventies can still seriously talk of a 2½ per cent

growth in industrial output per annum as a norm); that while there
are many firms that jog along in reasonable harmony with reasonable, or at least acceptable, productivity, the wild-cat strike, the
'confrontation' between management and union, the militant shop-
steward, are the main images of modern industry in the minds of
the public. Industry, and therefore management as its controlling
force, has big problems which are insufficiently understood. For a
problem to be understood it must be analysed and clearly stated.
It must be Mayo's chief claim to fame that he was the first to see,
to analyse and to state a new aspect of the problems of a modern
industrial civilization.

## The Human Problems of an Industrial Civilization

This, the first of Mayo's books published in 1935, gives an account
of the early researches into industry carried out at Harvard, and
draws some revolutionary conclusions. Although it is overtaken and
much further developed by his second book, on social problems,
its interest and importance lie in the fact that it is such an early and
revolutionary step in the development of ideas about management.

Quite apart from breaking entirely new ground, Mayo's work at
this stage is of vital importance because of the basic philosophy
behind it. The idea is not his own (it had been implicit in the work
of the Harvard School of Business before he went there), but he
states it explicitly. There are, he says, two forms of knowledge:
knowledge of and knowledge by acquaintance. Knowledge of is
obtained by reading books, by discussion, by imaginative thought –
it is essentially theoretical and secondhand. Knowledge by acquaintance, on the other hand, is obtained only by personal experience,
by living with and through the facts to be studied. As a basis for
real understanding of practical problems, for the development of
answers, knowledge of is too remote, too far removed from reality
to be of any use. Only knowledge by acquaintance, acquired in the
clinic and developed in the laboratory (to use Mayo's own metaphor), is of any use. Harvard were following this idea by using only
real live business situations to study and teach management. Mayo
bases all his statements of problems, his tentative conclusions on
field research, on real live business. Here is no empty theorizing,

but a statement of what has actually happened and the conclusions thereby reached.

It is not intended in this book, even if there were room, to go into the detail of the experiments and investigations recorded. Essentially the purpose is to re-state the problems tackled by Mayo. Mayo states as his starting point that 'The human aspect of industry has changed very considerably in the last fifty years.'[1] Research into this began with the Health of Munitions Workers Committee in Britain in 1915, and continued with the Industrial Fatigue Research Board. In 1930 this Board significantly changed its title to 'Industrial Health Research Board', and this change was indicative of the extension of the work of the Board into more general aspects of working conditions and their effects.

The studies of fatigue, its causes and results are well documented by Mayo, but in the end he is forced to the conclusion that fatigue itself is a term with so many meanings as to defy neat definition, and that the subject is infinitely more complicated than the researchers had supposed. From a purely physical point of view it is possible to postulate what he calls a 'steady state' in which organic processes balance the output of energy required, and therefore it could be assumed that work under these conditions could be continued indefinitely. This, however, does not happen. Even under these conditions workers slow down or stop, and as this is not due to internal biological conditions it must be due to external conditions. So from this early start, based on the assumption that a simple physical phenomenon, fatigue, causes falling output, research is forced into a complex multi-factor situation in which physical, mental and organizational aspects must all be considered.

An early offshoot of the study of fatigue was the conclusion that boredom could have similar effects to fatigue in slowing down work, but that its causes were quite different and needed separate study. Increasing specialization in industry and the continued further breakdown of individual jobs into smaller and narrower content produces inefficiency up to the point where it requires so little attention as to release the worker for day-dreaming and/or social conversation. The worst possible combination is where the work requires just enough attention to prevent the worker from occupying his mind with other things, not enough to provide interest, and is physically so situated as to prevent contact with other workers. These are just the conditions which scientific management had produced in the name of greater efficiency.

In addition, boredom is a function of the intellectual capacity of the worker. The higher his intellect the more easily he becomes bored with routine, repetitive work. There is also the very import-ant point that boredom is no more easily defined than fatigue, and that what may be considered boring by one man will not be by another.

Mayo quotes from the Industrial Fatigue Research Board Paper No. 56 (1928) by Wyatt and Fraser the conclusions that monotony is related to the conditions of work and is less likely to arise when

(i) the form of activity changes from time to time;

(ii) payment by results is used;

(iii) work consists of self-contained tasks rather than continuous performance of the same small bit;

(iv) workers are compact social groups and not isolated indivi-duals;

(v) rest pauses are allowed.


These conclusions more or less confirm research work which Mayo himself carried out in 1923 into the incidence and causes of very high labour turnover in the mule-spinning department of a cotton mill at Philadelphia. In addition he concluded that other causes may operate to prevent incentive schemes raising or even maintaining output, that sincere and genuine interest shown by the management in the workers and working conditions is a consider-able incentive, and that consultation with the workers or, better still, self-determination by the workers themselves can do nothing but good.

Together these two sets of conclusions can be taken as an early statement of the fact that any one single factor in the work/ managerial situation cannot be studied in isolation. It is one aspect only of a complex situation in which many factors are interrelated and interdependent.

The significance of these conclusions was confirmed and extended by the results of the classic Hawthorne investigations, which took place over a period of about five years from 1928. For a detailed account of the research itself the reader is referred to F. J. Roethlisberger and W. J. Dickson's book *Management and the Worker*, published by Harvard University Press in 1939. At this point we are concerned only with the conclusions drawn in 1933.

In the relay test-room experiments a long series of deliberate and carefully planned and controlled changes in working conditions led to a continuous rise in output. Speaking of the time when production reached a new peak, Mayo says:

> Many changes other than those in production had been observed to be occurring; up to this time it had been possible to assume for practical purposes that such changes were of the nature of adaptation to special circumstances and not necessarily otherwise significant. Equally it had been possible to assume that the changes recorded in output were, at least for the most part, related to the experimental changes in working conditions – rest pauses or whatnot – singly and successively imposed. At this stage these assumptions had become untenable – especially in the light of the previously expressed determination not to test for single variables but to study the situation.[2]

The results of the experiment are given as

  (i) A continued rise in output of the group over the whole period, independent of changes in working conditions.

  (ii) The reduction in fatigue is not related to increased output.

  (iii) Increased contentment among the girls concerned.

  (iv) Large decreases in absenteeism, both voluntary and due to sickness.

  (v) Output more related to type of working day than to whether 5 or $5\frac{1}{2}$ days worked.

  (vi) Although output vastly increased operators working within their capacity and able to maintain higher rates indefinitely.

  (vii) Increased eagerness on the part of operators to come to work.

  (viii) While not really sure of the reasons the operators feel that the increase in output is due to 'pleasanter, freer and happier working conditions'.

(ix) Increased social contact between operators at work and outside work.

These changes point not just to increases in output but to fundamental changes in the total situation, with the emphasis on attitudes and social aspects. The cause of the changes is not the single factor of changing hours and working conditions but a complex combination of this, of changed methods of supervision which are felt by the workers to put them under less pressure, of a feeling of importance and recognition on the part of the operators, of conditions which support and encourage the growth of internal group solidarity, and of co-operation between the group and the management. In brief, the true complexity of the work situation is being shown for the first time.

The massive interview programme at Hawthorne in which 20,000 workers were enabled to talk freely and confidentially added further insights. The first experimental interview programmes forced management to question '. . . whether industry really knew anything whatever about appropriate working conditions or proper supervisory methods'.[3] And this was in a company which would have stood very high in a league for competent, modern and far-sighted management!

One very important conclusion from the programme was that the opportunity to talk freely and confidentially, to 'get things off your chest', was by itself of great value in improving the work atmosphere. Another was the vital need for training managers to understand and cope with the 'all-too-human situations' which the interviews showed existed.

One particular part of the programme raised the suggestion that '. . . the locus of industrial maladjustment is somewhere in the relation between person–work–Company policy rather than in any individual or individuals'.[4] Put in the language of later years, this meant that people could become bored, disinterested, obstructive and even bloody-minded, not because they were made that way, but because the working conditions did not meet their psycho-sociological needs, because of conflict between individual and Company aims, or because group formation and group functioning was inhibited. Truly this is a massive insight and one which is still far from fully appreciated or acted upon today.

Moving on from Hawthorne, Mayo devotes a chapter to a review of the work of sociologists on the possible breakdown of society due to the growth of industrial cities and the consequent loosening of social ties, and another to the problems of government having to take over functions previously exercised by self-controlling, smaller societies. While they are interesting, they only contribute very indirectly to thinking on management except to suggest that the logical processes of management and the increasing sophistication of techniques are trying to function in a world in which the old stability and social health of the community is breaking down, and 'The belief of the individual in his social function and solidarity with the group – his capacity for collaboration in work – these are disappearing, destroyed in part by rapid scientific and technical advance.'[5]

He concludes, in a chapter entitled 'The New Administrator', that the growth of science and technology has not been matched by any growth in understanding of the human problems brought about by the changes, and that a new management élite raised by a new and broader type of training is essential if industrial civilization is to survive.

## The Social Problems of an Industrial Civilization

Twelve years after writing on human problems Mayo produced his book *The Social Problems of an Industrial Civilization*. While it is to some extent a recapitulation of the earlier book, its ideas are based on a programme of continuous research which had been carried on at Harvard for the whole intervening period.

Mayo starts by repeating his thesis of the disruption of society in a chapter entitled 'The Seamy Side of Progress'. Quoting mostly the same authorities he comes rapidly to the conclusion that society must, whatever its type of culture, meet and solve two problems. These are providing for economic needs and maintaining spontaneous co-operation. Modern industrial society, he says, is geared entirely to the first objective and not at all towards maintaining co-operation. This is shown, he says, by the prevalence of absenteeism, labour turnover and wild-cat strikes. The problem is sociological, and due to the transition from an established society which altered slowly to an adaptive society where technological change is taking place much faster than our ability to cope with it is increasing. Instead of co-operation between groups we have animosity, suspicion and even outright hatred. Instead of easy, effective communication within small groups we have the complete breakdown of communication between large specialized groups, especially between management and workers, which has led to conflicting aims and interminable misunderstanding.

A further difficulty arising from scientific and technological progress is that it threatens the security of the individual. No longer can anyone be sure that the skills in which he was trained and which provide his livelihood will be needed tomorrow. He may well be faced, perhaps even more than once in a lifetime, with having to learn new skills and a new job or being thrown on the industrial scrap-heap.

Modern industry and economic theory have grown up together and it is plausible to assume that economics provide the rationale of industrial organization and practice. Mayo's second chapter, 'The Rabble Hypothesis', is a devastating attack on the fundamental bases of classical economics. Behind it, he says, lie two basic assumptions. The first is the physiocrats' concept of *laissez-faire*: that the greatest good for the greatest number will be achieved if everyone has the maximum freedom to pursue his own self-interest. The second is the fundamental concept of scarcity, that wants are unlimited and that there are never enough resources to go round.

These two assumptions, he maintains, are inadequate and irrelevant to modern industrial society, and a theory which is built on them is more than misleading: it is positively dangerous. It assumes that society consists of a rabble of individuals, each fighting for what he sees as his own best interest. But the reality is that modern society, if it is to survive, must consist of co-operating groups.

Politics, too, comes in for its share of criticism. As society moved from small, self-controlling groups, so the politics of the State developed. Behind the theory of the State is the concept of a 'community of individuals'. Mayo says, 'Both these theories foreclose on and discourage any investigation of the facts of social organization',[6] and '. . . for so long as these topics are allowed to be a substitute for direct investigation of the facts, the total effect will be crippling for society.'[7]

Returning to the research work which was the topic of *Human Problems*, Mayo has nothing new to say on the textile mill at Philadelphia. On the Hawthorne Experiments he does develop some fresh insights. The first was implied earlier but not, perhaps, so clearly stated. It is that:

In modern large-scale industry the three persistent problems of management are:
 1. The application of science and technical skill to some material good or product.
 2. The systematic ordering of operations.
 3. The organization of teamwork – that is, of sustained co-operation.
The last must take account of the need for continued reorganization of teamwork as operating conditions are changed in an *adaptive* society.[8]

The third, he repeats, is almost wholly neglected despite the fact that the larger the organization the more important it becomes.

Further conclusions which were developed between the end of the Hawthorne experiment and the writing of this book were:
 (i) The importance of the supervisor in this situation and the problem which he faces in setting up proper relations with a constantly changing team.
 (ii) The loss of feelings of security and certainty by the individual worker.
 (iii) The importance of the primary or natural group in the work situation and of the standards and customs which the group establishes for itself.
 (iv) The real need for an effective way of moving individuals

when necessary from one group to another and making it possible for them to integrate rapidly into the new group.

(v) The interview technique properly used has tremendous value in helping both the individual and the group situation.

(vi) Interview programmes provide management with a new, effective and vital channel of information on the work situation which they would otherwise not get.

Comments on further researches carried out at Harvard between 1933 and 1943 emphasize previous conclusions and bring some new ones to light. One which, when it is baldly stated, appears so obvious as to be almost trite, is that there is an enormous difference between managing a business employing up to 500 persons and one employing 2,000 or more. But the simple fact is still observable today that it is in the larger businesses that the problems, the difficulties and the troubles arise. The significance of the statement and the need to find the answer at the human level still seems to escape us.

A fairly long account of researches into absenteeism in different factories leads to confirmation and extension of earlier findings. Absenteeism and the general morale and attitudes of workers are favourably influenced when foremen are trained not only to be technically competent but also to handle human situations; when foremen are relieved of routine duties so that they have adequate time to devote to human problems; when work is so organized that team spirit and group responsibility are given the chance to grow. Technological reorganization, when it adversely affects these conditions, will show in a general deterioration in the situation. The small, natural group of up to ten or twelve people is the key factor in the situation. Finally the person in authority must deliberately and consciously work to create the right conditions for co-operation.

*Conclusion*

Mayo's work marks a very big step forward in what was, for its time, an entirely new and important direction. While he left the detailed analysis and presentation of the results of research to his colleagues, he himself painted the broad picture of the problems of modern industry.

At the time when management itself was really beginning to develop new techniques of management, and putting the emphasis on systems as the way to better management, he was questioning the whole basis on which industrial performance rests – the need for and the ability to get willing co-operation.

From the early part of the twentieth century the moral, scientific and philosophical 'certainties' of the Victorian era had been disintegrating one by one. At the same time the very structure of society had begun to change at a phenomenal rate. Sociology as a developing science was turning its attention to these changes, their effects, and the search for new and more meaningful explanations of social phenomena. Mayo and his co-researchers were the first sociologists to turn their attention to the conditions in twentieth century industry.

For this they must be given full credit. That they erred, if erred is the right word, in concentrating on one aspect of the total management complex is beyond doubt. But all fields of knowledge as they develop involve more and more specialization on particular aspects. That their results and conclusions are related only to the particular and special circumstances of exceptional cases may be open to argument.

There are those who maintain that the mere presence of an observer or researcher in a human situation alters the very situation itself and therefore prevents valid conclusions about the original situation being drawn. Does this invalidate the whole structure of Mayo's work? Probably not, but allowance must be made for it.

Again, it is possible to argue that in practice the majority of firms carry on day after day, year after year with reasonable efficiency and make reasonable profits. It is tenable that only the few have the major problems and that the attention they get in the newspaper headlines is out of all proportion to their real significance in the total situation. But this may be the argument of complacency, an appalling ability to be satisfied with what is and a complete inability or unwillingness to see what could be.

Time alone will show the true value of Mayo's work, and whether he opened up a trail which leads to the promised land or one which leads to nowhere in particular. On balance the odds would seem to be that he set management thought off on a new trail which is of vital importance to modern industry.

## References

(1) Mayo, Elton, *The Human Problems of an Industrial Civilization* (The Macmillan Co., New York 1933), p. 1.

(2) ibid., pp. 63–64.

(3) ibid., p. 87.

(4) ibid., p. 116.

(5) ibid., p. 166.

(6) Mayo, Elton, *The Social Problems of an Industrial Civilization* (Routledge and Kegan Paul, London 1949), p. 49.

(7) ibid., p. 49.

(8) ibid., p. 61.

## Bibliography

BOOKS BY ELTON MAYO

*Democracy and Freedom* (Macmillan and Co., Melbourne 1919).

*The Human Problems of an Industrial Civilization* (The Macmillan Co., New York 1933).

*The Social Problems of an Industrial Civilization* (Division of Research, Harvard Business School, Boston 1945; Routledge and Kegan Paul, London 1949).

*The Political Problems of an Industrial Civilization* (Harvard University Press, Boston 1947).

# 14

# J. A. C. Brown
# 1954

*Introduction*

The earlier psychologists who concerned themselves with industrial
problems were, with the exception of Mary Follett (*see* Chapter 12)
dealing mainly with such things as the effects of surroundings, of
welfare work, and industrial fatigue. Mayo's work (Chapter 13),
although carried out in the early nineteen-thirties, for one reason
and another did not really become known until the late nineteen-
forties.

J. A. C. Brown, having worked as a psychiatrist before the war
and with the Forces during the war, joined an industrial firm afterwards and became directly involved in industrial problems. Seven
years of this convinced him of two things: that if people are
mentally sick the cause is likely to lie in the society in which they
live and work, and that within the work situation the small group is
probably of greater importance than the individual. The direct
result of his experience and ideas was the book *The Social Psychology of Industry*, published in 1954. It can be said to follow Mayo
in that it deals primarily with groups, but it is broader in outlook and
deals with people in the normal rather than the experimental
situation.

Starting with a brief historical review of the development of
industry and its effect on work he leads on to a criticism of the
assumptions on which the scientific management school of Taylor,
Gilbreth and their followers was based. These are given as: the
natural, fixed characteristics of men are those that make them dislike work, become lazy and get only one satisfaction from work, i.e.
money. Management is assumed to be concerned with man only as

a machine to do as he is told and without a brain – or if he has one management does not want him to use it. It can be argued that this is over-stating the case against the original exponents of scientific management, but in general it is a close approximation of how things have worked out in a large number of cases.

In contrast Mayo is quoted with approval. The man (or woman) at work is not an isolated individual reacting as a machine. The results he or she produces depend on the motivation to work, the state of morale, and the group to which he or she belongs. These factors and the resulting behaviour are largely affected by the assumptions management makes and the way it operates. If things don't work out, if workers are lazy or 'couldn't care less' then management should look at its own practices rather than blame the worker for being stupid, 'bolshie' or even bloody-minded.

In more general terms the questions the social psychologists should be concerned with are:[1]

(1) What is the nature of man as an individual, and what, if any, are his basic needs?
(2) What is the nature of man as a social animal, and how does he relate himself to society?
(3) What is the nature of industry, and how far does it fit in with what we know of man as a human being both socially and individually?

Industry, it is suggested, has gone badly astray. It ignores the real nature of man by creating conditions in which he surrenders himself to work so that he can 'live' when not working, in which he is expected to exercise few of his faculties, in which he becomes the hostile, passive element in the work situation. The psychology of man is ignored, the organization is the key factor. While these statements are obviously not true for all work, and probably all of them together are not true for any work, they state a problem which is almost certainly the major one facing industrial society today. The way out cannot be backward to an idyllic age of simplicity and craftsmanship: it must be forward, to an adaptation of industry to the nature of man.

## Human Nature and Society

The real starting point here is the key to the rest of the book. Man is not simply a biological animal reacting to innate and inborn needs. He is much more complex, and his pattern of needs and his behaviour to meet them arise in part from innate qualities, which provide a base, but, more importantly, from the society of which he is a part. Human nature is not fixed; it is fashioned by environment, it is the result of the relationships which relate the individual to society. And one of the most important of these relationships is that between the individual and the small, natural primary groups to which he belongs. In the work situation the primary group of up to a dozen is probably more important as the basic unit than the individual.

Society, then, is not a mob or rabble of self-centred and self-concerned individuals, but an organism with a structure of individuals combined into groups, and a pattern of relationships between groups. To effect change we have to alter the group, its ideas, its relationships. The nature of the group will be the result of the culture or sub-culture of the society in which it exists. Modern Western industrial society has developed so fast technologically and in formal organization that its social structure has failed to keep up. The difference between the two is the crux of the industrial problem.

## The Formal Organization of Industry

An understanding of the formal pattern or organization of industry and the way it works in practice is essential to see where things have gone wrong. Fundamental to the system is the concept of concentration of power at the top and its delegation in the form of authority through the various steps of a hierarchy down to the foreman, charge-hand or supervisor. This hierarchy provides, in theory at least, a channel for communication downwards and upwards. In general it is an inefficient means of communication, and information, where it is required for decision-making or for understanding, is often missing or incorrect.

Movement of the individual up the hierarchy, while usually supposedly on merit, may have many other causes, and for the majority may be impossible. Workers tend to regard it with suspicion.

In theory at least formal organization is quoted[2] as having three characteristics:

(1) It is deliberately impersonal.
(2) It is based on ideal relationships.
(3) It is based on the 'rabble hypothesis' of the nature of man.

The behaviour of one person to another, then is supposedly based rationally on function and status and not on personal likes or dislikes. The 'rabble hypothesis' of individuals each concerned only with himself, again in theory, gives the organization the necessary flexibility. The system of the hierarchy provides position, status, defines the individual job, and sets up the pattern of relationships.

Cutting across the levels formed by the hierarchy (known as line structure) are two other patterns of organization. The first is given the term 'functional', where different types of work are separated into different hierarchies with one common point at the very top, for example the sales function and the production function. A more difficult problem arises with what Brown calls 'staff organization'. (Both 'functional' and 'staff' are used by some other writers with quite different meanings.) This staff organization consists of specialists who either are advisers to line managers in their specialized form of knowledge, or work in departments which themselves do specialized work, for instance accounting or buying. Difficulties have always arisen in fitting the first type into the formal organization structure.

There are two basic weaknesses in formal organization structures. The first arises as soon as a total job starts to be split into parts, i.e. organized. This is inherent and fundamental. The purpose of the business is a whole, a unity (or it should be!). But it is carried out by separate divisions, departments, sections, groups and individuals. The weakness lies in co-ordinating these separate parts so that they work together to the same end. The basis of co-ordination is effective communication, so that people can know on the one hand what is required of them and on the other what is happening. Really effective communication is very difficult to achieve because of problems of time, of space, of sectionalization, and of unwillingness for one reason or another to pass on information correctly or even at all.

The second difficulty arises from the 'formal' nature of formal organization. It must of necessity be based on one of two assumptions: either all men are alike and interchangeable, or every man can and *will* adapt to fit a formal position and a formalized set of relationships. Both are manifestly untrue, and formal organization falls down when it meets the reality of human nature. The inevitable result is conflict between the requirements of the organization and those of the groups and individuals that comprise it. While this is true in general, especially in competitive industries where there is pressure for results from management, it is not universally true, and some firms or organizations might and do take personal factors into account.

Formal organizations, then, is a necessity. Inevitably it forms a parameter within which human behaviour is determined. For a number of reasons, of which the techniques of scientific management, growth in size and complexity, distance from top to bottom, ineffective communication, and the conduct of pressure-orientated managements are some, that behaviour has become more and more one of apathy and/or conflict.

## *The Informal Organization of Industry*

Unless a formal organization structure has been carefully and deliberately designed to meet the human and psychological needs of the people who form it, an informal organization is bound to exist alongside but not parallel with the formal one. The basis of this, which, in contrast to the formal organization, is built up from the bottom, is the natural or primary group. This usually consists of between six and twelve people bonded together as a group by common purpose, common ideals, common interests, or just sheer physical proximity. Each informal group will have its own leader, and these leaders themselves form into their own primary groups, and so on. The leader acts as the link-pin (as Likert calls him) between the group which he leads and the higher one of which he is a member.

What happens then depends on circumstances. If the aims and objectives of the primary groups coincide with those of the formal organization there will be a well-integrated, effective firm achieving its objectives with the minimum of internal friction and difficulty. For this to happen the formal goals must, whether management likes it or not, be acceptable to the primary groups. If they are not and differences arise between primary group and formal aims then it is the latter which will suffer, and conflict and friction will ensue.

There are many other implications of the primary group in the industrial setting. It provides the individual very largely with his attitudes, opinions, ideas and goals (at the same time the individual may have an influence on forming these in the group). It may provide the discipline and control when formal control is lacking or can be overridden. When change, especially change in attitude, is required management must achieve that change through changing the ideas of the group, not the individual. Formal control works best when it can work in tandem with the informal control of the group. Quite apart from the need to attain specific goals, the primary group exists to serve the social needs of the individuals; it tends therefore to persist even when immediate goals are not pressing.

But while the primary group as described above is perhaps the most significant (and least understood) aspect of the firm's structure there are, says Brown[3], five other aspects of informal organization:

(1) The total informal organization of the factory, viewed as a system of interlocking groups of all types.
(2) Large groups which generally arise over some particular issue of internal politics within the factory ... A diffuse group of this sort may extend throughout all the departments of the factory, and is generally described as a 'crowd' or a 'gang'.
(3) The primary group formed more or less on the basis of a common job in the same part of the factory ...

(4) Groups of two or three particular intimate friends who may be members of larger cliques.

(5) Isolated individuals who rarely participate in social activities.

Well-integrated groups are unlikely to form where labour turn-over is high so that people don't have time to get to know each other, for instance where part-time female or casual labour is employed. They are most likely among skilled operators, in smaller communities, and in firms where employees are more or less permanent.

While mention was made a short while ago of the primary group leader as the link-pin with the next higher group, leadership in the primary group tends more to move around from one individual to another according to the needs of the moment. At one time it may be assumed by the man with most experience or knowledge, at another by the best talker or advocate, at another by the arbitrator, and so on. Leadership is not just a question of the individual, but of the individual and the group and the current situation.

The group provides the individual not only with his aims but also with his status, role and prestige. Status is his position and recognition within the group. Role is the part he is expected to play in furthering the aims of and maintaining the group. Prestige, which may be high or low or in between, comes from belonging to the group and is, in effect, a reflected glory.

In return for the benefits of membership the group expects certain things from its members. Conformity to its customs and ideas, both general and in relation to a particular role occupied, willingness to do a fair share of the work (as the shaving cream advertisement used to say, 'not too little, not too much'), loyalty to the group and the individuals who comprise it, are typical of most primary groups.

It is easy to think of the informal organization as being always in conflict with the formal one and creating chaos. At times it does create chaos. At other times, particularly when the formal structure is bad, inappropriate or out of date, it is the informal structure which gets things done and keeps them going by cutting corners, and by ignoring the 'rules' that could only lead to disaster. Such actions are influenced by the 'atmosphere' of the firm, the attitudes of the managers, and particularly those of the man at the top.

### Attitudes and Opinion Surveys

Seemingly out of context there follows a short chapter on this subject. Perhaps by now Brown has made his point that what people think and do will be profoundly influenced by their attitudes, and that formal lines of communication are the least effective way of discovering what they are.

Their importance to management lies in the fact that ' . . . what is forgotten is that the position of management in relation to workers is . . . that of the parent who takes his problem child to the Child Guidance Clinic and is distressed to find that the psychologist works on the principle that "there are no problem children, only problem parents".'[4] If a firm has poor attitudes among its workers the reasons for them will lie not with the stupidity, the ignorance, the selfishness of the workers but with the ignorance, the wrong attitudes and the bad practices of management. And these, however unpalatable, are things that management should know and put right. Formal communication channels and joint consultation will probably not bring them to light. The only way to discover them is by arranging an attitude survey, conducted in complete confidence by competent impartial outsiders.

Not only will this enable management, if it is mature enough, to put right its own mistakes, but it has other advantages. The mere fact of being able to 'let off steam' is itself the greatest safety valve. Many a problem which seemed enormous when 'bottled up' becomes insignificant after a good grouse about it. In other cases problems arise because of lack of information or explanation, and when brought into the open an honest explanation of the situation by management is all that is required.

### Work, its Nature, Conditions and Motivation

Like most modern psychologists, Brown disagrees violently with the view of industrial society that work is inherently something which people dislike and will avoid if they can. If this state of affairs does exist then it is due to psychological conditions associated with the work and not primarily to the fact of work. The management 'folk-lore' that people will not work willingly, that the pay-packet is the main incentive, that more paint, or brighter surroundings, or work study will by themselves improve output, is discarded *in toto*.

Instead he puts forward views on work which have become more or less standard among modern students of industry:[5]

(1) Work is an essential part of man's life since it is that aspect of his life which gives him status and binds him to society. Ordinarily men and women like their work ... When they do not like it, the fault lies in the psychological and social conditions of the job rather than in the worker. Furthermore work is a social activity.

(2) The morale of the worker (i.e. whether or not he works willingly) has no *direct* relationship whatsoever to the material conditions of the job ...

(3) There are many incentives, of which, under normal conditions, money is one of the least important. Unemployment is a powerful negative incentive, precisely because (1) is true. That is to say, unemployment is feared because it cuts man off from his society.

Perhaps one should add here that now, fifteen years later, these statements would be regarded as something of an over-simplification of a very complex situation. They were, however, nearer the truth than the assumptions on which management did and largely still does appear to rest.

Work in industry, suggests Brown, has a dual function – an economic one of providing the goods and services required and a social one of providing the necessary relationships for the individual. From these relationships he can get psychological satisfactions of belonging, status, respect and admiration, fulfilment and, in some cases, power. This, at any rate, is what should happen. It is because the social function is so seldom realized on the factory floor that trouble arises and it *appears* that man does not like work. (*see also* Chapter 16, on Douglas McGregor.)

One very important condition must be added. Everyone knows that different people can and do see the same set of circumstances in a different way and put different interpretations on it. People react to a situation and to their surroundings not necessarily as they actually are but as they see and interpret them.

Work and the conditions under which it is done must meet the needs of the worker if it is to be a source of satisfaction to him. Needs, as mentioned in considering human nature, may be innate but are also acquired from the social conditions in which the person grows up. Brown says that 'people define their needs in terms of the time and place in which they live'.[6]

Meeting some needs, mostly those which industry has tried so far to meet, gives only temporary satisfaction. Other kinds of needs, the psychological ones of status, satisfying inter-personal relationships, sense of achievement, do, when met, give long-term satisfaction. Generally at shop-floor level the work situation ignores these needs. Attempts to discover a general pattern of priorities had, up to the time when Brown was writing, generally failed. Work since then has thrown real doubt upon the possibility of ever getting a standardized list.

Work and motivation under modern factory conditions is dealt with in some detail. Leaving on one side the problem of detailed lists of motives, work can be performed (a) because of its own intrinsic value (as a craft), (b) because of satisfying conditions associated indirectly with the work; (c) because it simply supplies money which enables satisfactions to be obtained outside the work situation. Condition (a) is ideal, as anyone who has had the good fortune to have been in this situation will realize. Condition (b) is second-best, and may result in a generally satisfying work situation. In this category comes boring routine work where the attention is so little occupied that social chatter, gossip or even day-dreaming is possible. But near-routine work which requires just too much attention, or isolates the individual so that these conditions cannot be met, is psychologically the worst and least satisfying form of work. The third condition would appear to assume a near-schizo-phrenic personality.

*Leaders and Leadership*

Any psychological approach to industry and management must sooner or later tackle this, the most difficult of all areas. Almost equally inevitably the starting point is what leadership is not. A leader is not a person possessed of super-human qualities, or even of any particular list of qualities or traits. But Brown does quote with apparent approval W. Jenkins' conclusions that leadership is specific to a particular situation, and that a leader almost always has some superiority over the rest of the group in some way or other.

A necessary distinction is drawn between 'leadership' (which works) and 'headship' or formal position in the hierarchy, which implies a leadership position (but which may not work). Another distinction is made between the effective leader of a healthy group who is reasonably intelligent, well-balanced and can not only 'lead' the group his way, but can react to the feelings and needs of the group, and the ineffective leader who is too rigid, fixed and self-centred to react to the group.

When one considers that leadership should be a function of the situations in which it occurs, and that even with the same group situations change from time to time and/or because of outside influences, it should be obvious that an effective leader will change his immediate behaviour to meet the circumstances of the moment while maintaining a coherent, recognizable pattern of procedure which is acceptable to his group. Even so, Brown gives a classification[7] of 'types of leaders' which might be more usefully called 'styles of leadership'.

    A. *Autocratic leaders*
        (1) Strict autocrat
        (2) Benevolent autocrat
        (3) Incompetent autocrat
    B. *Democratic leaders*
        (1) Genuine democrat
        (2) Pseudo-democrat
    C. *Laissez-faire leaders*

Experimental work in psychology and in industry is beginning

# J. A. C. Brown

to show that genuine democratic leadership may be actually the most effective and satisfying form. (It might almost be true to say that any first-line supervisor who has held his job under post-war conditions of full employment *knows* that this is true.) The point is rammed home with the statement that however good a manager may be technically, if he is inefficient in the sphere of human relations he is 'a menace to the well-being of the factory'.[8]

## Frustration

It is suggested that frustration is something that everyone feels at times, that its effects may be small and unimportant but that under the conditions of modern industry it is often important enough to cause recognizable patterns of behaviour which the manager ought to understand.

Broadly, four general reactions to serious frustration occur – aggression, regression, fixation and resignation. Aggression may mean merely any attempt to fight for an improvement in an unsatisfactory situation, and all the technological and social improvements from prehistoric to modern times may be said to be its valuable results. But it may also take the form of a build-up of energy which cannot find an outlet in putting things right and so spends itself in 'taking revenge' on the person or persons causing the blockage, or possibly on some quite innocent person who just happens to be in the way. Such aggression may show itself in excessive criticism of management, putting forward superficial grievances, sabotage, militancy, absenteeism, and go-slow tactics. All of these are a form of revenge against management for blocking the desires and needs of the workers, and are danger signals that something is seriously wrong.

Reggressive behaviour, the second alternative, means reverting to a more immature form of behaviour. Two of Brown's versions of aggressive behaviour might, it is thought, be also forms of regression – sabotage and airing superficial grievances. He suggests as forms of regression a lack of critical faculty and receptiveness to suggestion also an excessive regard for the 'good old days', and an inability to face change.

Fixation is merely continuing with the same pattern of action although it is quite obvious that it will not and cannot produce the required results. Apathy, the attitude of 'couldn't care less' or resignation, might with some justification be said to be the disease of the twentieth century. 'The world [or the firm] is so big and I'm so small, management is so powerful [or so distant] and I'm so powerless, so why bother ? Do as little as possible, create no fuss, don't get excited – there'll be the pay packet on Friday, so what ?'

Lost output, accidents, absenteeism, strikes, neurosis, psychosomatic illness, and high labour turnover may all be attributed to frustration. If only their real costs could be shown as an item headed 'Frustration' in the Profit and Loss account, how quickly managements would wake up. Unfortunately they cannot.

## Conclusions

Brown's book is now almost twenty years old. It ought to be dated; in fact with the work that has been done in this field it ought to be *outdated*. It isn't. Some of its ideas may, perhaps, now seem a little crude and underdeveloped. Despite this it is still one of the best books in its field; it provides a general introduction to basic problems which every manager or student of management should read. It presents for all to see the trap that we are in, with our industrial society which cannot at present cope with the human problems it produces; a society which raises hopes and cannot satisfy them; a society split between those who have the power to control and do not know how to use it effectively (if indeed the knowledge is possible at present) and those who have the power only to disrupt. Can modern society accept his view that 'the changes suggested here go far beyond problems of industrial efficiency and production, since the social function of industry is no less important than its technical efficiency' ?[9]

## References

(1) Brown, J. A. C. *The Social Psychology of Industry* (Penguin Books, Harmondsworth 1954), p. 21.
(2) ibid., p. 105.
(3) ibid., p. 130.
(4) ibid., p. 165.
(5) ibid., p. 187.

(6) ibid., p. 200.
(7) ibid., p. 226.
(8) ibid., p. 241.
(9) ibid., p. 301.

*Bibliography*

BOOKS BY J. A. C. BROWN

*The Distressed Mind* (Watts, London 1946).
*The Evolution of Society* Second Edition (Watts, London 1949).
*Psychology* (Paul Elek, London 1950).
*The Social Psychology of Industry* (Penguin Books, Harmondsworth 1954; Baltimore 1961).
*Techniques of Persuasion* (Penguin Books, Harmondsworth 1963).

## 15

## Chris Argyris
## 1957

*Introduction*

That the developments in the behavioural sciences, particularly in the post-war period, were becoming accepted and used is recognized by Argyris in the opening words of the Preface of his book *Personality and the Organization*. But at the same time he recognized that the sciences were still in their relative infancy, fragmented and disconnected and often not directly related to the industrial situation.

This book is an early, if not the first, attempt to draw together the separate threads and to write for students and for managers a preliminary theory of behaviour in the industrial setting. He stresses that it is incomplete and that for several reasons, including the one that research itself is still too narrow, a complete statement is not yet possible. But a start has to be made somewhere.

Based on the existing knowledge of psychology and, to a lesser extent, sociology, the book attempts to set out an explanatory theory for human behaviour based on the characteristics of the individual, the work group and the formal organization. It is explanatory rather than prescriptive. When it comes to offering solutions Argyris admits he has little except a few generalities to put forward. This is the area where the practical manager who has found *ad hoc* solutions and the theorist must get together to see how and why the workable solutions do or do not match the theory. Up to the time of this book this was the last explored field of management.

*Basic Assumptions and Viewpoints*

The very first and most fundamental assumption lies in the subtitle of the book – 'The Conflict between System and the Indivi-

# Chris Argyris

dual'. While this assumption underlies the whole book the question can be raised 'Is it a valid assumption for all places and all time?' The existence of conflict in industry cannot be disputed. Every newspaper every day has its column of 'Industrial News', and always the news is of conflict, of strikes, sit-ins, walk-outs and arguments. But would a statement that 300 men had worked for 300 days without a dispute be newsworthy? Yet readers will know of, or may work for, a firm where open conflict seems non-existent. So some firms may already know the answers which Argyris seeks, but are they in fact, typical firms?

Conflict, it must be admitted, is typical of the larger firms, and as these employ the majority of workers the study of it is worthwhile and important. Perhaps not for all workers, but for a large enough number the assumption appears valid.

In a number of senses the viewpoint of the book is limited. As already said, it is concerned with the industrial work-situation, and only ideas from the behavioural sciences which specifically relate to it are included. Then only what Argyris calls systematic work from the social sciences is included – this is work which in his opinion passes the minimum scientific standards. Finally the work presented must be 'integrated' – that is, it must be sufficiently interrelated to present a reasonably coherent picture to the reader.

The scientist, and now the manager, need a coherent theory to understand, to predict and to control. The scientist may be concerned with the atom; the manager is concerned with human beings at work. The manager, if he is to understand human behaviour ' . . . *requires self-awareness*. We shall see later that *it is impossible to understand others unless we understand ourselves and we cannot understand ourselves unless we understand others*'.[1] But self-awareness is not sufficient – it needs the backing of principles.

Research suggests that industrial behaviour is caused by one or more of the following:

  (i) Individual, personality factors.
  (ii) Small, informal group factors.
  (iii) Formal organization factors.

Between them they require a knowledge of individual psychology,

205

social psychology and organization theory; more than that, they require a knowledge of the combination and interaction of them all.

While the scientist may be satisfied with the answer to the question 'Why?' the manager needs to go further. When he can answer the question 'Why?' (or even without the answer) he must attempt to forecast 'what'. To do this he needs a skill consisting of 'balanced growth and learning'.[2] And beyond that the manager needs a 'philosophy of life'[3] to guide him when principles have gone as far as they can, and he must then decide between 'good' and 'bad'.

The final assumptions are simple but essential: for a manager common sense is essential but inadequate by itself; experience is only of value if the manager has used and learnt from it; the human being is by far the most complex object existing on the face of the earth.

## The Human Personality

The personality of the individual is essential to the study as it is one of the three forces acting on and in a very complex situation. It is complex enough to form a study by itself, so Argyris limits himself to the basic generally accepted aspects which he feels the manager should know.

Personality consists of a series of parts which relate together to form an individual and unique whole. Not only the parts but the way in which they are combined, their relative strengths and weaknesses lead to the uniqueness which comprises the individual person. Consequently any attempt to change just one part or aspect must cause difficulties, because the one part cannot be changed without changing its relationships to others, and therefore to some extent the pattern of the whole.

Ideally the organization of the parts into the whole should present a two-sided state of balance, of adjustment internally between the parts, and of balance or adaptation of the whole to the external situation in which it exists. An integrated person is both well adjusted in himself and well adapted to his environment. Frequently this complete integration fails to materialize, and probably few people attain it in perfect form. In any case internal change is normal as a person grows from the immaturity of the child to the relative maturity of the adult. Also external change in the environment may arise from a myriad causes. The process then becomes the continuous one of a more or less reasonable state of balance or equilibrium forced into disequilibrium by change of one sort or another, followed by attempts to reach a new state of equilibrium in the new conditions. The attempts to move to a better state are, in fact, the behaviour of the individual, known technically as 'self-actualization'.

In order to behave, to create change, the individual is assumed to possess a source of energy. Opinions differ as to whether the total amount of energy is fixed or is dependent upon the mental state at the time. It has both a physical and a psychological form. Physical energy is used up by physical activity, psychological by creativity, conflict, frustration, and anxiety. Psychological and physical energy are closely related, and excessive loss of the former from whatever cause will reduce the available amount of the latter. For example laziness and physical inertia may be due not to physical causes but to frustration and anxiety states.

Considerable importance is given to psychological energy because it is regarded as the basis of behaviour. The following characteristics of it are important from the managers' point of view.

(i) All people possess it.
(ii) It is indestructible.
(iii) The amount used varies with the state of mind.
(iv) If its expression is temporarily blocked in one desired way it will try to find expression in some other way.
(v) If it is channelled into some form of unsatisfying activity people will try to find satisfactory expression elsewhere.

To understand psychological energy it is necessary to understand its source. Depending on the basic personality, its form of adaption internally, and the maturity of the individual, each person is assumed to have a pattern of wants or needs which require satisfaction. These needs release energy in order to obtain satisfaction. The deeper the need the greater the amount of energy it will release. The appearance of particular needs, their duration and intensity, will vary from one individual to another, from time to time, and as a reaction to changes in the total system. Although overt behaviour is the result of needs in action, the connection between need and action is by no means always direct, so that 'obvious' relationships are often dangerous and incorrect conclusions.

Needs can be classified into the inner needs of self-adjustment and its maintenance, and outer needs, which are less vital. Needs may be conscious and understood by the individual or unconscious, in which case, although they give rise to behaviour, the individual will be unable to explain them. Also there are social needs related to and conditioned by the society in which the individual lives, and physiological needs based on bodily comfort.

Needs have been dealt with at some length because they are vital to and underlie the whole of Argyris's book. They do not, however, tell the whole story of human personality. In addition the individual possesses abilities. The current suggestion is that abilities arise as a result of practice in satisfying needs. Needs may fuse together to become an interest. The repetitive attempts to satisfy this interest leads to skill in doing certain things, i.e. ability. Some few skills, however, may be acquired as the result of inheritance. Broadly speaking, abilities may be of three kinds – knowing or cognitive, doing or motor, and those of feeling or sensitivity.

Leading on from the ideas of needs, of abilities, and of a separate physical body is the concept of the 'self' as a separate individual. While this arises partly from the realization, to a greater or lesser extent, of the parts of the individual and their organization or structure, it is only completely possible within a society, so that the individual can differentiate between 'me' and 'others'. This is something which comes with experience and growth. The importance of the self lies in its reaction to outside events and ideas – that of accepting and incorporating them, ignoring them, or distorting them to make them fit the pattern of the self.

An important result of this concept of the 'self' is the behaviour pattern which results. The realization of its existence causes reaction to anything which appears to present a threat to the 'self'. In other words the maintenance of the 'self' is a prime need and a major cause of behaviour. This form of behaviour is known as a 'defence mechanism', and it can appear in many different guises. The different forms are the result of the different mental states which the threat may produce – anxiety, conflict, frustration, or failure.

Argyris gives a long list of defence mechanisms, and a summary can hardly do it justice:

   (i) Aggression, or attempts to injure or hurt the cause of the threat.

  (ii) Guilt when the threat is internal. Possibly because of some shortcoming, guilty feelings result and show as aggression turned back on oneself.

 (iii) Continuation, or avoiding direct conflict by a second-best choice, but continuing to wish for the original.

 (iv) Discriminatory decision, or resolving an internal conflict by conscious rational decision.

  (v) Denial, or remaining unaware of the facts of the threat.

 (vi) Repression, or refusing to allow oneself to recognize a threat and forcing it into the unconscious mind without realizing it.

 (vii) Suppression, or deliberately forcing the conflict into the unconscious mind.

(viii) Inhibition, or deliberately refraining from doing things.

 (ix) Conversion, or converting conscious fear into physical illness.

  (x) Over-compensation, or working so hard at overcoming an obstacle that one goes too far.

 (xi) Rationalization, or knowingly inventing an excuse for not being able to accept a situation.

 (xii) Identification, or overcoming the obstacle by copying some usually admired person.

(xiii) Projection, which may be either blaming others for one's own shortcomings, or ascribing to others fears and feelings of one's own.

(xiv) Vacillation, or constant switching from one solution to another.

 (xv) Ambivalence, or holding two opposite points of view at the same time.

(xvi) Slip of the tongue, or the unconscious revelation of the real situation.

With such a wide variety to choose from it should be obvious that the 'defence mechanism' behaviour often conceals more than it discloses, and makes the real need and motive very difficult to locate. From the point of view of management, which unfortunately is continually meeting defensive behaviour (usually as a reaction to its own behaviour!) a complex situation is made even more difficult to understand. But, if to understand others we must first understand ourselves, it would help enormously if managers recognised when they themselves were using defence mechanisms.

Finally, as the individual grows from childhood to being an adult, growth and experience tend to give him a greater degree of maturity. This takes place in several ways. The 'parts' of the individual become more numerous and more complex, the inter-relationship between them, i.e. their organization, becomes more complicated, and the relationship pattern between the individual and the society in which he lives also becomes much more complex. 'To summarize, man in his need fulfilling, goal directed behaviour is to some extent: "like all other men, like some other men, like no other men".'[4]

This development of personality towards maturity, while by no means equal in all men, is, nevertheless, an inherent need for all. In achieving this development people are assumed to tend to do the following:

  (i) Develop from passivity to increasing activity.
 (ii) Develop from dependence on others to relative independence.
(iii) Develop from a few restricted forms of behaviour to many varied ones.
 (iv) Develop from shallow to deep interests.
  (v) Develop from short- to long-term perspectives.
 (vi) Develop from subordinate to equal or superior positions.
(vii) Develop from lack of awareness of 'self' to self-awareness and self-control.

## Chris Argyris

One word of warning is necessary, however. The limitations of the society in which a person lives and the limitations of his own basic personality will always prevent the situation emerging where everyone achieves complete and ultimate maturity.

### The Formal Organization

In considering formal organization Argyris simultaneously reviews a 'model' based on the ideas and principles of 'classical' theory and the ways in which this conflicts with the nature of a 'model' personality, as discussed in the previous chapter. He admits that neither 'model' is really true to life but claims that they provide a yardstick by which reality can be measured. He also admits that in many cases management is trying hard to alleviate the worst features of the conflict between organization and personality.

For present purposes the principles on which organization should be based will be given first, and their overall effects summarized afterwards.

Basically all formal organizations are assumed to be rational, that is, they have a specified purpose or objective, and the structure of the organization is designed by intelligent minds to further the achievement of these objectives. Urwick's suggestion that this structure can be designed as a blue-print excluding consideration of personalities and individuals is quoted in support of this thesis; also Fayol's principle of order: 'a place for everything and everything in its place'. In practice, however, personalities must be taken into account and perfect order can only be an ideal, so the optimum rather than the ideal becomes the aim.

The first real principle is that of task or work specialization. Output will be increased and, therefore, objectives attained more economically if the individual concentrates on a narrow range of tasks, the narrower the better. This leads to Gilbreth's 'one best way' to do a job, the assumption that specialization increases skill and the further assumption that individual differences may be ignored because people will adapt to the situation.

Logically following on from specialization is the principle of 'Unity of Direction'. The individual having only a narrow task to perform can neither see nor comprehend the overall objectives. At suitable points in the structure leaders must be put in to define and direct the work of those under them so that it contributes its appropriate share to organizational objectives.

There is a limit to the number of people a leader or superior can control. This limit is known as the 'span of control' and is a fundamental principle of formal organization. The results of this is the hierarchy, or successive layers of management from the top to the bottom.

Putting the models of personality and formal organization side by side Argyris concludes that there are 'basic incongruities'[5] between the needs of the organization as they impinge on the individual and the psychological needs of the individual as he develops into a mature person.

The formal organization if ideally planned and worked produces a situation where[6]

Employees will tend to work in an environment where

(1) they are provided minimal control over their workaday world,
(2) they are expected to be passive, dependent and subordinate,
(3) they are expected to have a short time perspective,
(4) they are induced to perfect and value the frequent use of a few skin-surface shallow abilities,
(5) they are expected to produce under conditions leading to psychological failure.

In other words to conform to the organizational situation people should be immature psychologically. The requirements of the organization are that people should 'feel dependent, submissive and passive and to require them to utilize only a few of their less important abilities'.[7] The results are predicted as being frustration, conflict, feelings of failure, and short-term perspectives.

*Individual and Group Adaptation*

It is one thing to predict from an analysis of the situation that people working in organizations will suffer such psychological ills. It is another matter to show from actual behaviour patterns that in fact they do. Argyris turns to research into industrial behaviour to support his case. His case is, however, limited to adaptive behaviour by groups and individuals within the organization. Not enough research has yet been done to follow up the adaptation of the organization to external circumstances and the relation of this to internal behaviour.

Starting with conflict, this will arise where the individual finds he cannot at the same time fulfil his personal needs and meet those of the organization, for example the organization requires him to be dependent and submissive, while he wishes to exercise independence and to use his own intelligence.

From researches carried out there can be various reactions to this situation:

(i) Leave the situation: get another job, get promoted, take time off – the half hour for a smoke, the day or two without a doctor's certificate, longer with psychosomatic illness, day-dreaming when the work is sufficiently routine to allow it.

(ii) Push aside and ignore to a greater or lesser extent the organization's requirements – apathy, loss of interest, lack of loyalty.

(iii) Remain in conflict, with increasing tension which will eventually explode over some quite insignificant incident.

Frustration tends to produce more or less similar patterns of behaviour.

(i) Less mature behaviour.
(ii) Leaving the situation.
(iii) Aggression, hostility, and blaming others.
(iv) Remaining frustrated, leading again to more tension.

A sense of psychological failure also can produce various results:

(i) Loss of interest in work.
(ii) Loss of self-confidence.
(iii) Giving up easily – failure to try.
(iv) Lower work standards.
(v) A fear of change.
(vi) An expectation of still more failure.
(vii) Blaming others.

A short-term perspective leads to feelings of insecurity, with regressive behaviour.

The situation may well be that the worker feels not one but several of these pressures at once, and the resultant behaviour may be a combination of various types. In addition he may, consciously or sub-consciously, decide to substitute for his own needs or to compensate for the poor situation by demanding more money.

The detailed researches which Argyris quotes to support these hypotheses would be out of place in this book. Here it is sufficient to say that all the suggestions have some evidence to support them, although at times it is fragmentary. The situation, however, does look promising, and further research will quite possibly enable us to explain the real reasons behind worker behaviour and, more importantly, predict the likely results of managerial action.

In addition to individual behaviour there is also group behaviour to be considered. A good deal of the possible individual adaptive behaviour is 'anti-organization' and therefore runs the risk of punishment by management. This possibility leads to feelings of insecurity, and one of the main functions of the primary group is to provide a supportive situation by backing or even requiring this sort of behaviour. It is required by the group and the whole group are doing it, the individual member is not out on a limb. One way in which the informal group does this is by setting lower work targets or standards than management requires and insisting that the individual keeps to the group standards. Another more formal way is by working through the trade unions to decrease the real authority which management has and to transfer some of it to the workers as represented by the union. (It is true that the post-1945 situation has made this action much easier to accomplish.)

Finally there is the very practical point that if practising managers are asked 'what do workers want most?' the answer in ninety-nine cases out of a hundred will be 'more money'. How does this fit in with theories of adaptive behaviour? There are two possible answers, both supported by research. One is that the worker deliberately says to himself in effect 'To hell with the work situation. I'll put up with that so long as I can live better outside work.' To do this he needs and demands more money. Alternatively he may de-emphasize or even not be consciously aware of his real needs and so regard the wage-packet as the pre-eminent goal.

One thing at least can be said with absolute certainty. Worker behaviour and adaptation to complex, modern industrial situations are extremely complex, and any over-simplified generalization on the subject is certain to be wrong.

## Management's Reaction

A moment or two's thought about Mary Follett's principle of circular behaviour should lead to the realization that workers behave in this way not simply because this is how they are made, but because they are reacting to a situation set up by management and its relationship to their ideas. Management should, therefore, in its assessment of the situation include its own behaviour. Research shows that top management in particular does not. 'They observe their employees while at work and they conclude: (1) The *employees* are lazy. (2) The *employees* are uninterested and apathetic. (3) The *employees* are money crazy. (4) The *employees* create errors and waste.'[8] They conclude that these 'faults' are inherent in and part of the workers make-up and that therefore the workers must be changed if the organization is to succeed. (Compare McGregor's Theory X, p. 225.)

The logic of organization leads to three conclusions.

(i) Strong, dynamic leadership is important.

(ii) Logical, systematic control over employees' behaviour is important.

(iii) The communication of management thinking to employees is important.

Strong, dynamic leaders are those who can push or persuade workers to produce more, can get facts and make good decisions, know policies, can communicate effectively and evaluate performances strictly and honestly in accordance with management policies. They are, as Likert says, 'job oriented', pressure leaders. So management's first reaction to poor performance is normally to increase pressure, so setting up a vicious circle although, as Likert shows, pressure-orientated management may get good results for a time.

The second reaction is to install tighter control systems over ever more detailed aspects of work and to remove still more of any discretionary element left to the worker. This can only add to the sense of psychological failure.

In the 1950s one reaction which was very popular was what Argyris calls 'The Human Relations Fad'. For perhaps slightly different reasons Drucker is equally scathing about this. While few people can define the human relations approach adequately it seems to consist of: keeping people happy – the 'one big happy family' approach; 'selling' the company and free enterprise to the worker; great stress on communication downwards; creating enthusiasm in the worker. Again it seems that this approach must fail, if only for two reasons. It misses completely the real psychological problems at the root of the trouble. It is presented by management and if, as is only too frequently the case, the worker is already suspicious of management the most likely reaction is 'What are they up to, and who do they think they're fooling?'

A somewhat later aspect of the human relations approach is the democratic approach. If this is sincere and properly used it can help, but more often it is likely to be pseudo-democracy in which management go through the motions without real belief in what they are doing (as with much so-called joint consultation), or, even worse, management autocratically insists on democracy. It needs little imagination to realise that the last two approaches don't help! Their most likely effect is to decrease or distort even more such communication upwards as does occur.

All of the management reactions so far mentioned have this one thing in common – they isolate the manager still further from the real situation, and the higher up he is the greater the isolation and less likely he becomes to be able to initiate useful remedies. On this basis it is a dreary and pessimistic picture indeed.

## The First-Line Supervisor

All that has been said is this chapter up to now emphasizes the difficulty in the position of the supervisor. With the two camps of the management on the one hand and the workers on the other he is truly the 'man in the middle'.

Usually an ex-worker himself, his natural sympathies often lie with the men. But as 'one of the management team' his loyalty is to management, from whom his instructions come and to whom he must report. If he does his job properly he must pass on correctly to the workers management information which they will dislike and, probably, disbelieve, and if he accurately conveys to management the shop-floor situation he only gets a similar reaction. In fact, research seems to show that he does as little as possible of either and regards the main part of his job as trying to keep everybody happy. Unless the supervisor is in the fortunate position where the aims of management and the aims of the workers coincide he must inevitably be in a situation of stress and conflict.

This conflict becomes even worse for him when the trade union enters the picture. Workers now have union loyalties; shop-stewards are there to capitalize on every spot of bother and every complaint; shop-stewards and management often talk and arrange things directly between them, leaving the foreman out. He then learns from his subordinates on the shop floor what is going on.

Management, even if it realizes the foreman's problems, often does little to help. Much lip-service is paid to his being part of management without anything effective being done to make him part of it. In addition it often behaves as if the trouble was some shortcoming on the part of the foreman, and 'get-togethers', pep talks, and 'training' are used in the hope of improving *his performance*. In fact, management does anything except tackle the real, basic causes of the situation.

## Decreasing Incongruence

So far, on the basis of a theory of the individual and a theory of formal organization Argyris has predicted the probable outcome of the usual management practices and to a very considerable extent backed up his predictions by detailed references to research results. He has exposed and analysed the 'disease' of modern industry. Much more briefly he turns to the 'cures'.

On the basis that prevention is better than cure the first question is, how is it possible to decrease the incongruence between the formal organization and the healthy individual?

By 'healthy' he means reasonably mature, so that the question is not, as management seems to think, one of altering the individual but one of altering the conditions which make 'healthy' individuals behave in an 'unhealthy' way.

The first change suggested is job enlargement, i.e. a reversal of the process of 'scientific management'. Instead of cutting jobs down to the smallest possible element they should be increased in content and in variety. In so far as this can restore interest in and enthusiasm for work, give scope for some initiative and responsibility, it will help to remove the very conditions which create conflict, frustration, feelings of failure, and short-term perspectives. Where this can be and has been done it has produced very favourable results. The difficulty lies in the fact that where it is most needed it is technologically most difficult to achieve.

The second solution is to change to genuine participative or employeee-centred leadership. Much of the research quoted on this forms the basis of Likert's conclusions. The reader is referred to Chapter 17, and especially pp. 238–41.

Going still further along the line, participative leadership and management control is suggested. Again this comes up in Chapter 17 on Likert. Argyris, however, seems to have considerable doubts as to whether participative leadership would, in fact, work. To do so effectively it assumes mature individuals who can set their own goals and methods of achieving them, decide their aspirations, and behave in such a way as to maintain group cohesiveness. Where individuals or groups are not mature or have regressed into relative immaturity they may be unable to face the challenge involved.

Finally he mentions 'reality leadership'. Assuming that, as would seem realistic, owing to varying conditions, individuals and groups, there is no one best way to manage, then information, insights and knowledge must be used to discover which of many possible ways is the most effective way to manage in any particular situation. And just in case this should look too much like common sense let it be said that it is, *but* with a great deal of understanding rather than hunch to back it up.

*Developing Effective Executive Behaviour*

If the managers are to make the changes recommended in the previous section then the fact must be faced that it is the managers themselves who need to change and not, as they suppose, the workers. But how is the change to be brought about?

On this Argyris is not very specific. He quotes contradictory research results on leadership and, to be honest, finishes up with a few vague generalities.

(i) Developing managers must concentrate on development within and related to their particular organizational situation.

(ii) Certain basic skills are needed such as

(*a*) ability to diagnose correctly a complex situation.

(*b*) self-awareness.

(*c*) ability to help people to grow.

(*d*) ability to cope with lack of interest and apathy.

(iii) Of these skills the first to be learnt must be self-awareness, but Argyris makes no demand that he *must* then change himself. That is for him to decide in the light of his new viewpoint.

*Conclusion*

It would be unfair to end this chapter without giving verbatim what Argyris calls 'A Closing Note' to his book:

The objectives of this book have been to integrate the relevant behavioural science research by the use of a systematic framework in such a way that some insight can be obtained as to why people behave as they do in organizations, as well as to point out some possible areas for further research. No claim is made that the framework used in this analysis is 'the' framework. The best one can hope for is that some will find it useful and others will be inspired by its limitations to create newer and better frameworks. It can indeed be rewarding if a book is able to provide the impetus for research that soon outdates its conclusions.[9]

To this, perhaps, one or two final comments should be added. Argyris, if asked, would probably be the first to admit that his thesis is not universally true. He has postulated a 'model', admittedly scientifically based, of the worker, a 'model' of the manager and a 'model' of formal organization as his framework. His conclusions seem to have an air of pessimism, which is justified by research findings. They relate particularly to large-scale process industries although, in fact, he does not make this clear. He admits at one point that many managers by 'twisting the system or whatever' try to alleviate the conditions he describes, although probably without the knowledge to do it effectively. And everyone knows of some businesses, some large, some small, where management and workers do work in harmony.

But when all is said and done, at the time when the problems of managing, and particularly managing big business, seem to be getting more and more acute and intractable, Argyris's book must be regarded as a most valuable contribution to the subject, and the sooner it leads to the further contributions he hoped for the better.

*References*

(1) Argyris, C., *Personality and the Organization* (Harper & Bros., New York 1957), p. 6.
(2) Roethlisberger, F. *Training for Human Relations* (Harvard Graduate School of Business Administration, Boston 1954), p. 142.
(3) *Personality and the Organization*, p. 11.
(4) ibid., p. 48. The quotation is from *Personality Formation: the Determinants* ed. by Kluckhohn, C., and Murray, H. A. (Knopf, New York, 1949).
(5) ibid., p. 66.
(6) ibid., p. 66.
(7) ibid., p. 75.
(8) ibid., p. 123.
(9) ibid., p. 237.

*Bibliography*

BOOKS BY C. ARGYRIS

*Executive Leadership* (Harper & Bros., New York, 1953).
*Personality and the Organization* (Harper & Bros., New York 1957).
*Understanding Organizational Behaviour* (Dorsey Press, Homewood, Ill.; Tavistock Publications, London 1960).
*Inter-personal Competence and Organizational Efffectiveness* (Dorsey Press, Homewood, Ill.; Tavistock Publications, London 1962).
*Integrating the Individual and the Organization* (Wiley, New York 1964).

# 16

# Douglas McGregor
## 1960

*Introduction*

In the *Encyclopedia of Modern Knowledge* published by the Amalga-
mated Press in the late 1930s there is on page 596 (Volume II) a
photograph of the earliest wheels known at that time. Their date is
given as about 3200 B.C. To twentieth-century man life without the
wheel is completely incomprehensible, and yet it is only 5,000
years old.

Some poor but inquisitive Sumerian pulling a rough and probably overloaded sledge over rough ground must have asked the
question which man has been asking ever since he developed a
brain. 'Isn't there a better way?' Somewhere, perhaps, he had seen
a round stone rolling effortlessly along, but thought and ingenuity
were needed to recognize the possible connection between a round
stone and a section of tree trunk with an axle pin at its centre. To
make this connection he had to challenge all the preconceived
ideas of thousands of years, to suggest that some quite revolutionary
ideas might work better, and then with crude tools and implements
to make them work.

Such is progress that we have developed in only the last two
hundred years an industrial era with its pattern of very large, large,
medium and small firms. How far would it be true to suggest that
the 'modern' firm is still in the 'sledge era', with its own weight,
its load and every bump in the ground creating friction?

From many angles Part III of this book is representing ideas
which directly or indirectly challenge the basic theories on which
'sledge' organization is founded. Few have given a more direct

challenge or depicted more clearly the shape of the 'wheel' of industry than Douglas McGregor.

His book *The Human Side of Enterprise* is one long challenge to the basic concepts, ideas and assumptions on which current industry appears to be founded. That these ideas and assumptions are largely wrong he is in no doubt. In the conclusion he says:

> As Peter Drucker has pointed out, the modern, large, industrial enterprise is itself a social invention of great historical importance. Unfortunately, it is already obsolete. In its present form it is simply not an adequate means for meeting the future economic requirements of society.[1]

On the question of his own new ideas and assumptions (known as Theory Y) he is more modest. He says:

> It is not important that management accept the assumptions of Theory Y. These are one man's interpretations of current social science knowledge, and they will be modified – possibly supplanted – by new knowledge within a short time. It *is* important that management abandon limiting assumptions like those of Theory X [the present apparent basic assumptions], so that future inventions with respect to the human side of enterprise will be more than minor changes in already obsolescent conceptions of organized human effort.[2]

There, then, is the challenge. It remains to be shown how he develops it and the conclusions he draws from it.

*The Assumptions*
It is, perhaps, difficult for all of us to realize the extent to which our assumptions, whether consciously acknowledged or, more dangerously, unconsciously accepted, influence our ideas and our behaviour. Complete rationality of thought and conduct is much rarer than most of us would like to believe.

McGregor's first and basic point is that the manager today can, if he wishes, draw upon a 'reasonable and growing body of knowledge in the social sciences as an aid to achieving his managerial objectives'.³ Effective management, he suggests, depends on the ability to predict and control, and the extent of this ability depends on the accuracy and reliability of the basic ideas which lie behind it. While good management's ability in this direction is at present considerable, it falls well short of what it could be.

Two difficulties lie in the way of managers turning to and using the findings of the social scientist. The first is that of necessity they have had, as they have grown up and moved into positions of responsibility, a wide experience of dealing with other people, and almost inevitably they feel that this experience is an adequate guide. Deliberately or not this experience has been formalized into a personal orientation and set of assumptions which are a 'theory' on which conduct may be but is not always based.

The second difficulty lies in the nature of the control process – 'control' here being taken to imply managerial action with the purpose of achieving organizational ends. Control action must, if it is to be effective, be appropriate to the situation in which it is to operate. Much management action is ineffective because it runs counter to human nature, which is an essential factor in the total situation. But instead of questioning its methods, management looks for a scapegoat and blames people for their stupidity, unco-operativeness or laziness. The fundamental but 'revolutionary' question of why people behave like this is seldom asked.

Turning to classical theories of organization, McGregor finds that while on the whole they do not fit the general picture of industry as it is in practice, and that therefore managers have either rejected them or adopted some form of amalgam between them and their own ideas, yet some of the basic concepts, however inappro-priate, are still used as the foundation for organization and manage-ment practices.

The most fundamental of these concepts is that of authority as the basis of management. While most people, if not all, in positions of 'authority' know that the exercise of authority is by no means the only or even possibly the best way of getting things done, i.e. achieving control, yet most organizations are arranged as if the 'scalar chain' of Fayol were the bedrock of practice as well as theory.

Other ways of getting things done exist and are used, such as persuasion, consultation, discussion, and what McGregor calls 'professional "help".' But if control is to be effective the means selected must be the one most appropriate to the situation. In one set of circumstances a plain, unvarnished order may be right, in another a conversation which may start 'What do you think if . . . ' The other essential factor in the control situation is that the person or group to be controlled must to some extent be dependent upon the controller.

Changing conditions, especially since the end of the Second World War, have made authority far less effective than it used to be in earlier days. Alternatively it depends on the implied or actual threat of punishment, either by the imposition of sanctions such as dismissal or the withdrawal of privileges such as bonuses, or the approval of a superior. Certainly with social security, relatively full employment and greater mobility the threat of the sack has lost much of its power.

In addition the workers and their unions and frequently even managers have developed counter-measures and are only too ready to use them. Unwilling co-operation, the go-slow, low standards, protective behaviour, refusal to accept responsibility, the strike, the sit-in, are all used to a greater or lesser extent to combat authority.

McGregor suggests the situation is no longer one of dependence by the worker or manager on the firm for his survival but of inter-dependence. Top management is dependent on middle and lower management, and all management is dependent on the co-operation of the workers if it is to achieve its objectives. This fact is not recognized, he suggests, by conventional organization theory. This means that we must develop a new theory on which to base actions which are appropriate to modern conditions; to use his own metaphor, we must stop trying to make water run uphill. It means creating a theory and practices in which everyone can have sufficient independence to meet their essential psychological needs and yet be able to accept the necessary dependence on others without suffering undue frustration. It means a theory which can accept and explain changes in role from time to time by manager, specialist and worker, and the use in those roles of whatever means of exercising influence are, at the time, the most appropriate.

In order to do this McGregor develops two theories of behaviour. The first, known as Theory X, is based on the traditional view of direction and control. This theory states what are claimed to be the assumptions behind conventional organization theory and much of the earlier and current managerial practice. It consists of three propositions:[4]

1. The average human being has an inherent dislike of work and will avoid it if he can.
2. Because of this human characteristic of dislike of work, most people must be coerced, controlled, directed, threatened with punishment to get them to put forward adequate effort toward the achievement of organizational objectives.
3. The average human being prefers to be directed, wishes to avoid responsibility, has relatively little ambition, wants security above all.

It is claimed that, while many managers would disavow these assumptions in so blunt a form, the majority do, in fact, behave *as if they believed them to be true*, and that classical organization theory could only be based on the proposition that they are true. While there is a good deal in industry which cannot be explained in terms of Theory X, there is sufficient body of evidence to give it prima facie support.

After a short survey of the theory of motivation put forward by Herzberg (*see* Chapter 18) McGregor concludes, 'Theory X explains the *consequences* of a particular managerial strategy; it neither explains nor describes human nature although it purports to. Because its assumptions are so unnecessarily limiting, it prevents our seeing the possibilities inherent in other managerial strategies'.[5] In other words people behave in a way which appears to lend support to Theory X not because they are made that way but because such behaviour is a reaction to the practices of management. Instead of the nature of the worker being the cause of managerial strategy and practices it is the strategy and practices which cause the worker to appear and to behave as he does.

*A New Theory*

If, then, traditional theory and assumptions are to be so completely discredited, new and more appropriate ones are required. While admitting that many improvements in the workers' conditions and in worker–management relationships have occurred since the 1920s, McGregor maintains that these are still basically within the old set of assumptions and do not constitute a radical move forward. They are, in effect, only tinkering with the existing system.

A completely new approach is suggested in a set of assumptions called 'Theory Y'. These assumptions are, it is claimed, based on new information obtained about behaviour by the social sciences over the past half-century. They are:[6]

1. The expenditure of physical and mental effort in work is as natural as play or rest.
2. External control and the threat of punishment are not the only means for bringing about effort towards organizational objectives. Man will exercise self-direction and self-control in the service of objectives to which he is committed.
3. Commitment to objectives is a function of the rewards associated with their achievement.
4. The average human being learns, under proper conditions not only to accept but to seek responsibility.
5. The capacity to exercise a relatively high degree of imagination, ingenuity, and creativity in the solution of organizational problems is widely, not narrowly, distributed in the population.
6. Under the conditions of modern industrial life, the intellectual potentialities of the average human being are only partially utilized.

To elaborate and explain these assumptions a little he suggests that work can be a source of satisfaction or of punishment according to the conditions associated with it and under which it is performed. These conditions are controllable. It is agreed later that the extent to which control and variation is possible will depend on circumstances. Some work such as that of mass-production flow lines is so completely controlled by technology that variation may be difficult if not almost impossible in the present state of knowledge. Following Herzberg's theories on motivation, the more elementary and primary needs are generally being more or less adequately met for the majority of people in industrial societies today and therefore have ceased to be motivating forces as a rule. It is the higher ego and self-actualization needs which are now more significant. When work can be organized so as to meet these it becomes pleasure rather than a form of punishment, provides conditions where people will seek responsibility, will accept commitment to organizational objectives and be able and willing to utilize the highest powers of which they are capable. The real problem, therefore, is not human nature and its perversity but management's ability and ingenuity in providing the conditions which will allow the true form of human nature to show itself.

It is but a short step from there to a restatement in terms of Mary Follett's 'principle of integration'. 'The central principle which derives from Theory Y is that of integration: the creation of conditions such that the members of the organization can achieve their own goals *best* by directing their efforts towards the success of the enterprise.'[7] The difficulties, however, are not underrated. People are so accustomed to what is and to their attitudes and ideas about it that it is very difficult to see how things could be different. Things must, in fact, be what they are. The assumption that organizational objectives must take precedence over individual ones is another major stumbling block. Compare (Fayol's 'administrative duty': 'Ensure that individual interests are subordinated to the general interest').[8]

It is difficult to realize that if an integration is not possible, and McGregor admits that this can happen, then the enterprise may suffer if organizational goals are insisted upon at the expense of private ones. Yet surely everyone has seen cases where people forced to do things or accept them against their wishes have sabotaged, perhaps deliberately, perhaps unconsciously by lack of effort, the very results the organization has set out to achieve.

Another difficulty, which McGregor does not mention directly but which seems obvious, is that certainly the 'practical manager' will claim that Theory Y presupposes a collection of perfect human beings, whereas he lives and works in a very imperfect world. Faced with this challenge McGregor's answer would certainly be that the 'practical manager' is a prisoner of Theory X and his own ideas, assumptions, and attitudes, which prevent him from seeing anything other than what he already believes. Blinkers ensure that horses can only see forwards!

The claim for perfection actually is not even made. In other sciences the development of theory precedes what is immediately practical, and so it is with Theory Y. It opens up a whole range of possibilities for management to provide something better than now exists. It will take time, maybe decades; it requires changes of attitudes on the part of managers, unions, and workers, and these are not achieved overnight. Perfect integration is not a realistic objective, but 'we seek that degree of integration in which the individual can achieve his goals *best* by directing his efforts towards the success of the organization',[9] and that is a very different matter. 'Best' means not perfect but more attractive than present alternatives and therefore more likely to be adopted.

This statement of the theory concludes by suggesting that as many people have said, the progress of technology has gone so far and so fast that we can cope on that side and that the next half-century must be devoted to the 'human side of enterprise'. He is very pessimistic about this if management continues to manage on the assumptions – tacit or explicit – of Theory X. Theory Y opens up new possibilities and is 'an invitation to innovation'.[10] It remains to be seen how far management generally will accept the challenge of the invitation.

### The Evidence

Like a good counsel handling a difficult brief McGregor presents his case simply and briefly and allows his evidence to perform the job of convincing the jury. The case against Theory X and for Theory Y occupies only about one-fifth of his book. The rest is given over to evidence, to demonstrating where current management practice based on Theory X falls short, and where such practices as we can find which consciously or not appear to go along with Theory Y seem to do better.

The evidence presents a powerful case, and readers who are interested are recommended to read it in full in the original. Here it is only possible to touch on brief aspects of the main points.

His first target is management by objectives. At the time his book was written this was very much the current 'fashion' in American management. As generally used he regards it merely as 'no more than a new set of tactics within a strategy of management by direction and control',[11] which explains why it has not generally been as successful as its proponents maintain it should be. Then follows an illustration of the same technique, used deliberately by senior management to produce involvement, determination of and commitment to objectives by the lower level of management, and opportunities for the junior manager to exercise self-direction, self-control, and achieve satisfaction of ego and self-actualization needs. The illustration, given in full detail, appears fictional, but it obviously has a factual basis as McGregor quotes managers who have used the Theory Y approach.

Frequently related to and used with management by objectives is the performance-appraisal technique, where a manager and his subordinate review the latter's performance over a period of time. Again the evidence points in the same direction. The technique can be, and usually is, used as a means of control, with the assumptions of Theory X predominant. This way it is seldom a success. At best it is an embarrassing chore for the senior manager. At worst it is a real disincentive to the junior manager.

It fails because

(i) It is generally based on formal job-descriptions which are usually irrelevant. Many variables make the tightly defined job-description a travesty of what the job really is.

(ii) It depends too much on the subjective evaluations of the superior manager.

(iii) The performance of the junior manager is itself in part a function of the performance of his senior.

(iv) Communication of performance is effective in inverse proportion to the subordinate's need to hear it. If the junior does want to know how he is thought to be doing by his boss it may well be for the wrong reasons.

(v) Appraisal will only improve performance if the junior being appraised accepts the criticism and *wants* to improve.

(vi) Feedback on performance should immediately follow or be concurrent with performance, not be given months later when details and circumstances may have been forgotten.

(vii) Senior managers tend generally to dislike doing appraisal interviews, and seldom do them well.

This, then, is the Theory X approach of imposition from above. If, on the other hand, objectives are set by the junior manager for himself, performance results are fed to him and he makes his own appraisal of himself, all with the genuine help of his superior, i.e. the technique is based on Theory Y assumptions, it can produce excellent results.

Salaries and promotions come under very heavy fire. Promotions often fail to achieve anything like the best possible result because they are arbitrarily determined by senior management with only organizational objectives in mind, and the personal objectives of the man to be promoted are ignored. There is no attempt to achieve an integration of the two sets of objectives. In his new job the man may feel less than fully committed to its objectives; he may even suffer open conflict between his personal and organizational objectives, and consequently his performance is below standard.

Salary administration, especially the question of increases, is generally based on unrealistic judgement by superiors who are incapable of making the necessary fine discriminations. The use of relatively small increments of salary as a means of control and of encouraging greater effort is an inappropriate tool under the assumptions of Theory Y. Under Theory X it defeats its own purpose.

At the time the book was written the Scanlon Plan, which McGregor quotes next, was probably the best piece of evidence in support of Theory Y. Its methods, the underlying assumptions on which it appeared to be based, were so close to the Theory that its success was almost proof of the Theory in itself. In brief, the financial rewards to all levels of management and workers were directly linked to and an incentive to achievement of the business's objectives in that they were related to cost-savings and payable promptly, so that cause and effect could easily be seen. But the plan went further than this in that it gave everyone from the most lowly operative to top management the chance to become directly involved in the contribution of ideas and the setting of targets at all levels. Direct and genuine participation was the result, with the opportunity for everyone to experience satisfaction of higher psychological needs. The other result was a genuine working together of line and specialist management in order to achieve overall as distinct from sectional goals. But the Scanlon Plan is not just a formula or a set of techniques. It is a 'way of life' adapted to the needs of the company concerned, and based on a new way of thinking, which corresponds to the assumptions of Theory Y.

As McGregor points out, the very success of the Scanlon 'way of life' raises important problems. It has been applied generally to small or medium-sized companies. Is it possible to apply it to the typical large and/or automated plant of today? This surely was, and still is, the $64,000 question facing management. Is it possible to reconcile the mammoth size said to be required for marketing, for finance, for technology, for research, and, dare one say it, for the personal ego of the empire-building chairman, with the essential needs for the effective management of the human side of enterprise? The question is still unanswered.

Participation is briefly discussed on the lines that any form of participation under Theory X will tend to be minimal, unreal and ineffective. Under Theory Y it is essential, contributes to necessary personal and organizational goals, and must be properly used.

The subtle but all-pervasive effects of the 'managerial climate' come in for comment. This 'climate' will depend largely on the basic assumptions or, as Brech has called them, the 'mode of thought' which will control the thinking and actions of every person in the organization. Based on Theory X, they will produce a 'climate' of direction and control from above; based on Theory Y the 'climate' will be one of co-operation in a joint enterprise.

Staff–line relationships are discussed in terms of conventional organization theory, and constitute a problem which has probably produced more headaches for management theorists than any other aspect of management. What is needed, says McGregor, is 'a climate of mutual confidence around staff–line relationships which will encourage collaboration in the achievement of organizational objectives rather than guerilla warfare'.[12] Theory Y is briefly mentioned, but the argument is mainly concerned with a new role-relationship in which the staff become specialist advisers of their 'clients', the line management. It is an interdependent relationship in which the traditional question of authority becomes irrelevent.

*Developing Managerial Talent*

Finally, McGregor turns his attention to the development of managers. The starting point is an analysis of leadership. In view of the very considerable research done by social scientists since the 1930s, the traditional idea of a search for the qualities which should be possessed by a good leader is completely abandoned as irrelevant. In its place a number of generalizations are given which are taken to be supported by research. These can be summarized as follows:

(i) It is unlikely that there is any one pattern of abilities and personality traits which is common to all leaders.
(ii) The characteristics in the leader required for success are dependent on the circumstances in which leadership takes place.
(iii) Within limits weaknesses in one direction may be compensated for by strengths in another.
(iv) The skills of leadership can be learned or acquired and are not entirely inborn, natural characteristics.

The development of these ideas leads to the conclusion that 'leadership is not a property of the individual, but a complex relationship among these variables';[13] the variables being the leaders' own characteristics, the attitudes, needs and characteristics of the led, the organization, the task, and the general background.

If, then, effective leadership is dependent on a complex of forces which varies from time to time and place to place, there is no future in management-development programmes which try to produce stylized leaders to a preconceived pattern. The only hope is to produce as wide a variety of potential leaders as possible and hope that the variety will be wide enough to cope with the range of future, unforeseeable circumstances. To do this there is one way only – to provide situations in which all those with potential talent can develop in their own way and not to a regimented pattern.

McGregor uses a delightful and highly illustrative metaphor for the two approaches to the question of management development. The first is the 'engineering' approach, in which specialists (the trainers) are given the task of 'designing' an effective manager, producing the 'detailed drawings' (training programmes) which specify his characteristics and then 'manufacturing' him (putting him through the programme). It goes without saying by now that this method does not meet with approval! The alternative 'agricultural' approach provides the soil, temperature, climate and fertilizer (background conditions) in which the seed or seedling (latent talent) can develop in its own way, but with constant attention to whatever its needs may be at any particular time to enable maximum growth to take place. This is a much more difficult and complex way. It means considering the individual, his strength and weaknesses and potential. It means that every manager who has one or more subordinates must regard 'farming' as an essential part of his job. It means deciding on an individual basis what experience, what internal training, what external courses are next required. It is, maintains McGregor, the only effective way.

## Conclusion

At the beginning of this chapter McGregor's own words from his own Conclusion were quoted – 'It is not important that management accept the assumptions of Theory Y.'[14] Perhaps not. Perhaps many people will honestly believe that they are too idealistic, too unrealistic. But is is important that they are considered alongside the other new ideas which are being developed. Few people today seriously accept the Victorian economist's idea of 'economic man' as a rational explanation of behaviour. Is Theory X equally irrational?

One thing is certain, and that is that the human side of industry and commerce has been ignored for too long; now it is time to redress the balance if possible.

*References*

(1) McGregor, D. *The Human Side of Enterprise* (McGraw Hill, New York 1960), p. 245.

(2) ibid., p. 245.

(3) ibid., p. 3.

(4) ibid., pp. 33–34.

(5) ibid., p. 42.

(6) ibid., pp. 47–48.

(7) ibid., p. 49.

(8) Henri Fayol, *General and Industrial Management* (Pitman, London 1929).

(9) *The Human Side of Enterprise* p. 55.

(10) ibid., p. 57.

(11) ibid., p. 61.

(12) ibid., p. 157.

(13) ibid., p. 182.

(14) ibid., p. 245.

*Bibliography*

*The Human Side of Enterprise* (McGraw Hill, New York 1960).

*Leadership and Motivation. Essays of Douglas McGregor* ed. Bennis, W. G. and Schein, E. H. (M.I.T. Press, Cambridge, Mass., 1966).

*The Professional Manager* ed. Bennis, W. G. and McGregor, C. (McGraw Hill, New York 1967; London 1970).

# 17

# Rensis Likert
## 1961

*Introduction*

If scientific method is accepted as a major basis of a science then the team headed by Rensis Likert at the Institute for Social Research, Michigan, has done more than most to make the study of management into a science. From 1947 onwards they have applied the scientific method of research into facts, development of hypotheses, and testing these hypotheses by further research and experiment to the study of management in practice. In doing this they have built up the framework of what Likert calls 'a newer theory' of management. This theory is set out in Likert's book *New Patterns of Management*, published in 1961.

Likert himself would be the last to claim that his version is final; in fact, he says in his book that 'There is no doubt that further research and experimental testing of the theory in pilot operations will yield evidence pointing to modifications of many aspects of the newer theory suggested in this volume.'[1]

In the present state of knowledge, with each approach vying for supremacy over the others, there are, of course, authorities who reject the work of Likert and similar researchers out of hand. The main argument against the psycho-sociological school is that when field research and experiments are carried out the mere presence of an outside observer is itself a factor which alters the total situation and which therefore renders the findings invalid. If the observer had not been there then the situation and the results would have been different.

There is a good deal of plausibility in this argument and, it must be admitted, it is only too easy for a researcher to influence the situation, deliberately or unwittingly, and so the result and the conclusions. Any managerial or work situation must consist primarily of people, of managers and workers. Putting a practical test or experiment into the situation must be dependent upon an outside researcher. The way he approaches people, puts forward his ideas and puts over the test or experiment must, to some extent, influence the reaction of the people involved.

The *possible* truth of this argument is obvious and it would be foolish to deny it. The danger is there, but to abandon all study of people at work because of this would be a policy of despair. The fact that we are now trying to study people as the most important factor in the managerial situation gives the greatest hope for the future. But those who are doing it must always be aware of its dangers, take steps to minimize them, and allow for the possibility of distortion in presenting their results.

Although Likert himself does not specifically mention this point it is difficult to imagine that he and his fellow-researchers were not fully aware of it and that the greatest care has not been taken to avoid distortion. On balance it seems fair to assume that *New Patterns of Management* presents a very considerable advance in the state of our knowledge.

### Methodology

A few words about the basic ideas and methods behind this work are called for before an attempt is made to present the results. Basically the whole discussion stems from the simplest of questions: Why do some managers get better results than others? This leads to further questions such as: What do good managers do that bad managers don't? and vice versa; How can we measure what is a good or a bad manager? What criteria exist or can be developed for measuring results? Are objective, factual measures sufficient in themselves or are they misleading?

In the research at Michigan to answer these and other questions the basic fundamental scientific method was used throughout: first the question, followed by the collection and analysis of as much information as possible. From the analysis a hypothesis was developed to explain the results and to serve as a basis for forecasting.

This hypothesis was then tested, by application to further facts as they were collected and/or by deliberately setting up field experiments to show whether or not the hypothesis worked.

This sort of painstaking development of a theory had been carried out by a team of about forty researchers over a period of fourteen years prior to the appearance of *New Patterns of Management*, and it has continued since. The work has been done in a wide variety of places, in industrial and commercial firms, in railways, in hospitals, schools, and voluntary bodies. In many cases the collection of information and the carrying out of experiments has extended over months and even years. Nowhere else, so far as is known, has work on this scale been carried out so far.

*Changes in Management Practice*
Likert starts his book by suggesting that significant changes in management practice are, in fact, being made by some managers, possibly owing to self-criticism and a realization that things might be better, and to the pressure of changes which are occurring in society.

While these changes in society are given by Likert as applying to the United States it seems probable that they do apply more or less throughout the Western industrialized world, and are worth bearing in mind in any consideration of management practice. They are:

(i) Increasing competition from an ever-growing number of other industrialized nations.

(ii) Changes in peoples' ideas and backgrounds which make them less willing to accept pressure and close supervision.

(iii) Greater individual freedom and initiative, leading to expectations that this will be carried over to the work situation.

(iv) Higher educational levels in society in general and among the so-called working classes in particular.

(v) Greater concern in society generally about the increasingly recognized problem of mental health.

(vi) Dissatisfaction on the part of a considerable number of managers with currently accepted ideas.

(vii) More complex and larger business units.

He claims that the changes in management practice can be assessed and their results measured by the social sciences of psychology and sociology, and that from a study of these changes he and his co-workers have developed a 'newer theory' of management. It is significant that this newer theory, far from being an over-simplified abstraction is, in fact, much more complex than anything that has appeared before, and probably much more realistic.

*Leadership and Performance*

The concept of leadership put forward by the theory resembles very closely that of Mary Follett. Likert quotes, presumably with approval, from a study on leadership by Jenkins the following:

> Leadership is specific to the particular situation under investigation. Who becomes the leader of a given group engaging in a particular activity and what the leadership characteristics are in a given case are a function of the specific situation including the measuring instruments employed. Related to this conclusion is the general finding of wide variations in the characteristics of individuals who become leaders in similar situations, and even greater divergence in leadership behaviour in different situations.[2]

Based on a very considerable study of the leadership practices of managers and supervisors, the theory divides leaders into two broad groups – employee-centred supervisors and job-centred supervisors. The term 'supervisor', wherever used in Likert's work, appears to include 'manager'.

Job-centred supervisors are described as those whose pattern of leadership concentrates on the work to be done, on 'keeping their subordinates busily engaged in going through a specified work cycle in a prescribed way and at a satisfactory rate as determined by time standards'.[3] Actually this definition is narrower than appears to be intended, as job-centred supervisors are shown as being in charge of all sorts of work, not just that which has been or can be work-studied. The essential point is that in their supervision they are concerned primarily with the work and only secondarily with the people who do it. Employee-centred supervisors, on the other hand, '. . . focus their primary attention on the human aspects of their subordinates' problems and on endeavouring to build effective work groups with high performance goals.'[4]

In measuring the performance of groups supervised in different ways a number of criteria are used. These go well beyond the usual measures of performance traditionally used by managers at present. In fact one of the main points of the new theory is that traditional measures may well provide misleading information. The measures used and developed include productivity per man-hour, job and other satisfactions, labour turnover and absenteeism, scrap and reject work, costs and motivation factors. Some of these are more or less objective facts obtainable from normal records; others are subjective measures and require special methods for their assessment.

On the basis of measurements such as these supervisors are divided into two groups, those with high-producing sections and those with low-producing ones. In general the practices of supervisors with high-producing sections tend to show the following characteristics:

(i) Employee-centred supervisory practices.
(ii) Supervisor sets high goals of performance and gets them accepted.
(iii) Supervisors exert little pressure on subordinates.
(iv) Supervisors earn and get the confidence and trust of their subordinates.
(v) Supervisors exercise general rather than close supervision.
(vi) Supervisors allow freedom to subordinates to set their own pace of work.
(vii) Supervisors are helpful when mistakes and problems occur.

On the other hand the practice of supervisors with low-producing sections tend to show exactly the opposite characteristics:

(i) Supervisors favour job-centred supervisory practices.
(ii) Supervisors exert heavy pressure to get work done.
(iii) Workers show little confidence in the supervisor.
(iv) Supervisors exercise close, detailed supervision.
(v) Little freedom is allowed to subordinates.

(vi) Supervisors are punitive and critical when mistakes occur.

The question of cause and effect is then taken up. Briefly it can be put this way. Does a high-producing supervisor use the practices manifested *because* he has a high-producing section and is therefore able to 'ease up', or are his practices the cause of high production? Similarly, does a low-producing supervisor have to use his practices *because* he has a low-producing section, or do his practices cause low production? The answer to the question was found by a series of experiments in which high- and low-producing supervisors were switched into each others' jobs. Almost invariably it was found that the high-producing supervisor taking his normal practices with him raised the output of a low-producing group over a period of time, while a low-producing supervisor would lower the output of a high-producing group, again over a period of time.

The theory, then, proves that in general the ways in which supervisors carry out their jobs are major determining factors in the standard of performance achieved by the group. Where discrepancies between the theory and practice were found it was usually discovered that they were due to inaccuracies in the measuring devices used, or to other factors which would affect the situation but which were outside the supervisor's control. One by-product of this research was the discovery that a number of the factors normally assumed to have some bearing on performance, such as attitudes to the company, welfare schemes, and merit-rating, do in fact have very little effect.

Finally, this experiment shows that the allocation of sufficient time for achieving results is supremely important, so as to allow supervisory practices to make their mark. For a change in practice to work its way through to results may take up to two years. While this process is going on it is possible to get very misleading results. For instance, heavy pressure exerted by a supervisor may and often does produce high-performance results for a period of time. But it will produce them at the cost of the demoralization of the group, and there will ultimately be a marked drop in performance. The real significance of this is still to be appreciated while the tendency is for managers to be promoted or to move on every two years or so.

It means that a pressure-orientated manager can produce good results for two years, get promoted on the strength of them and move on, leaving someone else to 'clear up the mess'.

*Groups*

In common with all sociologists Likert stresses the importance of the group in the work situation, and the theory next turns its attention to group processes.

> Research in organizations is yielding increasing evidence that the superior's skill in supervising his subordinates *as a group* is an important variable affecting his success: the greater his skill in using group methods of supervision, the greater are the productivity and job satisfaction of his subordinates.[5]

The first point made is that favourable attitudes to the job on the part of subordinates tend to be linked with the practice of the supervisor of holding frequent meetings at which he hears and uses the ideas of his subordinates. It is essential that the supervisor is genuinely interested in his subordinates' views and that as far as possible he makes use of them.

A supportive attitude on the part of the supervisor is essential to develop 'group pride and loyalty'.[6] A supportive attitude means that the supervisor considers his subordinates as individual people and that when problems arise for them he identifies himself with them, or with them *and* the company. The supervisor must also have the ability to generate in his group a sense of pride in itself and a conviction of its own ability to accept and achieve high productivity targets.

While high group loyalty, that is, of the members towards the group, is essential to attain group objectives, these objectives do not necessarily have to be directed to high achievement. A group might, for instance, set itself the goal of defeating organizational objectives by every means in its power. In general, however, where group loyalty is high [to quote[7]]:

> ... the members of the group are more likely to have

1. greater identification with their group and a greater feeling of belonging to it
2. more friends in the group and in the company rather than outside it
3. better interpersonal relations among the members of the work group
4. a more favorable attitude towards their jobs and their company
5. higher production goals and more actual production with less sense of strain or pressure.

Group loyalty will tend to be lower when the supervisor deals always with his group as individuals and not as a group. In order to obtain high production the supervisor must learn and exercise those practices which will promote and use group loyalty.

*Communication and Influence*
The theory stresses the need for effective communication in all directions and for people at *all* levels to feel that by communicating they are able to exert influence on the situation, either directly or upwards through the usual channels. In fact, however, communication between individuals and between groups frequently breaks down, and either the message does not get through or it arrives in a distorted form. Such breakdowns arise from

(i) difficulties involved in the actual process, methods, or machinery of communicating;
(ii) the variety and complexity of information to be communicated: this becomes more complex as organizations get larger and themselves more complex;
(iii) emotional blockages and distortions due to unfavourable attitudes and/or the nature of the ideas themselves, which may arouse hostility or suspicion. On this point unreasonable pressure by the supervisor is quoted as a very real cause of the blocking of communication to and from subordinates.

Great stress is laid on the need for upward communication, from workers to supervisors, from supervisors to managers, and so on. For effective performance it is necessary for the subordinate to feel completely free to pass on any ideas, complaints, or suggestions to his superior. How free he will feel will depend on the customs and practices of the organization, on the attitudes of his superior, and on his own expectations as to his superior's likely behaviour. Where from previous experience he expects his superior to act in a hostile or punitive way then the process of 'selective filtering' will occur. This means that either only information which the superior is expected to approve is passed up, or the information is coloured, biassed and twisted so that it meets with approval. Few managers seem to realize how necessary a helpful, supportive attitude is if they are to receive effective communication which gives them a true picture of what is going on. In general, too, research has shown that superiors more often than not have a wrong idea of how free subordinates feel to communicate. Generally superiors think that their subordinates feel much freer than they actually do. Similarly there is frequently misunderstanding between superior and subordinate as to what the latter's job does actually consist of and what the limitations on him are.

In brief, the effectiveness or otherwise of the communication process within the organization is directly related to the effectiveness of performance. The possibility of being able to bring influence to bear on a situation in order to be able to improve it is similarly related to performance. At all levels, but particularly at the lower ones, people need to feel two things. First, that they themselves can communicate ideas, suggestions, complaints and grievances upwards *and that when this is done something will be done about it*. It follows from this that if the immediate superior is unable to do anything about it he will pass the information upwards, and that this process will go on until it reaches a level where something can be and is done. Secondly, they need to feel that the people above have power to influence situations, and that this power is used purposefully and not just as a reaction to outside circumstances.

*Measurements of Performance*
On the question of the measurement of supervisory performance the theory has two main things to say. The first is to challenge the effectiveness of measures as generally used, and the second is to suggest what should be measured.

To begin with it must be accepted that effective high-producing supervisory performance is a long-term process, and that short-term results may often be different from long-term ones. For instance, in one deliberate experiment on the introduction of change, parallel groups were set up using supervisory practices consistent with the new theory while other groups used old-fashioned methods of supervision. In the short period the old-fashioned groups produced better results measured in terms of output and so, if only the short-term results were considered, old-fashioned supervision would appear to be the better. In the long run, however, the new processes far outstripped the older ones both in performance and in attitudes.

The normal measures used, such as output per man-hour, costs, sales, profit, relate to what are called 'end-result variables'. These are susceptible to both short- and long-term influences. In the short term pressure-orientated supervision, especially if linked with high technical competence, can and frequently does produce good results measured in these terms. On the other hand supervisory practices based on the new theory take time to produce better results, again in terms of these measures. Managers are, therefore, misled into assuming that pressure-orientated practices pay, and, as they often do not stay long enough to see the long-term results, they have no reason to challenge this view.

But, it is suggested, other factors, not normally measured or even taken into account, will influence the end-results in the long run. These factors are given as loyalty, skills, motivation, effective interaction between people and between groups, communication, and decision-making. These factors are susceptible to the kind of supervisory practices used but do, in fact, only change relatively slowly. While their influence on end-results is vital it is slow to operate, so that one can have high output as an end-result of pressure-orientated supervision while, at the same time, factors such as loyalty, motivation, interaction, communication and decision-making are deteriorating. Eventually this deterioration will catch up and produce a marked drop in end-result variables such as production and costs.

In order to measure supervisory effectiveness properly one should have measures not only of the immediate end-results but also of trends in these intermediate factors, as these will show by their improvement or deterioration what is likely to happen to end-results at a later date. And, if a long-term view of effectiveness is taken, it is the changes in these intermediate factors which are the more important. So far measures of the intermediate factors have been lacking. The development of the attitude survey and of methods of group communication provide means of measuring them. In addition the hidden costs of labour turnover, absenteeism, and strikes should be set against the different supervisory practices in determining their effectiveness.

## Some General Trends

While the researches of Likert and his co-workers have produced a new theory from a study of what *some* managers do, Likert himself says that a review of the general trends of management in the United States shows very different results. It is stressed that what follows is a generalization and that many exceptions may exist. There seems little reason to doubt that the same generalization would apply to Great Britain.

First a broad division is made into two types of work:

 (i) machine-paced and assembly-line work, and detailed clerical work, which can be and is highly sub-divided and closely controlled;

 (ii) non-repetitive work, which cannot be divided easily and cannot be closely controlled.

These two types of work tend to produce different systems of management. The first lends itself to use of the methods of scientific management as developed by Taylor and the 'techniques' protagonists. Pressure-orientated methods of detailed targets, times, methods, and standards have been shown to produce effective short-term results in terms of cost, output and scrap. The fact that these methods have been clearly defined in book after book has made it easier to accept and apply them, especially as for fifty years they were not effectively challenged except by Follett, Rowntree and one or two others. Also, up till now, there have been no effective methods for measuring the intermediate factors and, in any case, in the short run there seems to be little if any correspondence between such factors as job attitude and output in this type of work. There has, therefore, been no challenge to this type of management for this type of work, and it has become self-perpetuating.

For non-repetitive work the detailed methods of scientific management are unsuitable and incapable of application. A style of management has therefore been developed which relies on the use of personality, attitudes, and motivation to get things done. But, lacking a basis of theory and set principles as guide-lines, the development of this style has been more haphazard and its effectiveness has not been appreciated.

It is suggested that the most effective management would arise from the use of suitable techniques from scientific management, but applied in a completely different way so as to eliminate the pressure orientation and use participation at all levels to a maximum. The effective use of these techniques linked to the processes, techniques and attitudes of employee-centred supervision would provide the best of both worlds.

## *Effective Supervision*

Starting from the point that the training of supervisors is often a disappointing process, Likert goes on: 'One of the difficulties appears to be a widespread but erroneous assumption that there are specifically "right" and "wrong" ways to supervise',[8] and also 'Supervisory and leadership practices, effective in some situations, yield unsatisfactory results in others.'[9]

This might lead to the assumption that there can be no basic principles or practices of supervision which are generally applicable, and, if this is so, then Likert's 'newer theory' is hardly worth the paper on which it is printed and certainly not worth the effort which has gone into producing it.

There is, of course, a misconception here. While the newer theory develops a set of principles, which appear at present to have much to commend them, it does not lay down the details of how to apply it to any given situation. This, to use Likert's phrase, is 'an adaptive and relative process'. This means that the application must be different in each case in that it must adapt to and be related to each particular situation. So, although the principles remain the same, the application must vary from case to case.

Some reasons for this variation are given as:

(i) The responses of different subordinates to the same supervisory act will vary from each other.

(ii) Different subordinates will perceive the same situation differently.

(iii) The expectations, norms and values of different people and groups are not the same.

(iv) Differences in personality.

(v) Differences in past experiences and traditions.

(vi) The supervisor's own personality.

(vii) The amount of influence the supervisor has or feels he has with his own superior.

(viii) The effectiveness of the inter-personal skills available.

To summarize in Likert's own words, 'Supervision is, therefore, always a relative process. To be effective and to communicate as intended, a leader must always adapt his behavior to take into account the expectations, values, and inter-personal skills of those with whom he is inter-acting.'[10]

*An Integrating Principle and an Over-view*
As the basic principle which the theory elaborates and extends Likert propounds the following:[11]

> The leadership and other processes of the organization must be such as to ensure a maximum probability that in all interactions and all relationships with the organization each member will, in the light of his background, values and expectations, view the experience as supportive and one which builds and maintains his sense of personal worth and importance.

To summarize the difference between the pattern of operations of high-producing and mediocre or low-producing managers he says that the high-producing managers' patterns more often show the following characteristics:

(i) A preponderance of favourable attitudes on the part of all members to all aspects of the job. These attitudes include identification with the organization and its objectives and a sense of involvement towards achieving them.

(ii) All major motivating forces are harnessed together and pulling in one direction towards achievement of organizational objectives.

(iii) The organization is a tightly knit, effectively functioning social system with high interaction skills.

(iv) Communication is efficient and effective.

(v) Decision-making is based on a sharing of all the necessary measurements and information.

(vi) The systems of scientific management are used, but in a different way so as to reinforce rather than destroy motivation.

Also the superiors who have the most favourable and co-operative attitudes in their groups display the following characteristics:

(i) Their attitudes and behaviour are seen by their subordinates as

(a) being supportive, friendly, helpful, fair but firm, and serving the interests of subordinates as well as those of the organization;

(b) having confidence in the ability, integrity and motivation of the subordinates;

(c) having high expectations of performance level;

(d) providing adequate training for the job and for promotion;

(e) providing special coaching for subordinates below standard.

(ii) The direction of work by the superior is based on

(a) planning, scheduling, training, attention to the provision of materials, tools etc.;

(b) adequate technical competence.

(iii) The group is a working team with high group loyalty using group participation and group leadership techniques.

## Conclusion

In the space available the above account of Likert's work is all that can be given. The remainder of his book deals mainly with testing the new theory, and describes further work on groups, interaction influence systems and measurements. It is thought that enough has been given to set out the essentials of the new theory.

It is possible to say that it contains nothing new, that it merely summarizes what *good* managers have been doing since time immemorial. Taking the narrow point of view there is some justification for this argument, but the simple fact is that he has developed a theoretical background, a set of principles which show why the practices used by the better managers do, in fact, produce better results. Perhaps even more important, they show why the better practices and better results have not been recognized for what they are and why they have not been universally adopted. As such the theory seems to be a great step forward.

What still remains to be done, more than ten years after the theory was first put forward in its entirety, is for it to be appreciated and applied on a wide scale. It would seem that in many cases practising managers are so conditioned by what is that they cannot see what could be.

## References

(1) Likert, R. *New Patterns of Management* (McGraw-Hill, New York 1961), p. 97.

(2) ibid., p. 90. Likert's quotation is from an article by W. O. Jenkins, 'A review of leadership studies with particular reference to military problems', *Psychol. Bull.* 1947, vol. 44 (1), pp. 54-79.

(3) ibid., pp. 6-7.

(4) ibid., p. 7.

(5) ibid., p. 27.

(6) ibid., p. 28.

(7) ibid., pp. 35-36.

(8) ibid., p. 89.

(9) ibid., p. 89.

(10) ibid., p. 95.

(11) ibid., p. 103.

## Bibliography

BOOKS BY R. LIKERT

*Behavioural Research* (U.N.E.S.C.O., Paris 1957).

*The Psycho-Sociological Approach*

(With S. P. Hayes, Jr.) *Some Applications of Behavioural Research* (U.N.E.S.C.O., Paris 1957).
*New Patterns of Management* (McGraw-Hill, New York 1961).

# 18

# Frederick Herzberg
# 1959

*Introduction*

Herzberg, Mausner and Snyderman, in their book *The Motivation to Work*, follow the pattern and the mood of management thought in the late 1950s. The pattern or trend of the decade was a move away from the rounded generalizations of earlier years towards the reporting of painstaking field research from which tentative conclusions were drawn. The mood was one of real dissatisfaction with the often pseudo 'human relations' ideas of the earlier 1950s, which had so obviously failed to produce the expected miracles.

In common with many other writers and researchers in the psychological schools of thought, Herzberg starts from the assumption that the individual is the centre of the work–managerial situation. With the individual as the starting point of the study the first fact about individuals at work is so obvious as to be a truism. For the minority their daily work is something which fills their lives with real, deep satisfaction, something which they enjoy and which provides them with feelings of self-fulfilment. For the majority there are many shades of grey, from toleration of a job which provides the means to enjoy life 'off the job' to anger, frustration and boredom endured only because no other alternative is available.

That these differences so obviously exist in all modern industrial societies can lead only to the one question – 'Why?' To this question there can be three possible answers:
  (i) Differences in people themselves.
  (ii) Differences in work itself.
  (iii) Differences in the conditions under which the work is performed.

Herzberg uses the last two, work and working conditions, as the basis for his research and findings. In making this distinction between work and conditions he is breaking new and seemingly fertile ground.

Before starting the research project on which the book is based Herzberg claims that he had carried out an exhaustive review of the research and literature on motivation at work. While not completely condemning it out of hand he is obviously dissatisfied with much of it as being too shallow, fragmentary, and often contradictory. Certainly to his mind it did not produce answers which could be used by practising managers to get better results. To provide these answers was the purpose of his research.

*The Research*

The basic idea behind the research was the hypothesis that if anything meaningful was to be found out about motivation the question of factors–attitudes–effects must be studied as a whole and not as isolated items. For the individual at work it was assumed that there would be periods of time during which he had experienced definite feelings about his job. It was assumed also that he would be able to identify these times, the factors both in the work and its surroundings which were operating, the feelings and attitudes which resulted, and the effects which these had.

The method of research was based on obtaining information on these points from a sample of middle-managers. Semi-structured interviews were used in which the manager was asked first to describe some time at which he had felt particularly good or bad about his job. Two necessary conditions for acceptance of the experience were that it had been caused largely by factors at work, and that it had had a recognizable duration, with a beginning, a middle, and generally an end, but it was allowed to be an experience still continuing at the time of interview.

After the initial starter question on the lines 'Can you remember some time when you felt particularly good (or bad) about your job? Please tell me about it . . .', the interviewee was then left to talk as he wished, except that leading questions could be used to ensure that relevant information on feelings, attitudes and results was not omitted.

Obviously with an interview programme of this kind a number of queries come to mind. The first is that it is entirely dependent upon the ability of the interviewees to recall events and feelings which had happened in the past, perhaps even the quite distant past. Given that these could be remembered, the reliability of the information given then depended on both the interviewee's ability to verbalize and convey it accurately and on his 'honesty' in supplying all the information and not consciously or sub-consciously suppressing items which might have reflected badly on him or on other people.

Herzberg does admit that the number of instances of poor work, slowing down on the job and so on was smaller than might have been expected, and that this was probably due to suppression, whether deliberate or otherwise. Apart from this he claims that the difficulties just suggested did not, in fact, materialize.

To return to the interview programme, after two pilot surveys the main programme was intended to produce detailed information under five heads:

 (i) The actual occurrences in the sequence of events, especially those which caused changes in attitudes. These were called first-level factors.

 (ii) Reasons given for feelings and attitudes which arose from the interviewee's own mental outlook – second-level factors.

(iii) Changes in attitudes during the sequence.

(iv) The durations of the sequence of events and of the effect on feelings and attitudes.

 (v) How critical or important the whole sequence and its effects were to the person concerned.

## The Analysis

Analysing the masses of differing data produced by unstructured or even semi-structured interviews is always a herculean task. Herzberg and his associates resolved this by producing a large series of 'thought forms' which enabled them to classify the content of what had been said, and from this classification to quantify it for analysis.

The first approach shows what are called 'first-level factors'. These consist of occurrences in the situation which led to recognizable good or bad feelings about the job. No less than fourteen such factors are identified. They are

(i) Recognition
(ii) Achievement
(iii) Possibility of growth
(iv) Advancement or promotion
(v) Salary
(vi) Interpersonal relations
(vii) Supervision – technical
(viii) Responsibility
(ix) Company policy and administration
(x) Working conditions
(xi) The work itself, its nature, ease or difficulty, etc.
(xii) Factors in personal life
(xiii) Status
(xiv) Job security

As mentioned earlier, the next objective of the survey was to identify 'second-level factors', that is, those causes which arise from a self-examination of one's own values, ideas and orientation. They could produce new feelings, attitudes or behaviour as a result of interaction with outside events. They are given as feelings of recognition, achievement, possible growth or blocks to it, responsibility and changes in it, belonging to or isolation from groups, interest or lack of it in the job, changes in status, changes in security, fairness or unfairness, pride, inadequacy or guilt, and salary.

It is, perhaps, necessary to emphasize the difference between first- and second-line factors. First-line factors are outside events and occurrences, second-line are internal feelings and reactions. Both, however, are motivators of conduct, often, but not necessarily, reinforcing each other. Finally, an analysis was made of the effects, as the third aspect of the 'events–attitudes–effects'.

Effects on performance are classified as generally better or poorer work, increased rate of working, specifically improved or worsened quality, and claims of a refusal to allow changed feelings or attitudes to affect performance standards. In addition, changes could take place in what might be called the desire to stay in the job. This could be increased where neutral feelings or pre-existing thoughts of leaving were converted to a positive wish to stay. On the other hand negative changes could range from thoughts of leaving, to looking for opportunities to leave, to actually getting another job.

In many cases the effect was shown in a change in mental health. A few showed improvement; the greater number showed deterioration in the form of anxiety, nervous tension and related minor physical symptoms, and even major pathological illness in a few cases.

Another area in which marked effects were shown was in interpersonal relationships. Obviously these could be both cause and effect. They have already been listed as first-level factors in causing feelings about the job, but it is equally apparent that a change in the job or its conditions could alter the man's relationships with others, both at work and at home.

Finally, effects in the shape of changes in attitudes to the job, to fellow workers, to management, and to the company as such could be identified.

## The Results

The factors–attitudes–effects sequences which formed the basis of the enquiry could obviously be analysed in different ways. The most important was the distinction between what are called 'high' sequences, giving rise to 'good' feelings, and 'low' sequences, resulting in 'bad' feelings. Other sub-divisions were between long and short sequences, and between those which produced long-term effects and short-term ones. Within these divisions there could be all sorts of possible combinations, with the exception that long-term sequences rarely if ever resulted in short-term effects.

In Herzberg's book the results are displayed in great detail, showing the effects of different combinations. The reader who is interested in detail should refer to the book itself. For our purposes it is probably enough to state the broad outline of the main results. Essentially it comes to this. The factors which cause high job-attitudes and good performance are quite different from those which cause low job-attitudes and poor performance. These are called respectively motivating factors and hygiene factors, or satisfiers and dissatisfiers.

To spell it out in a little more detail, let us assume a norm of average performance and attitudes which is not being particularly influenced in either way. If, then, the motivating factors come into operation favourably, attitudes and performance will rise above the average. If they are absent they do not often cause a comparable fall below the norm. On the other hand the hygiene factors seldom operate to cause performance and attitudes to rise above the norm, but if these factors are not seen as being satisfactory then both attitudes and performance will drop below the norm.

Out of a list of sixteen first-level factors only six have a significant effect as motivators. These are achievement, recognition, the work itself, responsibility, advancement, and salary. Apart from salary, all of these are directly connected with the job itself, its content and performance. Of these six achievement and recognition are the most important, with achievement having a very clear lead.

The hygiene factors are greater in number and more evenly spread in influence. The more important are company policy and administration, supervision–technical, salary, inter-personal relationships with superiors, working conditions, and inter-personal relationships with equals. All of these relate to conditions surrounding the job rather than to the job itself. Additionally, when things go wrong with the motivating factors of recognition, the work itself, and advancement, they may have significant effects in producing low attitude–performance results.

At the second level of factors, that is, the feelings and attitudes of people as causes of change, the most significant factors in causing high sequences are feelings of recognition, achievement, responsibility, and feelings about the work and work group. The factors bringing about low sequences are feelings of unfairness in treatment, impossibility of growth, lack of recognition and of achievement, and inadequacy.

Trying to summarize the findings may well have made them seem more difficult to understand. It is possible to put the results even more briefly and perhaps with greater clarity as follows. Achievement and recognition act most frequently as motivation factors or satisfiers more usually over short periods. The work itself, responsibility and advancement act most frequently as long-period motivation factors. All when satisfactory lead to good attitudes and high performance. Company policy and administration, supervision–technical, salary, inter-personal relations with supervision, working conditions, are hygiene factors, are most frequently wrong, act as dissatisfiers, and lead to poor attitudes and low performance.

## Implications

One of the major, if not the greatest, problem facing management in the post-1940 period has been to find an effective substitute for the work drives of the 1930s and before. Unemployment, poverty, the fact that the boss could always sack and replace a worker easily ensured a motivation to work, albeit a negative one. The post-war economic and social revolutions have not only removed these spurs but have gone further and made them socially and morally unacceptable for the future.

This alone was enough to make management's job of securing effective performance more difficult than ever before. But the explosive growth of technology, the wider acceptance of the ideas of scientific management and the development of the very large business unit have conspired to make the individual at work and his contribution in so many cases so insignificant that a whole new range of problems add even more to management's problems.

Particularly in the United States the investigations of the psychologists and the sociologists, their writings and hypotheses, the practices of management such as the welfare and human relations programmes, the supervisor-training blitzes, the psychological testing of managers and so on were all ultimately directed at this problem of restoring adequate motivation. None of them seem to have been wholly successful. Many were complete failures.

Herzberg's theory does, if it is right, show why. The main emphasis in welfare, human relations, and similar programmes has been on the conditions surrounding work. Improving these conditions would at best reduce or eliminate negative motivation, it would not produce positive motivation to perform well.

Management must, according to Herzberg, realize that motivation to work is not a single entity but has two distinct aspects, which both require separate attention. The conditions in which work is performed should be kept at least at an adequate level to prevent the 'dissatisfiers' from operating. But also, and more important, the 'satisfiers' or motivators must be built into the work itself to get performance above the mediocre average. People must get from their work situation an intrinsic sense of satisfaction from the work itself, a real sense of achievement, recognition from superiors and equals for work well done, the chance to grow and develop, and a financial reward which they feel is fair and just.

## Conclusion

Progress in ideas in any field sometimes comes from the blinding flash of inspiration. More often it comes from dissatisfaction with existing knowledge which fails somehow to explain adequately what is happening. Herzberg and his associates have worked from the second approach and have produced a theory which seems to offer a better solution to existing problems.

It is impossible, however, not to have one or two doubts. The research and consequently the conclusions are based on a sample of middle-management people, engineers and accountants. Their background, education, value systems must inevitably be different, probably very different, from the mass of shop-floor workers. For the man who pushes a truck all day or watches a near-automatic machine, who has grown up in this atmosphere since he was a small boy, whose father did the same sort of work, is it appropriate to talk of a value concept of achievement? If he has or understands such a concept, does it correspond to that of the accountant?

Then, again, is the conflict between scientific management, mass production, mass markets, modern technology, and the human, psychological needs inevitable and insoluble? How can one build satisfaction and achievement into endlessly tightening the same four nuts with a power-driven spanner day in and day out?

Herzberg suggests what should be done: structure jobs to provide goals for achievement, to provide opportunities for growth; match abilities to jobs; teach supervisors to do these three things, to give real, not pseudo, recognition to workers and to encourage workers to decide the best way of doing their own jobs.

He tells us *what* to do. Is it unfair comment to add that like almost all writers of the psycho-sociological school he stops short of telling us *how* to do it?

## Bibliography

BOOKS BY F. HERZBERG

*Work and the Nature of Man* (Staples Press, London 1968).

(Jointly)

*The Motivation to Work*, by F. Herzberg, B. Mausner and B. B. Snyderman (Wiley, New York 1959).

## 19

# D. Cartwright and A. Zander
## 1953

*Introduction*

Cartwright and Zander's book *Group Dynamics: Research and Theory*, published in 1953, is not primarily a book on management, but parts of it are of more than passing interest to the student of management.

The purpose of the authors was to bring together much of the research and theorizing carried out by many people in the field of sociology. In particular it aimed to show the position at the time of the work on human groups, their characteristics, structure and behaviour.

While much of the book concerns social and experimental groups, there is a good deal about industrial groups which is of direct concern to managers, who, after all, probably spend at least as much time and thought dealing with groups as with individuals. In many cases even the experimental groups set up solely for research purposes have considerable relevance to the management situation. A short chapter picking out the highlights of this work seems to be called for.

Cartwright and Zander are careful to point out right at the beginning that there are many approaches to the problems of sociology, most of them specializing in some particular angle and producing results which may appear to be contradictory. They prefer the word 'complementary' because so often two or more researchers approaching the same aspect, let us say leadership, do so from different angles with different aims in mind. Sociology had not twenty years ago, and still has not, produced an overall, comprehensive theory. With a subject as complex as human beings and their behaviour this is hardly surprising.

## D. Cartwright and A. Zander

*What is a Group?*

Various views of the approaches to groups are given:

(i) The view that the study of groups should be based on
   (a) the characteristics of the individuals in the group;
   (b) the internal behaviour of the group;
   (c) the performance of the group as a whole.

(ii) The view that the real substance of groups is the interaction between the people forming the group, leading to ideas of status, control, and the action on the group of outside forces.

(iii) A third school has approached the group through studying problems of leadership and organization within the formal group. This has led to studies of the formal pattern of duties, responsibilities, and relationships, and comparison between the formal pattern and what actually happens in practice.

(iv) Psychological aspects of dependence and hostility within the group form the fourth approach.

(v) Finally there is the approach which starts from the premise that a group consists of people drawn together by free and spontaneous choice. But some groups (for example in industrial organization) are imposed on people, and it is suggested that these would be much more effective if they could be allowed to be spontaneous free-choice groups.

It is emphasized that these are by no means the only approaches. A little thought will show that each of them has something to tell the manager about his day-to-day job. What determines the behaviour of a group and whether its attitude is friendly or hostile to management? What effect will managerial action have on the groups who may regard it as 'outside pressure'? What, if any, is the relationship between the formal organization as laid down by management and the spontaneous informal organization? How much does practice differ from theory? Would it be better if we scrapped all our ideas on formal organization and started afresh? The list of questions could go on and on. Enough has been said, however, to show that group dynamics is not an abstract subject for University theorists but one of very real concern to any manager who wishes to do more than manage by rule of thumb.

*Group Cohesiveness*

The ability or otherwise of a group to stick together, to maintain its aims and purposes in the face of pressure, hostility and difficulty is an aspect on which little work had been done up to the time that Cartwright and Zander's book was published. Its importance for the manager is considerable. What is the extent of cohesiveness in his formal departments and sections? Will they hold together under stress or will they break up? What splinter groups exist and what is their effect? Where informal groups exist in parallel with formal ones, which group will hold the loyalty of members?

Social groups tend to arise when the means of easy meeting and communication exists and the formation of a group will further the aims of the individuals. Membership of a group is affected by the attractiveness of belonging, and favourable friendly treatment will encourage belonging and cohesiveness. A threatening and unpleasant environment, on the other hand, generally reduces the attractiveness of the group, but it may also weld them together in opposition and aggressive behaviour. Difficulties and frustration tend to cause groups with low cohesiveness to break up. Highly cohesive groups may quarrel and disagree on how to tackle the problem because, having stronger group goals and more 'we-feeling' they feel frustration more strongly. But they are less likely to split up.

Within these obviously extremely abbreviated summaries there are lessons for management: the physical arrangement of desks and work-places, the effects of long production lines with the individual a more or less isolated unit, the effect of friendly or hostile management practices, the different reactions to difficulty, problems and frustrations.

*Group Pressures and Standards*

It seems that a lot of work has been done on the way the group influences the individual by setting its own standards and bringing pressure to bear on non-conformists. Group pressure may cause an individual to openly disavow what he really believes in, but it is an open question whether he really changes his mind. Whether he is a voluntary member of a group who can walk out or a compulsory member who must stay may also affect the pressure the group can exert. Another aspect of the same point is that a group with greater cohesiveness usually has greater power to influence its members. Deviant members who refuse to conform are likely to be rejected by the group.

Considerable work has been done, much of it in industry, on the relative effectiveness in changing behaviour of the decision imposed by authority and the self-imposed decision made by the group itself. The work shows clearly that group discussion followed by group decision is vastly superior as a means of introducing change and bringing about new behaviour patterns, and also maintaining the change once it has been established. The reason is, of course, that group discussion and decision changes the group norm of behaviour to which members of the group will conform. Instruction from above may well leave the group norm unchanged, with the result of no change in behaviour, or conflict in the individual between his loyalties to the firm and to the group to which he belongs.

Group pressures and standards are certainly an aspect about which management should know far more than it does.

*Group Goals and Locomotion*

Almost every book on management emphasizes the importance of the goals or objectives of the firm. Fayol stresses the importance of subordinating individual goals to the group goal. Likert regards as essential the coincidence of individual, group and company goals.

Cartwright and Zander start by suggesting that if a group has clear goals and is effective in reaching them, personal satisfaction of members and group morale are usually high. While this may be true of small, face-to-face cohesive groups it is much less likely for compulsory members of very large groups such as industrial companies. Here ignorance of or indifference towards company goals is much more likely to be the reality. If sociology can give real guidance to modern management to find its way out of this impasse, which has been caused partly by history and partly by sheer size, it will be performing a vital service.

The authors produce a list of 'working hypotheses' which they suggest managers and other leaders use in determining group effectiveness. It comprises:[1]

1. the extent to which a clear goal is present
2. the degree to which the group goal mobilizes energies of group members behind group activities
3. the degree to which there is conflict among members concerning which one of several possible goals should control the activities of the group
4. the degree to which there is conflict among members concerning the means the group should employ in reaching its goals
5. the degree to which the activities of different members are coordinated in a manner required by the group's tasks
6. the availability to the group of needed resources, whether they be economic, material, legal, intellectual or other.

In addition to these determinants the list would also certainly contain many items specifying required group structures and processes, such as effective communication, competent leadership, clear lines of authority and participation in decisions.

These practical views are stated by Cartwright and Zander to show little agreement among the 'experts' and less evidence for their justification. The job of sociology is to discover a firmer basis for the theory of goals and movement towards them.

To do so scientifically is admitted to be one of the most difficult areas of sociology because of the problem of defining the area to be studied and the terms to be used. One line of approach is to ask whether or to what degree a group has a goal; whether, if it has more than one, they conflict; whether, as a result of group activity, movement has taken place, and finally whether it is towards or away from the goals. From this approach progression can be made to asking what helps or hinders the setting up of goals and what conditions help or hinder movement towards them.

A second approach is to classify group goals into different kinds. As with individual goals they arise to meet needs, but as with individuals the needs differ. The first type is the group goal that is comprised of similar individual goals. Secondly there are group goals that consist of the individuals' ideas of what the group should be doing. Obviously this requires consensus of opinion. Then a group goal can be dependent on the interrelation between the motivational forces of the members. All personally want something different and the group goal in different ways meets their needs. Finally, when a group goal is established it can be self-perpetuating in that it exerts influence on members to support and sustain it.

While this may sound rather abstruse from a management point of view it has a good deal of significance when thinking about company, departmental and individual goals in the organizational setting; more so when the explanation is carried still further to suggest that the degree to which group goals become established and the influence they can exert on members probably depends on the amount of similarity in the personal goals of the members. It also suggests, what is perhaps obvious and yet not completely realized, that individual goals will affect the way the group functions. A greater understanding and awareness of individual goals, their causes, and the ways in which they can be influenced, would increase the effectiveness of many a manager.

On the question of locomotion or movement by the group towards the attainment of its goals it is suggested that each goal will have its own set of functions and that activity by group members must match these functions. Work on this is largely limited to experimental and discussion groups, but the suggestion that the functions may be directed to attaining the group goal, maintaining the group, and pursuing individual goals at the expense of the group goal has obvious parallels in business organization.

As movement towards group goals is dependent on the efforts of individual members or of sub-groups it is obvious that an additional function of co-ordination of efforts is essential. This raises questions of the functions and styles of leadership which are dealt with later. A further question on effective locomotion is that of the degree to which group goals are accepted by members. This can cover a whole spectrum from whole-hearted commitment, through acquiescence to flat rejection. The group's power to get members to accept group goals seems to depend on how far the members of the group like each other, how far the group itself meets personal needs, and on the prestige of the group itself. Here may lie the explanation of much of the current apathy among workers in so far as the work situation often falls very short on these points.

Group goals have been dealt with at some length because it is felt that in the more orthodox management literature they have received too little attention. The tendency has been simply to state that the business must have clearly defined goals and then to assume or imply that all other goals must become subordinate to these. The simple fact is that in real life they don't, and management is just burying its head in the sand in assuming that they will. At the time Cartwright and Zander wrote this book sociology was still in the very early stages of studying the problem, and much more work may have been done since then. The limits marked out for this book prevent us from going further, but enough has been said to show the need for integration between sociological and management studies.

*Leadership*

If there is one subject which gives rise to conflicting opinions, not only among laymen but also among sociologists, it is leadership. Two aspects seem to cause most of the trouble. The first is the ideological question of 'what ought to be?'; the second the difficulty of defining leaders and leadership precisely. Are the attributes those of an individual or a function of a group situation?

Differing viewpoints give the following as aspects of leadership:

   (i) Leadership is a function of the group and may be displayed by different members of the group in varying degrees and at different times.

  (ii) Leadership is the personal exercise of the functions of planning, decision-making and co-ordination.

 (iii) In addition to the items in (ii) the leader is an expert, external representative, controller of relationships, distributor of rewards and punishments, arbitrator, and father figure among other things.

## D. Cartwright and A. Zander

Two important conclusions which arise from the concept of leadership as a group function are that leadership may move around the group according to the particular function to be performed at the time, and secondly, as a sort of corollary, different situations may call for different types of and qualities in the leader, so that one leader may not be the best under all circumstances.

Another aspect of leadership as a group function is whether from the point of view of performance it is better concentrated in the hands of one person, or whether it is better spread or delegated. In a number of researches in the industrial situation it was found that although the leaders were imposed on the group from above, those who delegated group functions more widely tended to get better results, such as higher production, more friendly attitudes in the group, and more cohesiveness.

If on the other hand the formal leader fails to exercise his function adequately, either personally or by delegation, then informal leaders arise who tend to 'take over' his function of leading the groups.

### Conclusion

Cartwright and Zander take great pains to point out that at the time they collected this work together much of it was still in its infancy, with little more than a series of items of groundwork covered. While the really serious work on sociological aspects of the industrial situation has proceeded only slowly, there can be little doubt that it will provide one missing link in the science of management, and psychology the other. To an outsider from another planet it would surely seem odd that we have learned so much about machines, materials and methods and so little about ourselves who alone make the whole thing work.

### Reference

(1) Cartwright, D. and Zander, A. *Group Dynamics* (Tavistock Publications, London 1954), p. 305.

# Conclusion

Long, long ago in my youth the Saturday serial films always ended at the most exciting point – the heroine tied to the railway line, the hero in dire danger. It would seem that this book, too, does exactly the same. Just at the point where it appears that some real insights into and some understanding of the reality of management are taking place the book stops.

But now that I have spent two-thirds of my working life in industry and commerce and the last one-third in teaching and observing management it seems to me that much if not most of current management in practice still has to catch up with many of the ideas summarized in this book.

There have been, and still are, four different and, so far, separate approaches to thinking about management: the approach through a study of work, the approach through an analysis of experience, the approach through the application of psychology and sociology have been dealt with, however inadequately, within this book. The fourth approach, through the development of managerial techniques, is too vast and too detailed a subject to be included, and in any case it did not fit the general pattern of this book.

If one can draw a parallel, the study, science if you prefer it, of management in 1960 had reached the stage of development of medicine a century earlier. Perhaps it had done no more than to show us the extent of our ignorance. Management is and, despite all the forecasts of the 'systems men', will remain an art. But art must be based on understanding, on experience, on science. If this book only makes some small contribution to easier understanding and to a more thoughtful analysis of experience I shall be well satisfied.

# Index

# Index

# Index

Here in one volume are summarized the main contributions which these influential thinkers have made to management theory since 1900: Chris Argyris – Chester I. Barnard – J. A. C. Brown – Lord Wilfred Brown – D. Cartwright and A. Zander – Peter F. Drucker – Henri Fayol – Mary Parker Follett – Henry L. Gantt – Frank B. and Lilian M. Gilbreth – Frederick Herzberg – Rensis Likert – Elton Mayo – Douglas McGregor – James D. Mooney – B. Seebohm Rowntree – Oliver Sheldon – Frederick Winslow Taylor.

The book is organized into sections illustrating the three different approaches which these individuals have adopted. One group approached management through the study of work; a second through the analysis of managerial experience; and the third based itself on knowledge from the psycho-sociological sciences.

The choice of what to include in this book reflects the 'newness' and significance of the ideas at the time they were published. It takes the story down approximately to 1960 and the full references will lead readers back to the specific original sources.

This epitome of management thinking will be of direct interest to all students of management and business who require background knowledge of the main trends but who will not have time to read twenty or so original texts. The practising manager and his colleagues in the personnel, industrial relations, and employment fields will also benefit from this important new survey.